Quiet Water

NEW HAMPSHIRE AND VERMONT

AMC's Canoe and Kayak Guide to the
Best Ponds, Lakes, and Easy Rivers

JOHN HAYES AND ALEX WILSON

Appalachian Mountain Club Books
Boston, Massachusetts

The AMC is a nonprofit organization and sales of AMC books fund our mission of protecting the Northeast outdoors. If you appreciate our efforts and would like to make a donation to the AMC, contact us at Appalachian Mountain Club, 5 Joy Street, Boston, MA 02108.

www.outdoors.org/publications/books/

Front cover photograph © Brooks Dodge
Back cover photographs © iStock
All interior photographs © John Hayes and Alex Wilson
Maps by Nadav Malin and Vanessa Gray, © John Hayes and Alex Wilson

Book design by Eric Edstam

Library of Congress Cataloging-in-Publication Data

Hayes, John.
  Quiet water New Hampshire and Vermont : canoe and kayak guide / John Hayes and Alex Wilson. —3rd ed.
      p. cm.
  Rev. ed. of: Appalachian Mountain Club quiet water canoe guide, New Hampshire, Vermont / Alex Wilson, John Hayes. c1992.
  ISBN 978-1-934028-35-3
  1. Canoes and canoeing—New Hampshire—Guidebooks. 2. Canoes and canoeing—Vermont—Guidebooks. 3. New Hampshire--Guidebooks. 4. Vermont—Guidebooks. I. Wilson, Alex, 1955- II. Wilson, Alex, 1955- Appalachian Mountain Club quiet water canoe guide, New Hampshire, Vermont. III. Title.
  GV776.N4H39 2010
  797.1'220974—dc22
                                    2009049961

The paper used in this publication meets the minimum requirements of the American National Standard for Information Sciences-Permanence of Paper for Printed Library Materials, ANSI Z39.48-1984. ∞

Outdoor recreation activities by their very nature are potentially hazardous. This book is not a substitute for good personal judgment and training in outdoor skills. Due to changes in conditions, use of the information in this book is at the sole risk of the user. The author and the Appalachian Mountain Club assume no liability for accidents happening to, or injuries sustained by, readers who engage in the activities described in this book.

Interior pages contain 30% post-consumer recycled fiber.
Cover contains 10% post-consumer recycled fiber.
Printed in the United States of America,
using vegetable-based inks.

Mixed Sources
Product group from well-managed forests, controlled sources and recycled wood or fiber
www.fsc.org   Cert no. SCS-COC-002464
©1996 Forest Stewardship Council

FSC

10 9 8 7 6 5 4 3 2 1   10 11 12 13 14 15 16

MAP LEGEND

Tent site	
Lean-to	
Picnic area	
Campground	
Boat access	
Parking area	
Marsh	
Peak	
Interstate highway	
State highway	
Paved road	
Less traveled road	
Rough dirt road	
Foot path	
River	
Stream	

LOCATOR MAP: VERMONT

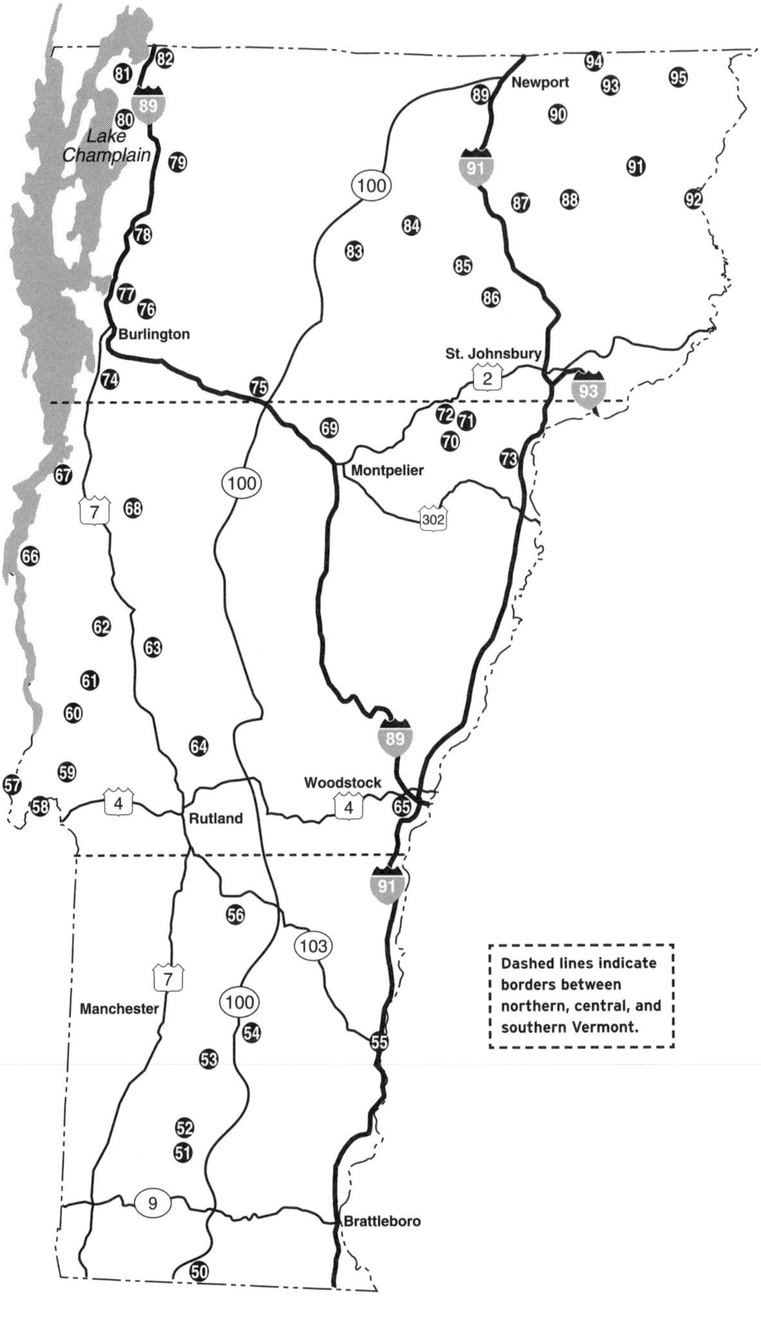

Lake Champlain
Burlington
Newport
St. Johnsbury
Montpelier
Woodstock
Rutland
Manchester
Brattleboro
89
91
93
100
2
302
7
4
103
9
50
51
52
53
54
55
56
57
58
59
60
61
62
63
64
65
66
67
68
69
70
71
72
73
74
75
76
77
78
79
80
81
82
83
84
85
86
87
88
89
90
91
92
93
94
95
Dashed lines indicate borders between northern, central, and southern Vermont.

LOCATOR MAP: NEW HAMPSHIRE

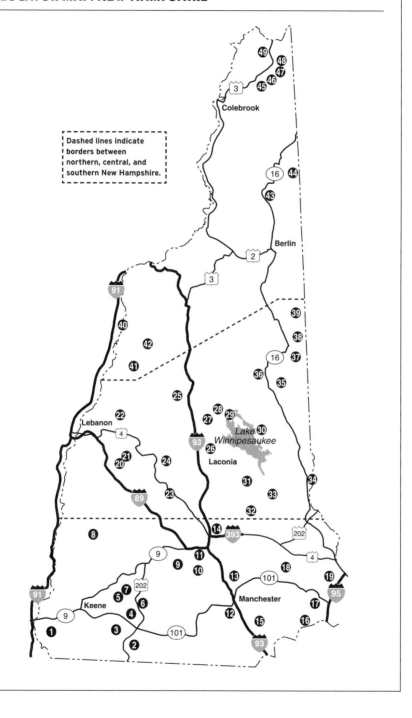

Contents

SECTION 1: SOUTHERN NEW HAMPSHIRE

SECTION 2: CENTRAL NEW HAMPSHIRE

SECTION 3: NORTHERN NEW HAMPSHIRE

SECTION 4: SOUTHERN VERMONT

SECTION 5: CENTRAL VERMONT

SECTION 6: NORTHERN VERMONT

NATURE ESSAYS

At-a-Glance Trip Planner

#	Trip	Page	Location	Area	Estimated Time
	SOUTHERN NEW HAMPSHIRE				
1	Pisgah Reservoir	2	Winchester	110 acres	3 hours
2	Hubbard Pond	5	Rindge	187 acres	3 hours
3	Mountain Brook Reservoir	8	Jaffrey	234 acres	3 hours
4	Edward MacDowell Lake	11	Dublin and Peterborough	165 acres	Half-day
5	Spoonwood Pond and Nubanusit Lake	13	Hancock and Nelson	144 acres; 645 acres	3 hours
6	Powder Mill Pond and Contoocook River	16	Bennington, Greenfield, and Hancock	419 acres	Half-day
7	Willard Pond	18	Antrim	98 acres	2 hours
8	Pillsbury State Park— Butterfield, May, Mill, and North Ponds	20	Washington	12 acres; 149 acres; 15 acres; 56 acres	5 hours
9	Stumpfield Marsh, Hopkinton Lake, and Everett Lake	23	Hopkinton and Weare	95 acres; 500 acres; 150 acres	All day

NOTES
*few motor boats
**no personal watercraft

Hiking Trails	Swimming	Motor Boats	Fee Required	Trip Highlights
Y	N	N	N	Pristine mountain lake with a backdrop of forested hillsides
N	N	N	N	Opportunity to see beaver, otter, osprey, and painted turtles
N	N	Y	N	Shallow, marshy pond with views of Mount Monadnock
Y	N	N	N	Opportunity for early morning paddlers to see beaver at work
Y	N	N	N	Deep, clear pond with nesting bald eagles
N	N	N	N	Shallow, marshy river backed up behind a small dam
Y	N	N	N	Clear pond protected by the Audubon Society
Y	N	N	Y	Wilderness ponds with on-site camping
N	Y	Y (none on Everett Lake)	N	Osprey, great blue heron, and ducks often visit these ponds

Hiking Trails	Swimming	Motor Boats	Fee Required	Trip Highlights
N	N	Y*	N	Pristine pond with extensive beaver meadow
Y	N	Y	N	Shallow, marshy ponds with long outlet stream on Turee Pond
N	N	Y**	N	Large, deep water-supply reservoir with protected coves and islands
N	N	Y*	N	Great blue heron rookery and a chance to study carnivorous plants
N	N	N	N	Opportunity to study ducks, geese, and other marsh animals and plants
N	N	N	N	Shallow, marshy pond with historic sawmill
N	N	Y*	N	Meandering stream with marshland species
N	N	Y*	N	Slow-flowing river with canopy of tall trees
Y	Y	Y	N	Large lake with coves, islands, and inlets; popular in summer
N	N	Y*	N	Large estuary formed by several inlet streams; extensive mud flats at low tide
N	N	Y*	N	Pristine marsh filled with wildlife
Y	N	N	N	A premier NH paddling destination; lots of islands and coves
N	N	Y	N	Shallow, out-of-the-way pond
N	N	Y*	N	Wide, slow-flowing river with minimal wind
N	N	N	N	Extensive marsh with abundant aquatic vegetation
N	N	N	N	Pristine bog with a view of the White Mountains

Hiking Trails	Swimming	Motor Boats	Fee Required	Trip Highlights
N	N	Y**	N	Small lake with marshy inlets, coves, and islands
N	N	Y	N	Shallow pond with marshy inlet and a good place to study ferns
Y	Y	Y**	N	Large, deep, scenic lake with many pairs of nesting loons
N	N	N	N	Shallow, marshy, pristine pond protected by Nature Conservancy
N	N	Y*	N	Opportunity to see frogs, turtles, and ducks
N	Y	Y	N	Deep lake surrounded by hills
N	N	Y**	N	Dammed river section with bays, inlets, and islands
N	N	Y	N	Meandering river; part of Merrymeeting River Wildlife Management Area
N	N	N	N	Marshy river forming boundary between New Hampshire and Maine
N	N	N	N	A paddle among bear oak and pitch pine barrens
N	N	N	N	Small, scenic lake near Mount Chocorua
Y	Y	Y**	N	Large White Mountains lake with many loons
N	N	Y	N	Shallow, marshy pond near the Maine border
Y	N	N	Y	Pristine mountain lake; requires hike in
N	N	Y	N	Scenic river sections backed up behind dams

Hiking Trails	Swimming	Motor Boats	Fee Required	Trip Highlights
Y	N	Y	N	Small lakes in the shadow of the White Mountains
Y	N	Y*	Y	Shallow wilderness pond in the White Mountains
N	N	Y	N	Reservoir with nesting bald eagles
N	Y	Y	N	Large lake on New Hampshire–Maine border, with nesting osprey, bald eagle, and loon
N	N	Y	N	Large, deep, remote lakes near Canadian border
N	Y	Y	N	Mid-sized lake with lots of wildlife
Y	N	N	N	Small, dammed stream; great place to see moose
N	N	N	N	Remote marshy pond set deep within moose country
Y	N	Y*	N	Deep lake near source of Connecticut River; close to Canadian border
N	N	Y* **	N	Pond with large floating island made of sphagnum and other bog plants
Y	N	Y**	N	Large reservoir in shadow of Mount Snow
Y	N	N	N	Marshy wilderness ponds in the Green Mountains
N	N	Y**	N	Possibility of seeing loon, beaver, mink, muskrat, and moose
Y	N	N	N	Shallow, marshy pond in Lowell Lake State Park
N	N	Y	N	Extensive marshy coves on the Connecticut River

Hiking Trails	Swimming	Motor Boats	Fee Required	Trip Highlights
Y	N	N	N	Wilderness pond in the Green Mountains; 1 mile hike in
Y	Y	Y	N	Narrow southern section with many inlets and bays
Y	N	Y*	N	Marshy river bounded by wildlife refuges; its mouth marks Lake Champlain's beginning
Y	N	Y (none on Half Moon Pond)	N	Large lake and three ponds in an area noted for its geology
N	N	N	N	Two small ponds covered with aquatic vegetation; waterfowl nesting area
Y	N	Y**	N	Wildlife-rich pond with historic covered railroad bridge
N	N	Y*	N	Slow-flowing river section through cedar swamps protected by Nature Conservancy
Y	N	N	N	Wilderness mountain lake; 0.6-mile hike in
Y	N	Y (none on Lefferts Pond)**	N	Large reservoir and small pond nestled below Green Mountain peaks
N	N	Y**	Y	Long, narrow reservoir at the foot of Quechee Gorge
N	N	N	N	Several dammed Champlain Valley creek sections loaded with wildlife
N	N	Y*	N	Lake Champlain estuary filled with waterfowl and other wildlife
N	N	Y* **	N	Marshy pond backed by scenic hillsides

Hiking Trails	Swimming	Motor Boats	Fee Required	Trip Highlights
N	N	Y**	N	Most interesting section is long, narrow inlet stream that ends in a waterfall
Y	N	Y (none on Osmore Pond)**	N	Great opportunity to see loon and beaver
Y	N	Y	N	Gorgeous setting makes up for some development and motorboat traffic
N	N	Y	N	Large pond with nesting loons and many beaver
N	N	Y (none on Upper Symes Pond)	N	Out-of-the-way ponds amid pointed spires of the northern boreal forest
N	N	Y	N	Pond used for environmental education; populated with rare ferns
N	Y	Y	N	Popular reservoir with 5 MPH speed limit on north end
Y	N	N	Y	Tiny pond, but a nice location for family trips
N	N	N	N	Winooski Valley Park District pond filled with wildlife
N	N	Y	N	Long, scenic Lamoille River reservoir with marshes on north end
N	N	Y **	N	Miles of pristine swamp with channels kept open by beaver
N	N	N	N	Small, marshy tributary streams to Lake Champlain
Y	N	Y	N	Huge wooded swamp at the northeast end of Lake Champlain
N	N	Y **	N	Possibility of seeing peregrine falcons

NOTES

*few motor boats
**no personal watercraft

Hiking Trails	Swimming	Motor Boats	Fee Required	Trip Highlights
Y	N	N	N	Vermont's premier paddling destination, with on-site camping
Y	N	Y **	N	Popular destination for multisport recreation in one of Vermont's most scenic areas
Y	N	N	N	Small, wilderness pond; 1-mile hike in
N	N	N	N	Remote pond filled with bog life
N	N	N	N	Little-known gem filled with wildlife
N	N	Y **	N	Clear, deep, picturesque lake with limits on motors
N	N	Y *	N	Huge marshland with open water and two long inlet rivers
N	N	Y * **	N	Slow-flowing river through Northeast Kingdom farmland
N	N	N	N	Small marshland in the heart of moose country
N	N	N	N	Shallow, remote marshland in the heart of the northern boreal forest
N	N	Y **	N	Long, narrow pond with several coves and inlet streams
Y	N	Y *	N	Ponds with marshy inlets within Bill Sladyk Wildlife Management Area
Y	N	Y **	N	Round, deep lake with excellent trout and salmon fishing

Preface

The first edition of *Quiet Water New Hampshire and Vermont*, published in January 1992, launched a series that now includes guides to Massachusetts/Connecticut/Rhode Island, Maine, New York, and New Jersey/Eastern Pennsylvania. John Hayes, co-author with Alex Wilson of the Maine and New York guides, has co-authored the second and third editions.

We took the opportunity in the second and third editions to add new material, nearly doubling the amount of water covered. The first edition contained 63 entries covering 74 bodies of water. For the second edition, we dropped six of those entries that covered eight bodies of water because of limited access, development, or overuse and added 55 new bodies of water, comprising 45 percent of the 121 total. For this third edition, we added Long Pond in Westmore, Vermont, and the lower section of the Poultney River where it flows into Lake Champlain. We also added Mountain Brook Reservoir in Jaffrey, New Hampshire. We also combined some entries: Branch Pond and Grout Pond, and Kettle Pond and Osmore Pond. We combined some new entries with first-edition entries: Hopkinton Lake and Stumpfield Marsh with Everett Lake, Lake Francis with First Connecticut Lake, and Bomoseen Lake and Loves Marsh with Glen Lake and Half Moon Pond. We also expanded some entries, adding another section to the Dead Creek entry and including a section of the Contoocook River in the Powder Mill Pond entry.

Because descriptions inevitably go out of date, we rechecked all bodies of water to make sure that new development had not crowded the shores, revised directions to reflect new road names, and added GPS coordinates to put-ins. When possible, we avoided places with substantial development, but we worried more about the effect of personal (motorized) watercraft and high-speed boating on safety, the quietwater experience, and the environment.

Acknowledgments

For the second and third editions, we owe special thanks to those who contacted us about new bodies of water to include, and to those who pointed out problems in the first edition. In particular, we thank Dick and Daniel Allen, Janet Brown, Bill Laliberte, Malcolm Moore, Linda Rice, Linda Robinson, and Peter Thompson of the Cornell University Geology Department. We thank Vanessa Gray, who did the cartography for the second and third editions, and the Spiral Shop Studios in Brattleboro for the photographic prints. We thank new paddling partners Philip Demay, Bob Engel, Vanessa Gray, and Andrew Hayes, and the AMC Books staff for their assistance in the preparation of this edition. Karen Klawiter, the former paddling co-chair at the AMC's New Hampshire Chapter, helped us determine whether any worthwhile bodies of water were missing from the last edition.

From the first edition (please note that many affiliations have changed) we thank Alex's family—Jerelyn, Lillian, and Frances Wilson—and other paddling partners (many of whom continue to paddle with us), including Sally Andrews, Betsey Copp, Jay Falk, Sumner Grey, Mark Kelley, Malcolm Moore, Ron Svec, and Jim Williams. For suggestions of lakes and ponds to explore, we thank Red Barber of the Vermont Department of Forests, Parks, and Recreation; Drew Gillett; Tom Howe of the Lakes Region Conservation Trust; Anne McCullough and Paul Doscher of the Society for the Protection of New Hampshire Forests; and David Sobel. For help with finding information, we thank Jerry Carbone at Brooks Memorial Library in Brattleboro, Vermont; Marc DesMeules at The Nature Conservancy, Vermont Chapter; Virginia Garrison and Susan Warren at the Vermont Agency of Natural Resources; Paul Wellenberger at the Great Bay National Estuarine Reserve; and helpful folks at both the Green Mountain and White Mountain national forests.

We are also indebted to Alex's business associate Nadav Malin, who produced the first-edition maps; Jennifer Ramstetter of Marlboro College, who reviewed the first-edition wildlife write-ups; Sheila Roth, a fine photographer in Brattleboro, for helpful photographic tips and the photographic printing; and Eric Edstam for the book design. Finally, we offer a special thanks to the Appalachian Mountain Club, and particularly to our good friend Gordon Hardy, who saw the potential in the series of quietwater paddling guides Alex envisioned and who carried out that vision in launching the series.

While we received a lot of help from these and other individuals, we accept responsibility for any errors. Please let us know of any problems so that we can correct them in future editions. Write to us care of AMC Books, 5 Joy Street, Boston, MA 02108. Thank you, and enjoy your paddling.

Introduction

Quiet waters—lakes, ponds, estuaries, and slow-flowing streams—receive much less attention than whitewater rivers. If you seek the adrenaline rush of paddling cascading rivers, there are plenty of excellent resources—but this is not one of them. The peaceful solitude of out-of-the-way lakes and ponds lures us to quietwater paddling. This guide will lead you to wood ducks swimming through early morning mists; to playful antics of river otter as you round a bend in a winding inlet channel; to the thrill of spotting a moose—mouth full of pondweeds—as it stands belly-deep in a bog; to old-growth white pine towering above crystal-clear ponds that help us imagine what our forests looked like centuries ago; and to the loon's haunting wail wafting off the water as afternoon settles into dusk.

With quietwater paddling, you can focus on *being* there instead of *getting* there. You do not need a lot of fancy high-tech gear—although a light canoe or kayak makes portaging over beaver dams a lot easier. Binoculars and field guides to fauna and flora make up our most important gear.

This guide will lead you to a body of water and describe why you might want to paddle it. Generally, we tried to include places that have abundant wildlife or extensive marshlands or beautiful scenery; most entries have all three. We hope that our research will allow you to spend your valuable time paddling instead of driving around for hours trying to find elusive accesses. We designed the AMC Quiet Water guides for paddlers of all experience levels, to help you better enjoy our wonderful water resources.

THE SELECTION PROCESS

This guide includes only about 10 percent of the nearly 1,000 lakes and ponds in New Hampshire and Vermont. In our selection process, we looked for great scenery; limited development; few motorboats and personal watercraft; a varied shoreline with lots of coves and inlets; and interesting plants, animals, and geological formations.

We include a variety of water types: big lakes and rivers for longer excursions and small, protected ponds and marshes for when you have limited time or when weather conditions preclude paddling larger bodies of water. We wrote this book not only for vacationers planning a weeklong trip hundreds of miles from home but also for local residents wanting to do some paddling on their afternoon off.

We asked people about the best places to paddle; we consulted maps from *DeLorme's New Hampshire Atlas & Gazetteer* and *Vermont Atlas & Gazetteer*; we bought other books about paddling; and we systematically examined the U.S. Geological Survey (USGS) 7.5-minute topographic maps of both states.

Although we tried to include the very best places to paddle, we doubtless have missed some really good locations. If you have suggestions of other lakes, ponds, and streams to include, please write to Alex Wilson or John Hayes, c/o AMC Books, 5 Joy Street, Boston, MA 02108.

SAFETY, EQUIPMENT, AND TECHNIQUE

We all long for the idyllic paddle on mist-filled, mirror-smooth surfaces of quiet ponds at daybreak. But if you spend any time paddling lakes and tidal rivers, you will also encounter far less tranquil conditions. Estuaries can have swift tides that, coupled with wind, can be very dangerous. On larger bodies of water, strong winds can arise quickly, whipping up 2- to 4-foot waves in no time—waves big enough to swamp an open boat. If you capsize in cold water even a moderate distance from shore, hypothermia—a cooling of the body's core that can lead to mental and physical collapse—can set in quickly. If you have just driven a long way to reach a particular lake and find it dangerously windy, choose a more protected body of water, or go hiking instead.

Safety First

All Northeast states require each boater to carry a U.S. Coast Guard–approved (Type I, II, or III) personal flotation device (PFD). A good PFD keeps a person's face above water, even if that person has lost consciousness. Children 12 and under must wear their PFDs, which must be the right size so that they will not slip off; adult PFDs are not acceptable for children. Although the law does not require adults to wear PFDs, we strongly recommend that you do so, especially when paddling with children. A foam- or kapok-filled PFD will also help keep you warm in cold water. If you do not normally wear your PFD while paddling, at least don it in windy conditions, when crossing large lakes, or when you may encounter substantial motorboat wakes. It could save your life.

You should also bring along a waterproof first-aid kit. The best kit is one that you assemble yourself; make sure that it has bandages or moleskin for blisters, an antihistamine for allergic reactions, sunscreen, an extra hat, a pain reliever, and any special medications that you might require.

As for clothing, plan for the unexpected. Even with a sunny-day forecast, a shower can appear by afternoon. On trips of more than a few hours, we bring along rain gear and dry clothes in a waterproof stuff sack as a matter of course. Along with rain coming up unexpectedly, temperatures can drop quickly, especially in spring or fall, making conditions ripe for hypothermia. Lightweight nylon or polypropylene clothing dries more quickly than cotton, and wool still retards heat loss when wet. Remember that heads lose heat faster than torsos—bring a hat.

Also bring a whistle, which you may need to use if you need help, since the sound of a whistle travels farther than the sound of a human voice, especially if it is windy. Bring enough food to maintain your energy level and carry one quart of water for short trips and two or more quarts for long trips. Avoid shallow, marshy waters during waterfowl-hunting season. For hunting-season dates, check the New Hampshire and Vermont fish and wildlife websites: www.wildlife.state.nh.us and www.vtfishandwildlife.com.

Other safety issues include:
- Getting off the water during lightning storms—lightning almost always strikes the highest object in the vicinity, which would be you in a boat out on a lake.
- Knowing what to do if you capsize and having experience doing it.
- Avoiding dehydration by drinking plenty of liquids.
- Avoiding areas with a lot of high-speed boating.
- Checking the weather forecast before going out.

Equipment

For quietwater paddling, avoid high-performance racing craft or tippy white-water models. Borrow a boat before buying; selection will be easier with a little experience. Whether you prefer to canoe or kayak, look for a model with good initial and secondary stability. A boat with good initial stability and poor secondary stability will tip slowly, but once it starts it may keep going. The best canoes for lakes and ponds have a keel or shallow-V hull and fairly flat keel line to help track in a straight line, even in a breeze. Kayaks perform extremely well in rough water, particularly if equipped with a foot-operated rudder and a sprayskirt to keep from taking on water.

If you like out-of-the-way paddling requiring portages, get a Kevlar boat if you can afford it. Kevlar is a strong, lightweight carbon fiber. We paddle a rugged, high-capacity, 18-foot, 4-inch Mad River Lamoille canoe that weighs just 60 pounds; a 15-foot, 9-inch Mad River Independence solo canoe that weighs less than 40 pounds; a 14-foot Wenonah Wigeon kayak that weighs 38 pounds; and a 14-foot Wilderness Systems Tchaika kayak that weighs 32 pounds. If you plan to go by yourself, consider a sea kayak or a solo canoe in which you sit (or kneel) close to the boat's center. You will find paddling a well-designed solo canoe far easier than a two-seater used solo. The touring or sea kayak—with its long, narrow design, low profile to the wind, and two-bladed paddling style—is faster and more efficient to paddle than a canoe.

A padded portage yoke in place of the center thwart on a canoe is essential if you plan on much carrying. With unpadded yokes, wear a life vest with padded shoulders. Attach a rope—called a "painter"—to the bow so that you can secure the boat when you stop for lunch, line it up or down a stream, and—if the need ever arises—grab on to it in an emergency. We both have embarrassing stories about not using a painter to secure the boat—wind can cause Kevlar boats to disappear very quickly!

Choose light, comfortable paddles. For canoeing, we use a relatively short (50-inch) bent-shaft paddle. Laminated from various woods, the paddle has a special synthetic tip to protect the blade. Bent-shaft paddles allow more efficient paddling, because the downward force converts more directly into forward thrust. However, straight-shaft paddles also work well. Always carry at least one spare paddle per group, particularly on longer trips, in case you break a paddle or a porcupine gets hold of one.

Paddling Technique

On a quiet pond, does it matter if you use the proper J-stroke, the sweep stroke, or the draw? No. Learning some of these strokes, however, can make paddling more relaxing and enjoyable. We watch lots of novices zigzagging along, frantically switching sides, shouting orders fore and aft. People have even told us about marriage counseling sessions devoted to paddling technique!

If you are new to the sport and want to learn canoeing or kayaking techniques, buy a book or participate in a paddling workshop, such as those offered by the Appalachian Mountain Club, equipment retailers, and boat manufacturers. We include recommend books on canoeing and kayaking in Appendix C.

Start out on small ponds. Practice paddling into, with, and across the wind. On a warm day close to shore, with your PFD on and others to help you out of difficulties, practice capsizing. Intentionally tipping your boat will give you an idea of how easily it can tip over. Try to get back into the boat away from shore. Getting the water out of a kayak while treading water is impossible without a hand pump; you can mount one permanently on your boat or carry a portable one. You should be able to right a canoe with two people, getting most of the water out (keep a bailer *fastened* to a thwart). Getting back in the boat is another story. Good luck!

PADDLING WITH KIDS

When canoeing with kids, try to make it fun and keep calm. Even though you may be plenty warm from paddling, children may get cold while sitting in the bottom of the boat. Remember that everyone should have PFDs on at all times, and PFDs will help keep children warm. Children also need protection from sun and biting insects. Watch for signs of discomfort. Set up a cozy place where young children can sleep; after the initial excitement of paddling fades, a gently rolling canoe often puts children to sleep, especially near the end of a long day. Also, for longer excursions, make sure to bring dry clothes for everyone in a waterproof sack.

How to Use This Book

For each trip in the book, we provide a list of basic information, a map, directions, and a short description of what you'll see.

TRIP INFORMATION

At the start of each trip description, we include location, DeLorme and USGS map information, area covered by the trip, an estimate of time required for a leisurely paddle, habitat type (i.e., type of environment you will encounter), types of gamefish, predominant animals and type of vegetation you should expect to see, contact information, camping information, and special notes about development or hazards to avoid.

Choose larger bodies of water and longer rivers when you have more time and a good weather forecast. Under windy conditions, paddle smaller bodies of water or rivers. Most entries include substantial shallow-water marshlands.

Campgrounds are public camping areas, keyed to the list in Appendix A. For information on private campgrounds, see the extensive lists in the DeLorme atlases.

MAPS

We recommend that you use the DeLorme Mapping Company's *New Hampshire Atlas & Gazetteer* and *Vermont Atlas & Gazetteer,* available at bookstores, outdoor retailers, and www.delorme.com. We key each entry to the respective DeLorme atlas, which divides each state into 36 detailed 10" x 15" maps at a scale of 1:100,000. The maps include most—but not all—access locations, campsites, road names, campgrounds, and parks, as well as other pertinent information. For more detail and information on topography, marsh areas, and so on, refer to the 7.5-minute, 1:24,000-scale USGS topographic maps listed in each section.

GETTING THERE

We give directions from the nearest city or major highway to the access. We provide distances between points, with the cumulative distance given in parentheses. We assume that you will use a detailed highway map, such as DeLorme's atlases. We also include GPS coordinates, taken on-site with a dashboard-mounted GPS unit; we report latitude and longitude values in degrees and decimal minutes, which is what our GPS units report.

WHAT YOU'LL SEE

The trip descriptions, each a few paragraphs long, give details about the area's natural features. Those details include birds, animals, and plants that you should expect to see on each trip, and in some cases we describe prominent geological features. Bringing field guides to birds, plants, and animals—along with waterproof binoculars—would be a great help in identifying and enjoying what you see.

Happy paddling!

Stewardship and Conservation

Diverse wetlands—among the richest, most readily accessible ecosystems—provide wonderful opportunities for paddlers to learn about nature. You can visit deep, crystal-clear mountain ponds, slow-flowing rivers, and unique bog habitats. You can observe hundreds of species of birds; dozens of mammal, insect, turtle, and snake species; and hundreds of plant species. Some quite rare species—such as a delicate bog orchid or a family of otters—provide a real treat when you observe them. But even ordinary plants and animals lead to exciting discoveries and can provide hours of enjoyable observation.

In the essays, we describe a few interesting plants and animals that you might encounter. We interspersed these descriptions—and accompanying pen-and-ink illustrations by Cathy Johnson—throughout. We hope that the information in these short essays will enhance your own observations.

DO WE REALLY WANT TO TELL PEOPLE ABOUT THE BEST PLACES?

People have asked us how we could, in good conscience, tell others about the more remote, pristine, unspoiled places—after all, increased visitation would make these places less idyllic. We spent many an hour grappling with this difficult issue as we paddled along. We believe that people who experience wild, remote areas firsthand will come to value them and build support for their protection

For many lakes and ponds, protection will mean purchase of fragile surrounding areas by state or local governments, or private organizations such as The Nature Conservancy. On other bodies of water, restricting high-speed boating offers the best form of protection.

Wetlands perform extremely important functions, such as recharging groundwater, helping control floods, supporting fishing and waterfowl hunting, and providing habitat for many rare and endangered species, as well as for hundreds of other species. Even low-impact uses such as canoeing or kayaking can substantially affect fragile marsh habitat. Paddling can disturb nesting loons and eagles, rare turtles, and fragile bog orchids. And even a canoe or kayak can carry invasive plants and other harmful organisms from one body of water to another; be sure to clean off your boat before you visit other water bodies.

You can go even further than the adage, "Take only photographs, leave only footprints." Carry along a trash bag and pick up the leavings of less thoughtful individuals. If each of us does the same, we will all enjoy more attractive places to paddle. While motorboaters tend to have a bad reputation when it comes to leaving trash, paddlers should have the opposite reputation—which could come in handy when seeking restrictions on high-impact resource use.

For information on low-impact camping and other uses of fragile habitats, see Bruce Hampton and David Cole's book, *Soft Paths: How to Enjoy the Wilderness Without Harming It*, 3rd ed. (Stackpole Books, 2003). Also, visit the website of Leave No Trace (www. lnt.org), an organization dedicated to teaching people how to have minimal outdoors impact.

Besides reducing our impact on the environment, we can actively work to protect fragile bald eagle, osprey, otter, loon, and other wildlife populations. If we want to preserve these species and their habitats for future generations, we will demand that elected and appointed officials make wildlife preservation and ecosystem protection a higher priority. We can also join conservation organizations—such as the AMC, Sierra Club, The Nature Conservancy, Audubon Society, and many others—so that when those organizations speak about preserving the environment, their voices carry the weight of tens of thousands of like-minded members.

Some of the waters featured in this book have more protection now than when the first edition was published in 1992. The state of Vermont banned water-skiing and personal watercraft and limited boating speeds to 10 MPH on Somerset Reservoir—one of the largest bodies of water in southern Vermont— and placed restrictions on personal watercraft and speeding on many smaller lakes and ponds. New Hampshire also banned personal watercraft from some important bodies of water. The land around a number of our most treasured water resources has received protection from development forever. While The Nature Conservancy and land trusts continue to protect more of the shoreline along a few key ponds and lakes, most other bodies of water suffer from continued development and more high-speed boating. When we update this guide in a few years, we hope to report a lot more progress in protecting these lakes and ponds.

We heartily applaud New Hampshire and Vermont for banning lead sinkers and jigs, fishing devices that the Tufts University Wildlife Veterinary Clinic has implicated in more than 50 percent of loon mortality in freshwater breeding grounds. Now we need to work on banning lead shot for waterfowl hunting.

THE AMC'S CONSERVATION EFFORTS

Because the lakes and ponds of New Hampshire and Vermont are beautiful, their real estate value is high, which can lead to excess development and harm to the environment. In response, the Appalachian Mountain Club has worked hard to protect the undeveloped shorelines of the Northeast. The AMC, with other environmental organizations and land trusts, has successfully secured millions of dollars in funding from federal and state budgets and bonds to protect critical lands with high aesthetic, recreational, and ecological waterfront values. The AMC has been a leader in protecting riparian lands during the licensing of hydropower projects, knowing that in return for using the public waters, the hydroelectric dam owners have an obligation to create shoreline management plans and mitigate their operational effects on the watershed. Some of the shorelines on trips listed in this book were protected by the AMC's involvement, including Lake Tarleton, Lake Umbagog, the Connecticut Lakes, and Somerset Reservoir. In addition, the AMC's recent purchase of more than 67,000 acres in Maine resulted in the protection of many miles of undeveloped lake, pond, and river waterfront for future generations.

PUBLIC ACCESS

Private land abuts many waterways. To ensure continued access, paddlers must respect private property. Never camp or picnic on private land without permission. In many places, adjacent landowners also own the riverbed or lakebed, which means that even if you have the right to paddle there, you may not have the right to fish there.

Both New Hampshire and Vermont have done a good job of providing public access to state waterways, either by establishing conservation easements or by purchasing land and water outright. We have listed only public access locations; however, private property bounds most bodies of water. Never launch your boat from private land without getting permission first, and do not get out along the shore on land posted as private. Cooperation will help keep bodies of water open to paddlers.

Fortunately, within the Green Mountain and White Mountain national forests and throughout the two states, several hundred thousand acres of public lands and many hundreds of bodies of water remain open for all to enjoy.

LEAVE NO TRACE

The Appalachian Mountain Club is a national educational partner of the Leave No Trace Center for Outdoor Ethics. The Center is an international nonprofit organization dedicated to responsible enjoyment and active stewardship of the outdoors by all people, worldwide. The organization teaches children and adults vital skills to minimize their impacts when they are outdoors. Leave No Trace is the most widely accepted outdoor ethics program used today on public lands across the nation by all types of outdoor recreationists. Leave No Trace unites five federal land management agencies—the United States Forest Service, National Park Service, Bureau of Land Management, the Army Corps of Engineers, and the United States Fish and Wildlife Service—with manufacturers, outdoor retailers, user groups, educators, organizations such as the AMC, and individuals.

The Leave No Trace ethic is guided by these seven principles:

Plan ahead and prepare. Know the terrain and any regulations applicable to the area you're planning to visit, and be prepared for extreme weather or other emergencies. This will enhance your enjoyment and ensure that you've chosen an appropriate destination. Small groups have less impact on resources and the experience of other backcountry visitors.

Travel and camp on durable surfaces. Travel and camp on established trails and campsites, rock, gravel, dry grasses, or snow. Good campsites are found, not made. Camp at least 200 feet from lakes and streams, and focus activities on areas where vegetation is absent. In pristine areas, disperse use to prevent the creation of campsites and trails.

Dispose of waste properly. Pack it in, pack it out. Inspect your camp for trash or food scraps. Deposit solid human waste in catholes dug 6 to 8 inches deep, at least 200 feet from water, camp, and trails. Pack out toilet paper and hygiene products. To wash yourself or your dishes, carry water 200 feet away from streams or lakes and use small amounts of biodegradable soap. Scatter strained dishwater.

Leave what you find. Cultural or historic artifacts, as well as natural objects such as plants or rocks, should be left as found.

Minimize campfire impacts. Cook on a stove. Use established fire rings, fire pans, or mound fires. If a campfire is built, keep it small and use dead sticks found on the ground.

Respect wildlife. Observe wildlife from a distance. Feeding wildlife alters their natural behavior. Protect wildlife from your food by storing rations and trash securely.

Be considerate of other visitors. Be courteous, respect the quality of other visitors' backcountry experience, and let nature's sounds prevail.

The AMC is a national provider of the Leave No Trace Master Educator course. The AMC offers this five-day course, designed especially for outdoor professionals and land managers, as well as the shorter two-day Leave No Trace Trainer course, at locations throughout the Northeast. For more information, see: www.outdoors.org/education/lnt.

For Leave No Trace information and materials, contact Leave No Trace Center for Outdoor Ethics at 800-332-4100, or visit www.lnt.org.

NORTHERN FOREST CANOE TRIPS

Several trips in the Northern New Hampshire and Northern Vermont sections of this book are part of the Northern Forest Canoe Trail (NFCT), a 740-mile inland paddling trail tracing historic travel routes across New York, Vermont, Quebec, New Hampshire, and Maine. NFCT connects people to the trail's natural environment, human heritage, and contemporary communities by stewarding, promoting, and providing access to canoe and kayak experiences along this route. The organization's website (www.northernforestcanoetrail.org) lists volunteer opportunities and events and offers a trip planner for finding maps, local outfitters, provisions, and lodging.

1 | SOUTHERN NEW HAMPSHIRE

The nineteen southern New Hampshire trips offer many types of paddling opportunities, ranging from small, marshy ponds—such as the 52-acre Kimball Pond—to the much larger 2,500-acre Lake Massabesic. The area also contains Great Bay, the only marine estuary in this book. The Lamprey, Squamscott, and Winnicut rivers flow together to form the 4,500-acre Great Bay National Estuarine Research Reserve, just west of Portsmouth. We prefer to use sea kayaks with spray skirts when paddling large bodies of water such as Great Bay and Lake Massabesic; we would use an open boat only if we were sure about favorable weather conditions.

The other seventeen trips include much smaller bodies of water. When it's windy, we head to these more protected ponds and rivers. Most include extensive marshy areas rich in plant and birdlife. Only two trips—Willard Pond and Spoonwood Pond—include deep, clear water. In New Hampshire's relatively flat, marshy southern tier, finding these two deep ponds is a bit of a surprise.

If you don't mind a steep hike to the put-in, you can visit the seldom-paddled Pisgah Reservoir. If you want to camp where you paddle, we recommend Pillsbury State Park, where you may hear coyotes and see moose. If you're looking for a marsh to paddle, we recommend Hubbard Pond, Edward MacDowell Lake, Stumpfield Marsh, Hopkinton Lake, Powwow River, Hoit Road Marsh, and Dubes Pond.

Although moose and loon remain relative rarities in the southern tier, bald eagle and osprey numbers are increasing. Beaver and muskrat occur in good numbers, and it's hard to avoid seeing plentiful great blue heron.

1 | Pisgah Reservoir

While paddling this pristine mountain lake with a backdrop of forested hillsides, you should see ducks and perhaps deer. Getting there requires a steep, half-mile, 30-minute hike.

Location: Winchester, NH
Maps: *New Hampshire Atlas & Gazetteer,* Map 19: G8; USGS Winchester
Area: 110 acres
Time: 30-minute hike-in, 3-hour paddle
Habitat Type: Small, pristine mountain lake surrounded by forested hillsides
Fish: Smallmouth bass, pickerel, crappie
Information: Pisgah State Park, 603-239-8153, www.chesterfieldoutdoors. com/plands/pisgah.html, www.nhstateparks.org
Camping: Monadnock State Park; see Appendix A, #1

GETTING THERE
From Hinsdale, at the junction with Route 63 north, go 2.6 miles east on Route 119, then turn sharply left onto Reservoir Road. Go 1.6 miles (4.2 miles) to the parking area on the left. Ruts and mud during wet weather can make passage difficult for low-clearance vehicles. *GPS coordinates*: 42° 48.600′ N, 72° 26.410′ W.

WHAT YOU'LL SEE
Hidden deep in the hills of 13,421-acre Pisgah State Park in the southwestern corner of New Hampshire, Pisgah Reservoir remains one of the most remote bodies of water included in this book. When you reach the end of Reservoir

PISGAH RESERVOIR

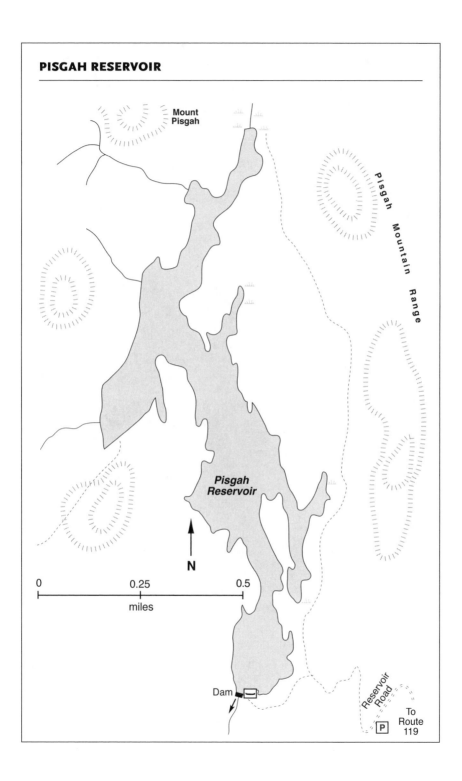

Mount Pisgah

Pisgah Mountain Range

Pisgah Reservoir

N

0   0.25   0.5
miles

Dam

Reservoir Road

P

To Route 119

Abundant aquatic plants dapple the sky's reflection on the placid waters of Pisgah Reservoir.

Road, you still have a steep half-mile carry with switchbacks. With a 40-pound canoe, the hike-in takes about twenty minutes. When you get to the very steep switchback, you are almost there. At the trail intersection, turn left to get to the dam for launching, or simply head through the woods to the reservoir, which you will see from the trail. All the hard work is worth it!

This gorgeous reservoir, small but highly varied, offers many islands, deep inlets, and hidden coves to explore. With a total length of about 1.5 miles, the reservoir offers more than 5 miles of shoreline to paddle—through quite deep, exceptionally clean, and unspoiled water. The surrounding heavily wooded shoreline supports hemlock and white pine as the dominant species, interspersed with various hardwoods, including red oak, beech, red maple, and yellow and white birch. At the water's edge, the banks often grow thick with blueberry bushes. The generally rocky shoreline gives way to marshy areas in the longer inlets, where you might see nesting ducks in spring. At the extreme northern end and in some of the shallow inlets, pond vegetation can grow fairly thick, but most of the lake remains open. In August, you will see extensive floating mats of purple bladderwort, an aquatic carnivorous plant, with occasional yellow bladderwort companions.

Besides the main reservoir, Pisgah State Park sports a number of smaller ponds—Fullam, Lily, Baker, Tufts, and Kilburn—located mostly in the northern half of the park, reachable via hiking trails or unimproved dirt roads. Access points to Pisgah State Park occur on all sides, with six parking areas at trailheads. Pick up a trail map in the mailbox at the end of Reservoir Road or at one of the other access points to the park.

2 | Hubbard Pond

This shallow, marshy pond sees few paddlers and offers a good opportunity to see beaver and otter. Also look for osprey and painted snapping turtles.

Location: Rindge, NH
Maps: *New Hampshire Atlas & Gazetteer*, Map 20: H5; USGS Peterborough South
Area: 187 acres
Time: 3 hours
Habitat Type: Shallow, marshy pond with inlets and islands
Fish: Smallmouth bass, pickerel
Camping: Monadnock State Park, Greenfield State Park; see Appendix A, #1, #2
Take Note: Access too difficult and water too shallow for motors

HUBBARD POND

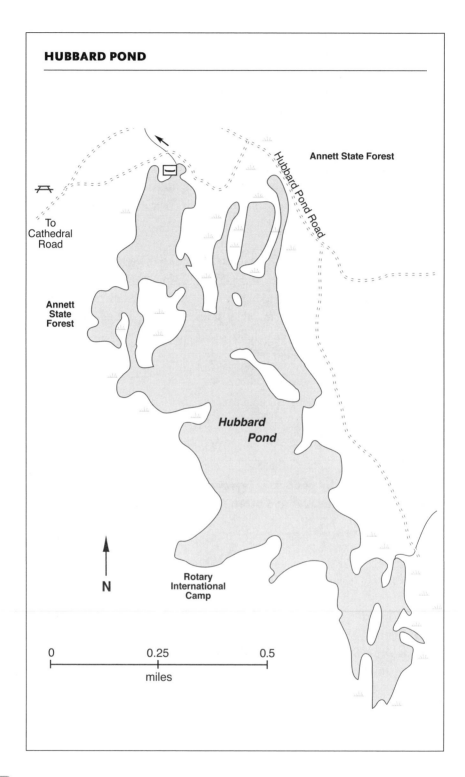

Annett State Forest

Hubbard Pond Road

To
Cathedral
Road

Annett
State
Forest

Hubbard
Pond

N

Rotary
International
Camp

| 0 | 0.25 | 0.5 |
miles

GETTING THERE

From Route 202 in Jaffrey, go 2.2 miles east on Route 124, and turn right onto Prescott Road. Go 0.6 mile (2.8 miles) to Squantum Road, and continue straight onto Cathedral Road. Go 0.7 mile (3.5 miles), turn left onto Fire Lane 222 when Cathedral Road goes sharply right, and go 0.4 mile (3.9 miles) to the access. The road may be difficult for low-clearance vehicles. *GPS coordinates*: 42° 47.066′ N, 71° 58.268′ W.

From Route 119 in Rindge, go 2.3 miles northeast on Cathedral Road, turn right onto Fire Lane 222, and continue as above.

WHAT YOU'LL SEE

Hubbard Pond, a hidden treasure in southern New Hampshire, offers much to the quietwater paddler. Surrounded on three sides by Annett State Forest, Hubbard Pond presents a wonderful place to visit in any season. We prefer spring and autumn, because wildlife viewing peaks in spring and fall foliage blends against the spectacular backdrop of Mount Monadnock—and you will not have to share the pond. You might want to visit in midsummer anyway, when the prolific highbush blueberries ripen.

Hubbard Pond's shallow waters offer a good opportunity to see snapping and painted turtles. You could also see an otter here.

Hubbard Pond's many marshy inlets and islands make the pond seem larger than it is. Weeds choke most of the shallow lake, making it a great spot for painted turtles, ducks, wading birds, beaver, and the occasional otter, which we have seen here in both spring and fall. In spring, we watched a pair of large snapping turtles mating and an osprey wheel overhead, searching the water for fish. By midsummer, though, vegetation can make paddling pretty difficult on the pond's shallowest parts.

White pine, hemlock, and other conifers dominate the wooded shoreline. Hummocks, covered with leatherleaf, also support lots of pitcher plant, tamarack, and black spruce, trees typical of more northerly locations. Despite some marshiness, the ground rises quickly on the eastern shore and most islands, so you can get up on solid ground for a picnic lunch. Up on the high banks, you will see plenty of evidence of beaver cutting saplings.

3 | Mountain Brook Reservoir

This shallow, marshy pond will take you away from busy Route 202 and offers great views of Mount Monadnock. Mountain Brook Reservoir is a good location to look for muskrat, wood duck, and deer amid the abundant aquatic vegetation.

Location: Jaffrey, NH
Maps: *New Hampshire Atlas & Gazetteer*, Map 20: H3; USGS Monadnock Mountain
Area: 234 acres
Time: 3 hours
Habitat Type: Shallow, marshy pond with inlets and islands
Fish: Largemouth bass, pickerel, yellow perch
Information: Town of Jaffrey, 603-532-7863, town.jaffrey.nh.us
Camping: Monadnock State Park, Greenfield State Park; see Appendix A, #1, #2

GETTING THERE
Route 202 access. From Route 124 in Jaffrey, go 0.9 mile south on Route 202 to the access on the right. The access is 3.1 miles north on 202 from Route 119.

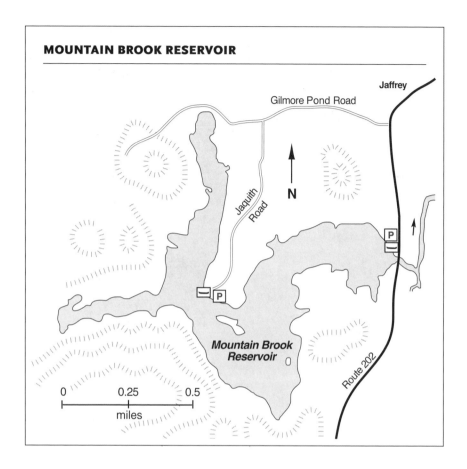

MOUNTAIN BROOK RESERVOIR

Jaffrey

Gilmore Pond Road

Jaquith Road

N

Mountain Brook Reservoir

Route 202

0   0.25   0.5

miles

High-ground-clearance vehicle recommended. *GPS coordinates*: 42° 48.215′ N, 72° 1.717′ W.

Jaquith Road access. From Route 124 in Jaffrey, go 0.4 mile south on Route 202, and turn right onto Gilmore Pond Road. Go 0.2 mile (0.6 mile), and turn left onto Jaquith Road. Go 0.8 mile (1.4 miles) to the access. *GPS coordinates*: 42° 48.104′ N, 72° 2.560′ W.

WHAT YOU'LL SEE

Mountain Brook Reservoir offers a beautiful paddling location, with arms extending east, west, north, and south from a central hub. The eastern extension, near the Route 202 access and outlet, has significant road noise and a number of houses impinging on the solitude.

Paddling away from 202, you quickly leave road noise behind. The southern shoreline offers a gorgeous view of Mount Monadnock (3,165 feet), one of the most climbed mountains in the world. The top remains barren because of

You may find a melting skim coat of ice if you paddle on a fall morning.

intentionally set fires in the early 1800s that destroyed the vegetation and topsoil. With binoculars, you may be able to see hikers on top as you paddle here.

The reservoir's western arm is the wildest, with most of the shoreline protected by the Monadnock Conservancy. In summer, paddling the shallow arms becomes restricted by extensive floating vegetation, including fragrant waterlily, yellow pond lily, water shield, and pondweed. If you can make it to the far western tip, you'll hear an inlet brook trickling over a small beaver dam.

Paddling along the northern arm, note that the vegetation on the west bank differs from elsewhere on the reservoir—with drier woodlands dominated by red oak. The arm eventually reaches two culverts through which Mountain Brook enters the reservoir. You can paddle through either culvert (be careful of some large rocks on the reservoir side) and into a small area thick with pickerelweed before reaching the rocky brook.

Extensive stands of pickerelweed, rushes, sedges, and grasses occur throughout the reservoir. In fall, you will see stands of winterberry with their bright red berries. We watched a deer browsing on these shrubs on the northern shore of the reservoir's eastern arm, where you may notice some tall tamaracks, which seem oddly out of place amid the white pine, maple, and oak. We saw evidence of beaver but didn't notice a lodge. We did get a great look at a muskrat, which used its strong tail to propel itself through the water, swishing it side to side. We saw mergansers when we paddled here in fall; earlier in the season, expect to see wood ducks.

4 | Edward MacDowell Lake

This small, marshy lake presents a great opportunity for early morning or evening paddlers to see beaver at work. Ducks, geese, and great blue heron also frequent the lake.

Location: Dublin and Peterborough, NH
Maps: *New Hampshire Atlas & Gazetteer,* Map 20: D4; USGS Marlborough, Peterborough North
Area: 165 acres
Time: Half a day, if you paddle the streams
Habitat Type: Small, marshy lake with beaver-impounded inlet streams to paddle
Fish: Largemouth bass, pickerel
Information: U.S. Army Corps of Engineers, www.nae.usace.army.mil/recreati/eml/emlhome.htm
Camping: Monadnock State Park, Greenfield State Park; see Appendix A, #1, #2
Take Note: Gasoline motors prohibited; several hiking trails begin at the end of Wilder Street

GETTING THERE
From Route 123 in Hancock, go 5.5 miles south on Route 137, and turn left onto Spring Road at a sharp curve. Go 0.3 mile (5.8 miles), turn right onto Richardson Road, and go 0.6 mile (6.4 miles) to the access on the right. *GPS coordinates*: 42° 54.176′ N, 71° 59.457′ W.

From Route 101, go 1.4 miles north on Route 137, turn right onto Spring Road, and continue as above.

WHAT YOU'LL SEE
Although Edward MacDowell Lake does not even appear on some maps, we found it a picturesque place with ample room to paddle, especially early in the season. Operated by the Army Corps of Engineers, the area consists of sinewy

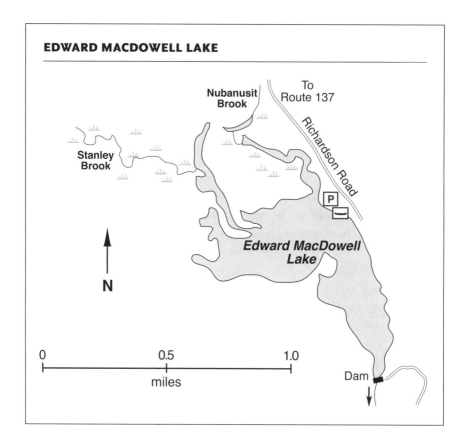

EDWARD MACDOWELL LAKE

channels that penetrate a shallow marshland with numerous floating islands, inlets, and channels to explore. The northern channels twist and wind with tight turns. We saw Canada geese, tree swallows, several great blue herons, wood duck, yellow pond lily, and some swamp rose. Fragrant waterlily, pickerelweed, and buttonbush line many of the channels.

If you paddle around to the right from the access, you come to a little water-fall and riffle with lots of rounded boulders. If you feel adventurous, carry up over this and paddle upstream a distance. You will come to some beaver dams that impound more water. Few people visit this very scenic area. You might regret trying to drag your boat through the riffle or through the poison ivy in the woods, but we felt it was well worth the effort.

The swampy, shallow, weedy nature of the place precludes much activity. We saw a few canoes and kayaks when we paddled here and felt it was quite easy to find solitude.

5 | Spoonwood Pond and Nubanusit Lake

Expect to see bald eagles on Spoonwood Pond, and in June, look for mountain laurel in bloom around both bodies of water.

Location: Hancock and Nelson, NH
Maps: *New Hampshire Atlas & Gazetteer,* Map 20: A3; USGS Marlborough, Stoddard
Area: Spoonwood Pond, 144 acres; Nubanusit Lake, 645 acres
Time: 3 hours on Spoonwood
Habitat Type: Clear, deep lake, forested hillsides
Fish: Smallmouth bass, perch, pickerel, smelt, landlocked salmon; brook, brown, rainbow, and lake trout (40-incher caught in Nubanusit in 2008)
Information: Harris Center for Conservation Education, www.harriscenter.org
Camping: Monadnock State Park, Greenfield State Park, Pillsbury State Park; see Appendix A, #1, #2, #3
Take Note: Personal watercraft prohibited on Nubanusit Lake; gasoline motors prohibited on Spoonwood Pond.

GETTING THERE

From Route 9 in South Stoddard, go southeast 4.7 miles on Route 123, and turn sharply right onto Hunt's Pond Road. Go 0.5 mile (5.2 miles), and turn right onto Kings Highway. Go 1.1 miles (6.3 miles) to the access on Landing Road on the left. Although there are many spots, parking is at a premium on weekends. *GPS coordinates*: 42° 59.793′ N, 72° 2.748′ W.

From Route 137 in Hancock, go 2.1 miles northwest on Route 123, turn left onto Hunt's Pond Road, and follow as above.

WHAT YOU'LL SEE

Nubanusit Lake would be one of southern New Hampshire's real gems if motorboating were more restricted. On summer weekends, the speedboats and water-skiers can be oppressive and even dangerous. The lake also can suffer from large wind-driven waves, so we do not recommend that you spend much time paddling there. Instead, paddle northwest from the Nubanusit Lake access and then around the bend to the southwest to reach comparative solitude. At the

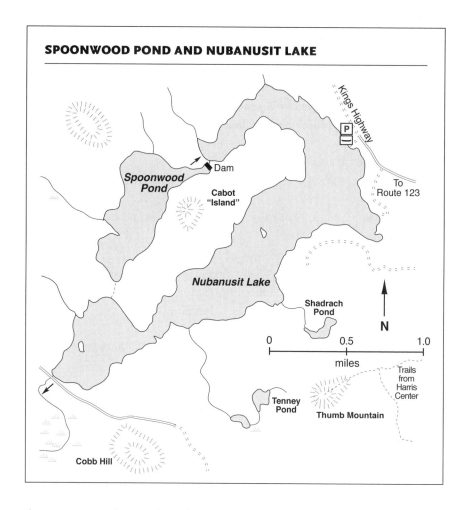

SPOONWOOD POND AND NUBANUSIT LAKE

Kings Highway

P

Dam

Spoonwood Pond

Cabot "Island"

To Route 123

Nubanusit Lake

Shadrach Pond

N

0   0.5   1.0

miles

Trails from Harris Center

Tenney Pond

Thumb Mountain

Cobb Hill

dam, carry your boat a short distance over to the outlet of Spoonwood Pond, and you are free at last.

Spoonwood Pond is well protected, inaccessible by car, and off-limits to motorboats. Like Nubanusit, Spoonwood has a rocky shoreline, and in some places giant slabs of granite extend down to and into the water. Large crystals of feldspar, mica, and garnet, along with iron deposits, poke out of the granite, making it look almost like a conglomerate rock. From Spoonwood Pond, you can hike through heavily wooded, rocky terrain on Cabot "Island" (really a peninsula), owned by Keene State College. You can cross over to the southern end of Nubanusit Lake if you want to watch motorboats, or you can stick to Spoonwood or hike on wilderness land managed by the Harris Center for Conservation Education.

Both Nubanusit and Spoonwood have exceptionally clean water. The considerable depth (96 feet in Nubanusit and 70 feet in Spoonwood) and lack of surrounding marshland make the waters oligotrophic (i.e., having very low biological productivity), allowing you to peer into their crystal-clear depths. The lakes show almost no evidence of tannic and other organic acids that result from plant decay and that turn the water yellow-brown. Both have excellent reputations for coldwater fishing, including for several species of trout.

In late June, mountain laurel blooms in huge, 10-foot-tall clumps, along with sheep laurel and many other densely packed shoreline shrubs. We saw a red-breasted merganser with a raft of young and watched two adult bald eagles fish Spoonwood Pond. Bald eagles did not nest in New Hampshire from 1949 to 1988; in 1989, eagles began nesting successfully on Lake Umbagog. Then in 1998 a pair started to build a nest near Spoonwood Pond. They hatched two chicks in May 1999, but the chicks fell prey to raccoons. In 2000, the chicks again failed to survive, this time succumbing to either a May heat wave or a winged predator, such as a great horned owl. However, eagles in recent years have had more success; in both 2004 and 2008, they fledged three young.

To visit the Harris Center for Conservation Education, drive a few minutes back along Kings Highway from the access. The Harris Center includes a network of hiking trails and a wonderful old estate where educational programs are held. A trail from the Harris Center leads to Thumb Mountain, which overlooks Tenney and Shadrach ponds.

Majestic bald eagles have nested near Spoonwood Pond since 1998. This is an important location in the recovery of this once-endangered species.

6 | Powder Mill Pond and Contoocook River

Look for muskrat on the shallow pond and meandering, slow-flowing river. Because of its clean water, this location is a good place to look for otter, and you might also see beaver.

Location: Bennington, Greenfield, and Hancock, NH
Maps: *New Hampshire Atlas & Gazetteer,* Map 20: B6; USGS Peterborough North
Area: 419 acres
Time: Half-day, more if you paddle the river
Habitat Type: Shallow pond with inlets, meandering river
Fish: Largemouth bass (6-pound bass caught here in 2008), pickerel
Camping: Monadnock State Park, Greenfield State Park, Pillsbury State Park; see Appendix A, #1, #2, #3
Take Note: Gasoline motors prohibited

GETTING THERE

Southern access. From Route 101 in Peterborough, go 7.4 miles north on Route 202, and turn right onto Forest Road. Go 1.3 miles (8.7 miles), crossing the covered bridge, to the access on the right. *GPS coordinates*: 42° 57.335′ N, 71° 56.414′ W.

Northern access. Go 2.2 miles (9.6 miles) north from Forest Road on Route 202 to the parking area on the left. Carry your boat across the road to the pond.

WHAT YOU'LL SEE

A dam on the Contoocook River in Bennington, New Hampshire, holds back unspoiled Powder Mill Pond. A few unobtrusive old farms front the pond's western shore. The main drawback: road noise from Route 202, which runs quite close to the pond at the northern end. Powder Mill Pond, a public water supply, enjoys exceptionally clean water, as evidenced by shells of freshwater mussels along the shore—probably left by raccoons or otters. You will find lots of deep inlets and marshy eddies to explore along the nearly 3-mile stretch from the covered bridge on Forest Road at the southern end of the pond to the dam at the northern end.

POWDER MILL POND AND CONTOOCOOK RIVER

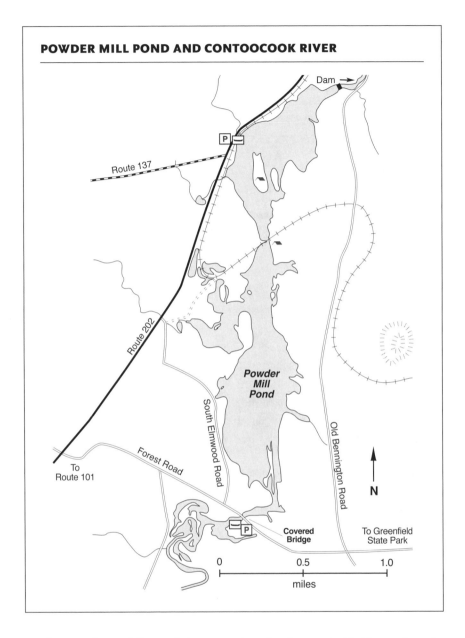

You can also paddle south (upstream) under the covered bridge and up the Contoocook River. This section of the river twists and folds tightly, leaving many islands and oxbow curves to explore. Red maple lines the shore, along with oak, hemlock, and other trees. Red maple always has red on it: red buds in winter, red flowers in spring, red stems on the leaves in summer, and red leaves in fall. Look for beaver activity in the swamps. We watched a muskrat harvest grass and saw several kingfishers. When you reach the point where the current picks up, some barely submerged boulders—hard to see and to avoid—will impede your progress.

7 | Willard Pond

Protected by the Audubon Society, the spectacular setting of this small, clear-water pond makes this an enticing destination. Look for loons here.

Location: Antrim, NH
Maps: *New Hampshire Atlas & Gazetteer,* Map 26: K4; USGS Stoddard
Area: 98 acres
Time: 2 hours
Habitat Type: Clear pond, forested hillsides
Fish: Brook and rainbow trout
Information: New Hampshire Audubon,
www.nhaudubon.org/sanctuary_antr.php
Camping: Monadnock State Park, Greenfield State Park, Pillsbury State Park; see Appendix A, #1, #2, #3
Take Note: Gasoline motors prohibited

GETTING THERE
From Route 137 in Hancock, go 2.9 miles northwest on Route 123, and veer right onto Davenport Road. Go 0.7 mile, turn right onto Willard Pond Road, and go 1.0 mile to the access. *GPS coordinates:* 43° 1.111′ N, 72° 1.233′ W.

From Route 9 in Stoddard, go southeast on Route 123 for 3.3 miles, turn left onto Willard Pond Road, and go 1.7 miles to the access.

WHAT YOU'LL SEE
Hidden in the southwestern part of New Hampshire, protected by a 1,400-acre Audubon Society preserve, Willard Pond is simply breathtaking. New Hampshire restricts fishing to loons, kingfishers, and fly fishers. The one privately owned house at the southern end of the pond, set back from the water,

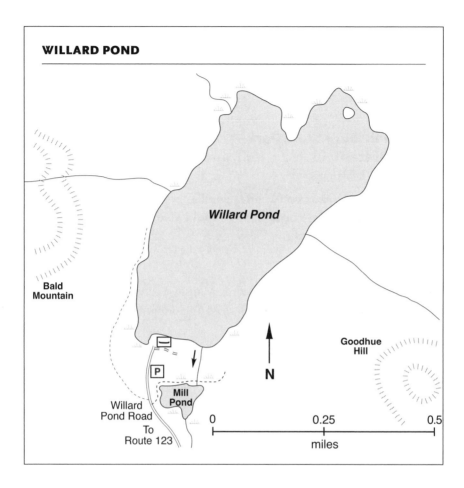

WILLARD POND

Willard Pond

Bald
Mountain

Goodhue
Hill

N

P

Mill
Pond

Willard
Pond Road

To
Route 123

0   0.25   0.5

miles

does not intrude on the pond. In 2009, New Hampshire Audubon purchased the last piece of privately owned shoreline

Moss-covered granite boulders dot the shoreline, and the forested hillsides harbor mountain laurel, aspen, yellow birch, beech, red oak, red maple, and white pine. The crystal-clear water allows you to see the bottom through at least 15 feet of water. The clarity of the water actually is disconcerting, because at first glance a boulder 2 feet underwater seems lodged just below the surface film—then you glide right over it.

A wildlife preserve owned and managed by New Hampshire Audubon nearly surrounds the entire area. In addition to observing birds from the boat, birders can make use of two trails that circle a substantial portion of the pond. The singing of warblers, sparrows, and a wide assortment of other songbirds makes the shore come alive. You may also hear the enchanting wail of the pond's nesting loon pair. (Be very careful not to disturb nesting loons.) Several marshy inlets provide ideal habitat for ducks and herons. The property obviously is well managed; in fact, we had a lot of trouble finding a piece of trash to take out.

8 | Pillsbury State Park— Butterfield, May, Mill, and North Ponds

These small wilderness ponds offer good opportunities to look for moose and to listen for coyotes. You should also see ducks, geese, loon, and great blue heron.

Location: Washington, NH
Maps: *New Hampshire Atlas & Gazetteer,* Map 26: D2; USGS Lovewell Mountain; AMC Southern New Hampshire Trail Map
Area: May Pond, 149 acres
Time: 5 hours to paddle all four ponds
Habitat Type: Small, wild, mountain ponds
Fish: Largemouth bass, pickerel
Information: New Hampshire Division of Parks and Recreation, www.nhstateparks.org
Camping: On-site camping; see Appendix A, #3
Take Note: No motors allowed, hiking trails

GETTING THERE
From Route 9 west of Hillsborough, go 13.5 miles north on Route 31 to the park entrance on the right. *GPS coordinates:* 43° 13.920′ N, 72° 6.258′ W.

From Route 10 south of Goshen, go 4.7 miles south on Route 31 to the entrance on the left.

WHAT YOU'LL SEE
Together, these four small ponds in Pillsbury State Park form the headwaters of the Ashuelot River and offer superb quietwater paddling, particularly if you camp here overnight. Butterfield Pond, the farthest downstream, extends from a dam next to Route 31. A narrow, rocky strait connects Butterfield to May Pond, the largest and deepest of the lakes. We saw loons on both Butterfield and May.

A dozen or so camping sites dot May Pond's northern shore, some beautifully

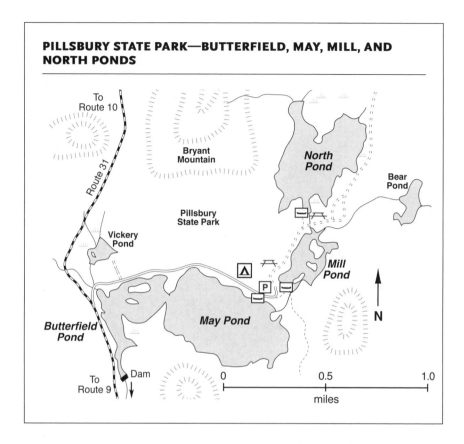

PILLSBURY STATE PARK—BUTTERFIELD, MAY, MILL, AND NORTH PONDS

To Route 10

Route 31

Bryant Mountain

North Pond

Bear Pond

Pillsbury State Park

Vickery Pond

Butterfield Pond

May Pond

Mill Pond

N

To Route 9

Dam

0   0.5   1.0

miles

situated on the water. They remain open year-round and are free of charge in the off-season. Listen for coyotes at night, and look for moose in the early morning or evening.

Near May Pond's eastern end, you can portage along an open trail and road up to Mill Pond, or you can drive. Aquatic vegetation covers much of Mill Pond's surface in summer, making paddling difficult. But you should see more wildlife here, such as the pair of hooded mergansers we watched feeding in late April.

The adventurous can take out on the right side of the inlet into Mill Pond and portage up to North Pond, the most remote of the four ponds. Carry a few dozen yards to the woods road, turn left (back toward the Mill Pond parking area), cross the bridge, and then take the trail to the right after 50 or 60 yards. This trail leads a few hundred yards to North Pond. You also can portage up from May Pond, with a longer carry.

North Pond, a rich fen, has the feel of northern Canadian wilderness, with birds galore and an interesting plant species: the northern pitcher plant

This picnic area near North Pond provides a pleasant view.

(*Sarracenia purpurea*). Look for these insect-eating reddish plants on the numerous low islands, sphagnum-moss hummocks, or shoreline amid the dense, creeping cranberry bushes and other heaths. Like Mill Pond, North Pond sports a fairly thick mat of summer vegetation, but that should not stop you from enjoying this bit of wilderness.

When you tire of paddling, you can enjoy some of the wonderful trails around these ponds and through the hills, including hikes to the smaller Vickery and Bear ponds. Pick up a map at the park office, just as you turn into the park from Route 31.

9 | Stumpfield Marsh, Hopkinton Lake, and Everett Lake

You will likely see osprey, great blue heron, and ducks on these ponds, which are largely covered by aquatic vegetation. In the early morning or evening, you have a good chance of seeing beaver and deer.

Location: Hopkinton and Weare, NH
Maps: *New Hampshire Atlas & Gazetteer,* Map 27: F11/H12; USGS Henniker, Hopkinton, Weare
Area: Stumpfield Marsh, 95 acres; Hopkinton Lake, 500 acres; Everett Lake, 150 acres
Time: All day
Habitat Type: Shallow, marshy pond and lakes
Fish: Largemouth bass (24-inch bass caught in Stumpfield Marsh in 2008), pickerel
Information: Army Corps of Engineers, www.nae.usace.army.mil/recreati/hel/helhome.htm
Camping: Greenfield State Park, Pillsbury State Park, Mt. Sunapee State Park; see Appendix A, #2, #3, #7
Take Note: Motors prohibited on Everett Lake

GETTING THERE

Stumpfield Marsh. From I-89, Exit 5, go west on Routes 9/202 for 1.7 miles, and turn left onto Stumpfield Road. Go 0.8 mile (2.5 miles) to the access on the right. From Henniker, go east on Routes 9/202. Turn right onto Stumpfield Road 2.2 miles after Route 127 goes left, and follow as above. *GPS coordinates*: 43° 9.998′ N, 71° 42.500′ W.

Hopkinton Lake. The access is on Stumpfield Road, 0.6 mile north of Routes 9/202. *GPS coordinates*: 43° 10.988′ N, 71° 43.325′W.

Everett Lake. Because Clough State Park is often closed, use the Mansion Road access. From Route 13 in Goffstown, go 1.4 miles west on Route 114, and turn right onto Parker Station Road. Go 1.2 miles (2.6 miles), and veer right onto Riverdale Road (River Road) at the sign for Everett Dam/Clough State Park. Go 2.6 miles (5.2 miles), and turn right onto Clough Park Road. Go 2.1 miles (7.3 miles) to the park entrance. Continue 1.2 miles (8.5 miles) on Everett Dam Road, and turn left onto Mansion Road (Ray Road). Go 1.9 miles (10.4 miles), and veer left just after passing through two stone walls. Go 1.5 miles

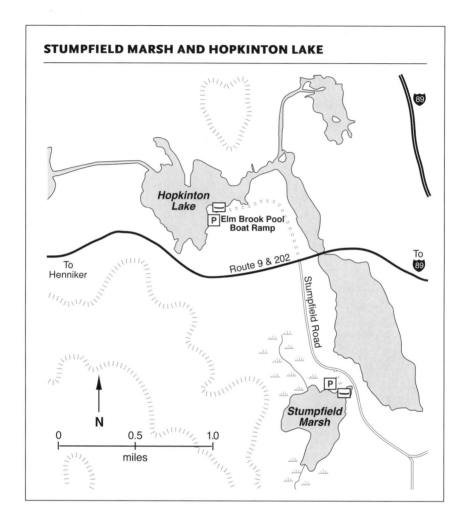

STUMPFIELD MARSH AND HOPKINTON LAKE

Hopkinton
Lake

P Elm Brook Pool
Boat Ramp

To
Henniker

Route 9 & 202

Stumpfield Road

To
89

N

0   0.5   1.0
miles

P

Stumpfield
Marsh

(11.9 miles), turn right, and go 0.1 mile (12.0 miles) to the access by the bridge. *GPS coordinates*: 43° 6.511′ N, 71° 39.689′ W.

WHAT YOU'LL SEE
Stumpfield Marsh

Of the three locations presented here, Stumpfield Marsh is the smallest and feels the most remote. No development encroaches on the layered hillsides surrounding this wide, shallow marsh. After banging into a few barely submerged stumps, paddlers will understand the reason for the marsh's name. Because the shallow waters support abundant vegetation, paddling here can be a challenge in summer and early fall.

EVERETT LAKE

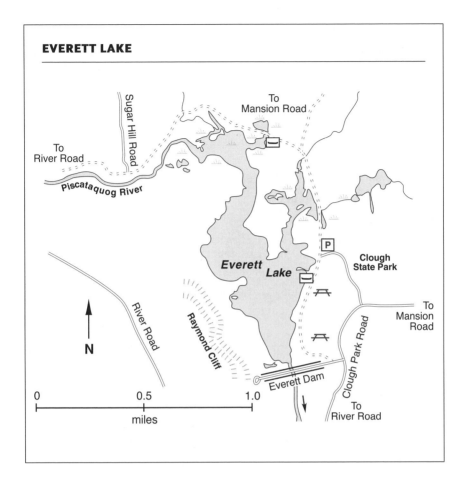

Standing at the access, note the dead trees with great blue heron nests out in the middle of the marsh; some of these trees have toppled, and eventually they will all disappear, absorbed into the marsh. We paddled here twice, once in late April (when herons were on their nests) and once in October. Although the foliage and the light-colored dead trees reflecting on the water make paddling here in fall gorgeous, we definitely prefer spring. Not only do you get to see the herons, but you can also paddle farther back into the marsh because of higher water and fewer aquatic plants.

We also saw many ducks and geese, with young in spring and during migration in fall. Mallards, red-breasted mergansers, wood ducks, Canada geese, and other waterfowl stop off here. Note the spent shells of huge aquatic snails in the shallows and the workings of the active beaver colony.

Hopkinton Lake

Hopkinton's varied scenery and forested hillsides, along with aquatic habitat diversity, make for enjoyable paddling, if you can ignore the noise from Routes 9/202 and I-89, which run close by. We prefer the northeast arm and the long connector that leads to it; we could hear I-89 off in the distance, but it did not disturb us—or the resident beaver colony—too much. Yellow pond lily and fragrant waterlily cover the shallow, marshy areas, along with pondweed and other aquatic plants. In the northeast arm, aquatic vegetation covered perhaps 50 percent of the surface area. We found quite a bit of buttonbush, other shrubs, and fern growing in the understory.

When we paddled here on a bright, sunny October day, we encountered only canoes, kayaks, and a lone eight-horsepower motorboat. Because of shallow water, barely submerged stumps, and abundant aquatic vegetation, this place does not suffer from too much high-speed motor traffic. Fishing must be good, with all of the drowned stumps providing cover.

Everett Lake

Created in 1962 when the Army Corps of Engineers built a flood-control dam on the Piscataquog River, Everett Lake offers pleasant paddling, picnicking, and swimming. Clough State Park manages the facilities and prohibits motors on the 150-acre lake; the only development consists of the dam and recreational facilities. Although the 250-foot-high dam looms over much of the lake, if you paddle north through the winding, marshy channels full of pickerelweed and waterlily, it will look and feel much more natural, with lots of nooks and crannies to explore.

On the marshy northeastern end, you should see great blue heron, painted turtles, and various ducks. On the larger, northwestern arm of the lake, you will find a sandy-bottomed inlet creek lined with alder and willow, but this creek is too shallow to paddle for more than a few hundred feet. Most of the lake shoreline is open and sandy, with white pine on the higher land. Many potential picnic sites dot the shores.

A common merganser casts a wary eye in our direction as we paddle past it. Use a long telephoto lens to take close-up photos without disturbing wildlife.

10 | Kimball Pond

This pristine pond located just outside Concord provides an opportunity to see raven, beaver, and various swamp species.

Location: Dunbarton, NH
Maps: *New Hampshire Atlas & Gazetteer,* Map 27: I14; USGS Goffstown
Area: 52 acres
Time: 2 hours
Habitat Type: Small, shallow, marshy pond
Fish: Largemouth bass, pickerel
Information: Forest Legacy program, www.na.fs.fed.us/legacy/legacy_places/nh/pdfs/nh_kimball_p.pdf
Camping: Greenfield State Park, Bear Brook State Park; see Appendix A, #2, #4

GETTING THERE
From I-89, Exit 1 southbound, go 5.8 miles south on Logging Hill Road (which becomes Bow Center, then Wood Hill, then Twist Hill roads), and turn right onto Morse Road. Go 0.7 mile (6.5 miles), and turn left onto Montelona Road.

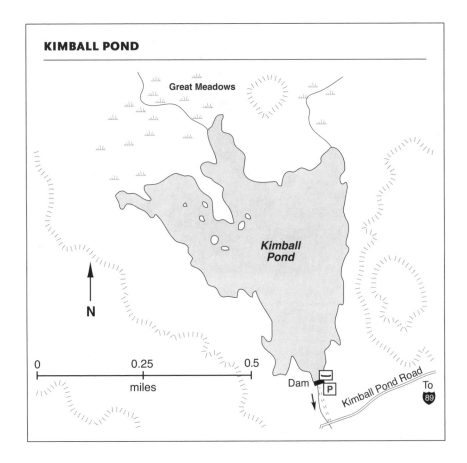

KIMBALL POND

Great Meadows

Kimball
Pond

N

0   0.25   0.5

miles

Dam

P

Kimball Pond Road

To
89

Go 0.3 mile (6.8 miles), turn right onto Kimball Pond Road, and go 0.8 mile (7.6 miles) to the access on the right. *GPS coordinates*: 43° 4.895′ N, 71° 34.520′ W.

WHAT YOU'LL SEE

This small, scenic pond, nestled among the hills just south of Concord, provides an outstanding place to paddle. Numerous marshy coves and islands await exploration, as does the Great Meadows marsh, which expands out to the north. Conifers dominate the wooded shoreline, with occasional red oak, white birch, and other deciduous trees. Conservation easements protect all of the woods surrounding the pond from development.

We portaged up into Great Meadows over a beaver dam and enjoyed the solitude, listening to ravens calling their hoarse cries off in the woods as a sharp-shinned hawk alternately flapped and glided overhead. Exploring here and in the marshy coves back on the main pond, expect to find waterlily, water celery, water shield, pickerelweed, arrowhead, and lots of other aquatic vegetation growing in profusion. Shrubs—including leatherleaf, sweet gale, buttonbush, and lots of sheep laurel—dominate the understory and the marshy islands. We found a large beaver lodge with many red oak cuttings.

We shared the pond with a couple of canoes and kayaks, but because of the islands and Great Meadows, you can get off by yourself to explore and to enjoy this wonderful, picturesque site.

11 | Turkey Pond, Little Turkey Pond, and Turee Pond

Of these popular destinations, Turee Pond receives the least traffic, and its outlet stream is a great place to look for beaver and other marsh wildlife.

Location: Bow and Concord, NH
Maps: *New Hampshire Atlas & Gazetteer,* Map 27: F14;
USGS Concord
Area: Turkey Pond and Little Turkey Pond, 339 acres; Turee Pond, 50 acres
Time: Half a day for all three ponds
Habitat Type: Shallow, scenic ponds; Turee Brook is marshy
Fish: Largemouth bass, pickerel
Camping: Greenfield State Park, Bear Brook State Park; see Appendix A, #2, #4
Take Note: Motors limited to 10 HP on Turee Pond

GETTING THERE
Turkey Pond and Little Turkey Pond, Stickney Hill Road access. From I-89, Exit 3 (northbound only), pass under I-89, and go 0.2 mile to the access, taking the second left onto Stickney Hill Road. Carry your boat along the hiking path, veering right just before the bridge, and head steeply down to the water. *GPS coordinates*: 43° 10.890′ N, 71° 37.752′ W.

Turkey Pond and Little Turkey Pond, Route 13 access. From I-89, Exit 2 southbound, go 1.1 mile south on Clinton Street/Route 13, and turn right into the unmarked access. *GPS coordinates*: 43° 10.121′ N, 71° 35.015′ W.

Turee Pond. From I-89, Exit 1 southbound, go 0.8 mile south on Logging Hill Road, and turn right onto White Rock Hill Road. Go 0.3 mile (1.1 miles),

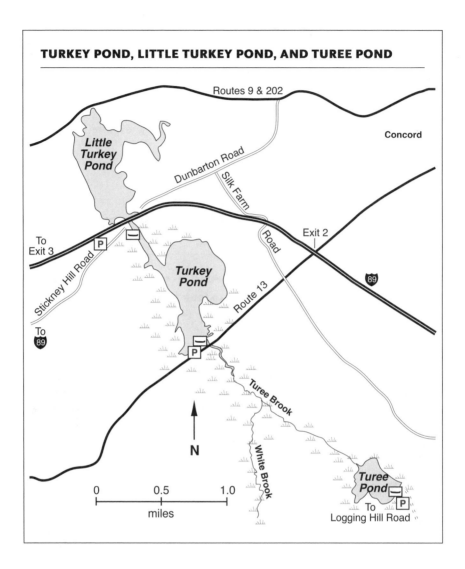

TURKEY POND, LITTLE TURKEY POND, AND TUREE POND

Routes 9 & 202

Little Turkey Pond

Dunbarton Road

Silk Farm Road

Concord

To Exit 3

Stickney Hill Road

Turkey Pond

Route 13

Exit 2

89

To 89

N

Turee Brook

White Brook

Turee Pond

To Logging Hill Road

| 0 | 0.5 | 1.0 |
miles

and turn right onto Turee Pond Road. Turn right into Bow High School, and keep right to the access. *GPS coordinates*: 43° 9.359′ N, 71° 33.046′ W.

WHAT YOU'LL SEE

Turkey Pond and Little Turkey Pond

This beautiful spot, where St. Paul's School protects much of the land on the east side, lies just outside of Concord. A wonderful biking and hiking path circles the ponds. Although I-89 bisects the ponds—and provides a fair amount of road noise—we still enjoyed paddling among the fractured granite boulders and tree-lined shores. Several tree-covered islands dot the waterways, adding to the ponds' picturesque beauty. You will find the occasional motorboat here, but we have encountered mostly canoes, kayaks, and rowing sculls at this popular recreational area during our visits.

We watched kingfishers dive for fish, fattening up for a soon-to-come journey, and studied flocks of ducks and geese that had stopped off in their fall migration. Various species of aquatic vegetation cover Little Turkey Pond, especially fragrant waterlily, yellow pond lily, and water shield.

Turee Pond

Although we enjoyed paddling on Turkey Pond and Little Turkey Pond, Turee Pond presents more of a wilderness-type experience for the adventurous paddler. At first glance, you see a small, round, seemingly uninteresting pond with lots of open water. Look carefully at the far shore, though—it is an extensive marsh with sphagnum hummocks covered with tamarack, black spruce, and red maple. If you hanker for a "wilderness" adventure right outside of Concord that includes portaging over several beaver dams, paddle northwest across the pond and down Turee Brook toward Turkey Pond, some two miles distant. We would not attempt this in times of low water.

Beaver lodges are a common sight along the shores of marshy ponds and streams.

You will paddle alone among the arrowhead and a diverse assemblage of shoreline shrubs. Red-winged blackbirds will accompany you for the distance, along with yellowthroats and swamp-loving sparrows. We hauled a large snapping turtle partially out of the water to check for leeches—it had two—and saw huge numbers of painted turtles. Several species of fern crowd the bank, along with sundew, leatherleaf, and sweet gale. One large beaver lodge we passed had so much brush stored for winter in the narrow channel that we could barely squeeze by.

As we paddled back to the access and then drove out the road, past a noisy soccer match, we reveled in the knowledge that such a wonderful and productive spot exists so close to Concord. However, do not go here unless you are willing to work at it—and probably get your feet wet.

12 | Lake Massabesic

This large, deep lake provides coves and islands for protected paddling areas. You should see loon and osprey here, and you may see beaver.

Location: Auburn and Manchester, NH
Maps: *New Hampshire Atlas & Gazetteer,* Map 22: A5; USGS Candia, Derry, Manchester North, Manchester South
Area: 2,512 acres
Time: All day
Habitat Type: Large, deep lake
Fish: Largemouth and smallmouth bass, pickerel, northern pike, perch; brook, brown, and rainbow trout
Camping: Bear Brook State Park, Pawtuckaway State Park; see Appendix A, #4, #5
Take Note: Swimming, personal watercraft, and water-skiing prohibited

GETTING THERE
From Route 101, Exit 1, go 1.6 miles south on Route 28 Bypass to the access on the left. There is also an access at the picnic area just south of the traffic circle (0.3 mile south of Route 101). *GPS coordinates*: 42° 59.281′ N, 71° 22.495′ W.

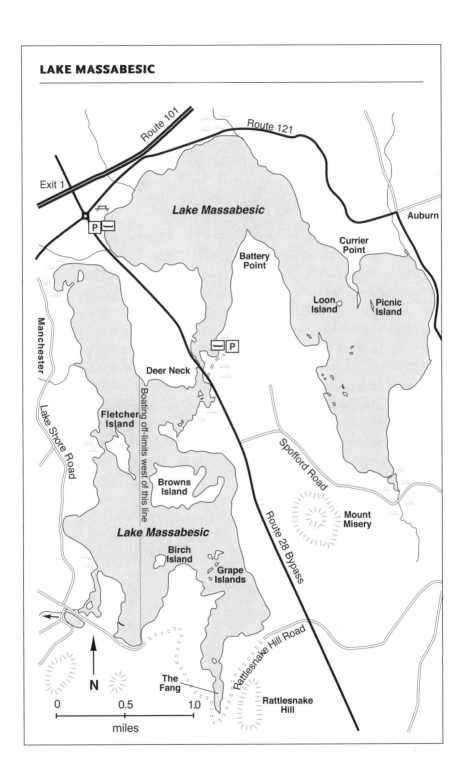

LAKE MASSABESIC

Route 101

Route 121

Exit 1

Lake Massabesic

Auburn

P

Currier
Point

Battery
Point

Loon
Island

Picnic
Island

Manchester

P

Deer Neck

Lake Shore Road

Boating off-limits west of this line

Fletcher
Island

Spofford Road

Browns
Island

Mount
Misery

Lake Massabesic

Route 28 Bypass

Birch
Island

Grape
Islands

Rattlesnake Hill Road

N

0   0.5   1.0

miles

The
Fang

Rattlesnake
Hill

WHAT YOU'LL SEE

Lake Massabesic—"the place of much water" to the Abenaki—serves as the water supply for the city of Manchester; consequently, the city prohibits swimming and water-skiing, and a portion of the lake remains off-limits to all boating. Despite this—and in part because of it—the lake offers superb paddling. The extremely clean and crystal-clear water, with its rocky bottom, supports an excellent smallmouth bass fishery. The limited development along the shore seems even less intrusive because of the prohibition on swimming. Indeed, it is a real surprise to find such a large and relatively pristine lake so close to New Hampshire's largest city.

Because of its smaller size and greater shoreline variation, we prefer paddling the lake's quieter southern section, which you reach quickly by paddling under the bridge. The generally rocky shoreline gives way to dense woods farther inland. White pine, red pine, red maple, white birch, and red oak dominate, but you will also see some black gum (*Nyssa sylvatica*) growing along the water's edge. One of the first trees to turn red in the fall, black gum's brilliant foliage really stands out. A few surviving American chestnut trees also grow here. If you visit in midsummer, you should find lots of highbush blueberry. Also keep an eye out for loons, which often nest here. Be careful not to disturb them.

The Grape Islands near the lake's southern end offer superb paddling, as does the deep cove at the southern tip called The Fang. You can also usually paddle a small marshy area near the inlet from the upper section of Massabesic, close to Route 28 Bypass. Look for great blue heron, wood duck, other assorted water birds, and possibly beaver here.

Because of the many motorboats and sailboats that ply Massabesic's waters, avoid the lake's upper end, especially on busy summer weekends. On a breezy day, explore the more protected southern end, or paddle one of the region's smaller bodies of water.

---

13 | Dubes Pond

One of the remote sections on this small, marshy pond has a great blue heron rookery. The pond also provides a great place to study carnivorous plants. Look for beaver here in the evening.

Location: Hooksett, NH

Lake Massabesic offers big waters for those seeking plenty of exercise. Do not paddle here when it's windy.

Maps: *New Hampshire Atlas & Gazetteer,* Map 28: I4; USGS Manchester North
Area: 111 acres
Time: 3 hours
Habitat Type: Shallow, marshy pond
Fish: Pickerel, perch
Camping: Bear Brook State Park, Pawtuckaway State Park; see Appendix A, #4, #5

GETTING THERE

From I-93, Exit 9 north, go 1.8 miles north on Routes 3/28, and turn right onto Route 27. Go 2.6 miles (4.4 miles) to the access on the left. Park on the opposite side of the road. *GPS coordinates*: 43° 3.984′ N, 71° 23.785′ W.

WHAT YOU'LL SEE

Dubes Pond, just a short distance from Manchester, can be described only as outstanding. The housing development along the western side that was under construction when we paddled here in April 2000 does not seem to have impinged much upon the pond. The houses perch well above the pond, with the woods as a screen.

Dubes Pond sees very little boat traffic, which is good, given the large great blue heron rookery that dominates the farthest reaches. If you paddle here when the herons nest, please stick to the edges of the pond, giving the stand of dead nesting trees in the middle a wide berth. The rookery is actually on a different pond, which has a small earthen dike separating it from the western arm of Dubes Pond. Out in the western pond, fragrant waterlily, water shield, and water celery abound in the clear water. We also saw a large snapping turtle.

Back on Dubes Pond itself, especially in the northwest, sphagnum hummocks support a large array of shrubs, but leatherleaf—with small, nondescript, bell-like flowers hanging down—appears to dominate. If you look carefully, you might find orchids growing on these hummocks. In other areas, granite boulders—some barely submerged, some out of water, some forming boulder islands—are the dominant theme. Some larger islands support stands of white pine, making this quite a picturesque pond. We found hours going by as we explored the many coves and islands.

If you paddle into the bay immediately to the right after leaving the access, you will find it choked with fragrant waterlily, with lots of round-leaved sundew

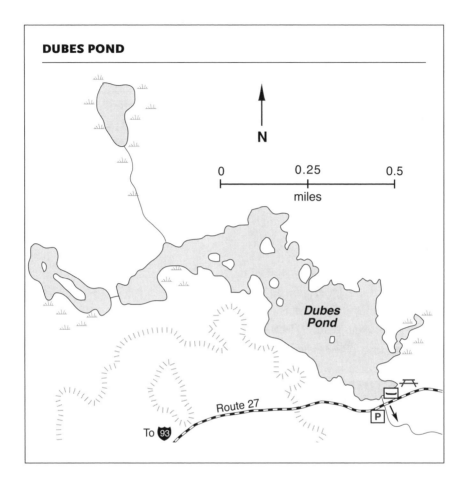

DUBES POND

0   0.25   0.5
miles

N

Dubes
Pond

Route 27

To 93

P

tufts on rotting stumps and small hummocks. The tiny carnivorous sundew, which grows in rosettes only a couple of inches across, captures hapless insects that alight on its glistening sticky hairs. The plant then secretes enzymes that help it digest the insects.

We saw another carnivorous plant growing here: yellow-flowered bladderwort. In contrast with sundew, bladderwort captures prey underwater in tiny air-filled sacs. Small aquatic organisms bump into the trigger hairs, and the sac deflates, sucking in the surrounding water and its prey.

On one excursion, as we paddled back to the access late in the day, watching beaver swim about and listening to rufous-sided towhees call from the brushy shores, we reveled in how this wild, pristine place can exist just 10 minutes from the center of New Hampshire's largest city. Let us hope that it remains wild for future generations to enjoy.

14 | Hoit Road Marsh

Maintained by New Hampshire Fish and Game, this small, shallow marsh offers a great opportunity to study ducks, geese, and other marsh animals and plants. You may also find beaver and a bald eagle here.

Location: Concord and Loudon, NH
Maps: *New Hampshire Atlas & Gazetteer,* Map 28: B1; USGS Penacook
Area: 101 acres
Time: 3 hours
Habitat Type: Shallow, marshy pond
Fish: Largemouth bass, pickerel
Information: Hoit Road Marsh Wildlife Management Area, www.wildnh.com/Wildlife/WMA_index.htm
Camping: Bear Brook State Park; see Appendix A, #4

GETTING THERE
From I-93, Exit 17, go 2.4 miles east on Hoit Road to the access on the left. Park across the road. *GPS coordinates*: 43° 17.544′ N, W71° 31.674′ W.

WHAT YOU'LL SEE
Although Hoit Road borders part of the marsh's southern edge, civilization all but disappears as you leave the access and paddle around to the left. A few cars pass at regular intervals, but they really don't intrude on the solitude once you have paddled off into one of the many arms of this wonderful and productive marsh.

Canada geese, wood duck, and possibly other ducks nest in this shallow marsh, maintained as a Wildlife Management Unit by the New Hampshire Fish and Game Department. The wetland also provides habitat for myriad other marsh birds, insects, mammals, and plants. Water shield, fragrant waterlily, pickerelweed, and other aquatic plants cover most of the surface. As these plants die back each fall, the decaying vegetation stains the water a yellow-brown. The many small islands harbor loads of sweet gale, purple iris, sheep laurel, and many other small shrubs. One large island on the northern end has a nice stand of white pine, and at the foot of the island we found a large new beaver lodge.

HOIT ROAD MARSH

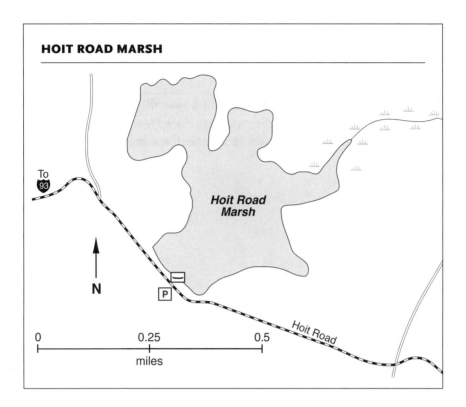

Besides numerous wood ducks, we saw a pair of Canada geese beginning to nest when we paddled here in spring. An adult bald eagle soared overhead, while numerous damselflies and dragonflies patrolled the surface. As we listened to the chorus of several frog species, we reveled in how special this place is—all the more remarkable because of its proximity to New Hampshire's capital. Its many nooks and crannies, wooded shoreline, and shrubby islands offer hours of exploration. Paddle here in the early morning or late evening when wildlife is active. Here you will be free from motorboats—and their noise, which dominates New Hampshire's larger lakes.

15 | Ballard Pond

At this small, marshy pond with a working sawmill you will find aquatic vegetation covering the pond's surface. You will likely see Canada geese, turtles, frogs, and other marsh species.

Location: Derry, NH
Maps: *New Hampshire Atlas & Gazetteer,* Map 22: E7; USGS Derry, Salem Depot, Sandown, Windham
Area: 89 acres
Time: 2 hours
Habitat Type: Shallow, marshy pond
Fish: Pickerel
Information: Ballard State Forest, Taylor Sawmill Historic Site, www.nhdfl.org/land-conservation/taylor-sawmill/
Camping: Bear Brook State Park, Pawtuckaway State Park; see Appendix A, #4, #5

GETTING THERE
From the junction of Route 28 and Route 28 Bypass just east of Derry, go 3.7 miles east on Island Pond Road to the access on the left at the old Taylor Mill. Park across the road. *GPS coordinates*: 42° 52.507′ N, 71° 14.356′ W.

WHAT YOU'LL SEE
The New Hampshire Division of Forests and Lands maintains the access at Ballard State Forest, Taylor Mill Historic Site. Ernest K. Ballard restored the site in 1940. Prior to 1865, Taylor Brook powered a reciprocating (up-and-down motion) sawmill here—later replaced by a more efficient circular saw, a technology invented by the Shakers. You may drop off your boat by the mill, but you need to park your vehicle back across the road. The second time we paddled here, we helped a small snapping turtle negotiate the traffic as we moved our vehicle.

When we paddled out on a perfectly still morning with glasslike water, a family of Canada geese cast rippling Vs as they beat a hasty retreat ahead of us. This wonderful spot, free from development, hosts many nesting waterfowl. The small millpond hides the main portion of the pond from view. Portage over

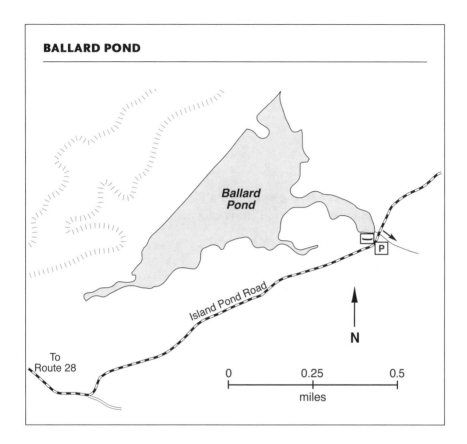

BALLARD POND

Ballard Pond

Island Pond Road

N

To Route 28

0   0.25   0.5

miles

the remains of an old concrete bridge at the end of the millpond and into a vast expanse of aquatic vegetation. We thought of Monet as we paddled through a sea of huge, fragrant waterlily blossoms during our late-August visit, but a thick carpet of aquatic vegetation hampered our explorations. Paddling here certainly would be easier in spring, before the emergent vegetation lays claim to the water's surface.

This shallow pond harbors huge amounts of aquatic vegetation that eventually dies back each fall, accumulating more rapidly than it can break down and settling to the bottom to decompose anaerobically. Your paddle may stir up methane-rich marsh gas and the sulfury smell of hydrogen sulfide. The decaying plant matter also releases tannic acids that stain the water a yellow-brown.

As we paddled by, large numbers of painted turtles and frogs dove for cover under the water shield, pickerelweed, and lily pads. If you paddle here midsummer, look for the meandering channel—most likely the old streambed that is too deep for pickerelweed—that wends its way back up the pond to the end. Finding this channel may take a few minutes, but it will make your paddling easier.

16 | Powwow River

A slow-flowing, meandering stream, the Powwow River is filled with marshland species. A rare stand of Atlantic white cedar lines the shore.

Location: Kingston, NH
Maps: *New Hampshire Atlas & Gazetteer,* Map 23: D12; USGS Kingston
Length: 2 miles one way
Time: Half a day
Habitat Type: Marshy, meandering stream, rare stand of Atlantic white cedar
Fish: Smallmouth bass, pickerel
Information: The Nature Conservancy, www.nature.org/newhampshire
Camping: Bear Brook State Park, Pawtuckaway State Park, Hampton Beach State Park; see Appendix A, #4, #5, #6

GETTING THERE
From Route 107 in Kingston, go 1.0 mile south on Route 125, and turn left onto New Boston Road. Go 0.3 mile (1.3 miles) to the access on the left. Park on either side of the road. *GPS coordinates*: 42° 54.940′ N, 71° 2.801′ W.

A cartop access is also available on Small Pox Road. *GPS coordinates*: 42° 54.756′ N, 71° 3.006′ W.

WHAT YOU'LL SEE
A sea of aquatic vegetation spreads out over a wide expanse of marsh. From the access just across the road from Powwow Pond, you can paddle a channel through the vegetation to Country Pond. Except for a power line, this marsh remains pristine, with much of the river frontage owned by The Nature Conservancy to protect a rare stand of Atlantic white cedar. The first time here, we paddled totally alone on a bright Saturday in mid-June.

It took us all morning to paddle up and back, mostly because we spent

POWWOW RIVER

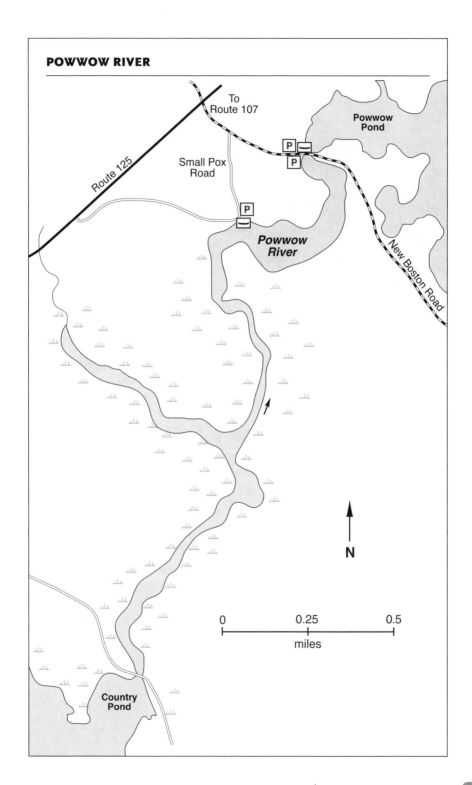

To Route 107

Powwow Pond

Route 125

Small Pox Road

P

P

P

Powwow River

New Boston Road

N

| 0 | 0.25 | 0.5 |

miles

Country Pond

A painted turtle basks in the sun's warmth to raise body temperature and boost metabolism.

time identifying much of the flora along the way and exploring side channels. Besides huge patches of fragrant waterlily, pickerelweed, water celery, water shield, and various species of sedge and pondweed, we found some nice patches of yellow crowfoot (*Ranunculus flabellaris*) in bloom. It typically has gorgeous yellow buttercup flowers, but the very finely divided underwater leaves look like those of water marigold (aster family) or coontail. In deeper water, we also found floating heart (*Nymphoides cordata*), a waterlily-like member of the gentian family, in bloom. What struck us most, perhaps, was the decidedly pinkish cast to the usually pure-white flowers of the fragrant waterlilies.

On this sunny day, painted turtles sunned themselves wherever they could clamber out of the water, and we spotted two water snakes (*Nerodia sipedon*), one of them very fat, out sunning. Bullfrogs tried to hide among the lily pads as we passed by. All the typical marsh birds appeared in profusion; we especially noted the large number of common yellowthroats calling from the brushy shores.

17 | Exeter River

Tall trees of many species form a canopy over this meandering waterway. Ducks nest in the adjacent marshes, and you may see beaver here.

Location: Exeter, NH
Maps: *New Hampshire Atlas & Gazetteer,* Map 23: B14; USGS Exeter
Length: 6 miles one way
Time: Half a day or more
Habitat Type: Meandering stream with tall deciduous canopy
Fish: Brook, brown, and rainbow trout
Information: Exeter River Local Advisory Committee, www.exeterriver.org/
Camping: Bear Brook State Park, Pawtuckaway State Park, Hampton Beach State Park; see Appendix A, #4, #5, #6

GETTING THERE
From Routes 27/101 in Exeter, go 0.7 mile south on Route 108, and turn left onto Bell Avenue. Go 0.3 mile (1.0 mile), turn left into Gilman Park, and continue to the parking area by the river. *GPS coordinates*: 42° 58.392′ N, 70° 56.579′ W.

WHAT YOU'LL SEE
Limbs of huge trees drape out over the water of this meandering, slow-moving stream. Neither we nor the several other paddlers who shared this water with us on a June Saturday could detect any current. We could not get over the size of the trees, particularly the white oak and white pine. Some of these stately trees certainly exceed 100 feet in height. High tree-species diversity kept us occupied as we identified red and white oak, basswood, beech, and shagbark hickory, among others.

Except for the campground along Route 108, which does not intrude all that much, the Exeter River corridor provides a pretty serene place to paddle. The lack of development here helps explain why we heard a continuous chorus of orioles singing their melodious song from the treetops as we paddled several miles upriver. Both the main and side channels provide opportunities for exploring.

We spotted a few different species of pondweed, one with a very long leaf lying flat along the surface of the water (look for brownish leaves with veins

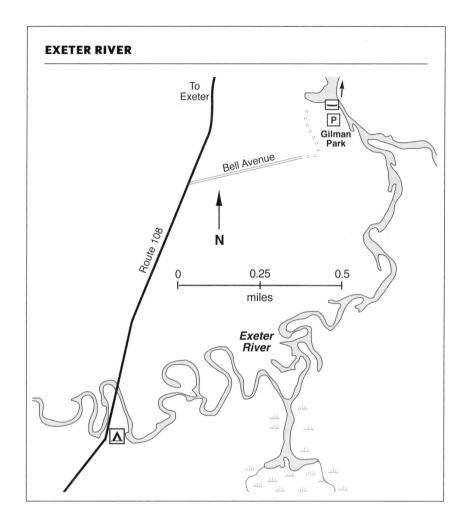

EXETER RIVER

To Exeter

Gilman Park

P

Bell Avenue

Route 108

N

| 0 | 0.25 | 0.5 |

miles

Exeter River

parallel to the leaf's long axis). Viburnum bloomed along the banks. Dead trees provided perching areas for birds and lent a somewhat somber character to the banks. Beaver cuttings crowded the shoreline in places. While pondweed seemed to dominate the water's surface near shore, buttonbush held sway on the banks. Up near Route 108, we found an escaped rose in electric bloom, with clusters of 25 or so blossoms at the end of each branch, some hanging over the water and some actually in the water. The small white blossoms of this truly gorgeous plant had a slight pink cast and a faint odor.

Bird-species diversity is also high along this lowland riverine area, so it would be a good idea to bring your binoculars, although you might have to crane your neck to catch a glimpse of the orioles and other treetop species.

18 | Pawtuckaway Lake

Despite the large number of visitors to this large lake at Pawtuckaway State Park, it is a nice place to go to see loon and great blue heron.

Location: Nottingham, NH
Maps: *New Hampshire Atlas & Gazetteer,* Map 29: I10; USGS Epping, Mount Pawtuckaway
Area: 903 acres
Time: Half a day on northern section
Habitat Type: Large lake with islands, shallow coves, and inlets
Fish: Largemouth and smallmouth bass, crappie, yellow and white perch, pickerel
Information: Pawtuckaway Lake Improvement Association, www.pawtuckawaylake.com/
Camping: On-site camping; see Appendix A, #5
Take Note: 6 MPH speed limit in Fundy Cove area; paddle elsewhere if it's windy; avoid on popular summer weekends; hiking trails, development on south end

GETTING THERE
From Route 27 in Raymond, go 5.4 miles north on Route 156, and turn left onto Deerfield Road. Go 1.9 miles (7.3 miles) to the access on the left. *GPS coordinates:* 43° 6.552′ N, 71° 8.868′ W.

WHAT YOU'LL SEE
Pawtuckaway Lake, a large body of water well known for bass fishing, boasts a highly varied shoreline with numerous coves, inlets, and islands to explore. Unfortunately, the eastern shore and the southern end suffer from heavy development and boat traffic. For the best paddling, stick to the northern end, especially Fundy Cove. There is no development in this cove and almost none around the northern end down to Log Cabin Island. South of the island, both seasonal and year-round houses dot the eastern shore and its numerous coves.

From the access, paddle south into Fundy Cove and then east into the main lake. White pine, red maple, white birch, and hemlock dominate the heavily

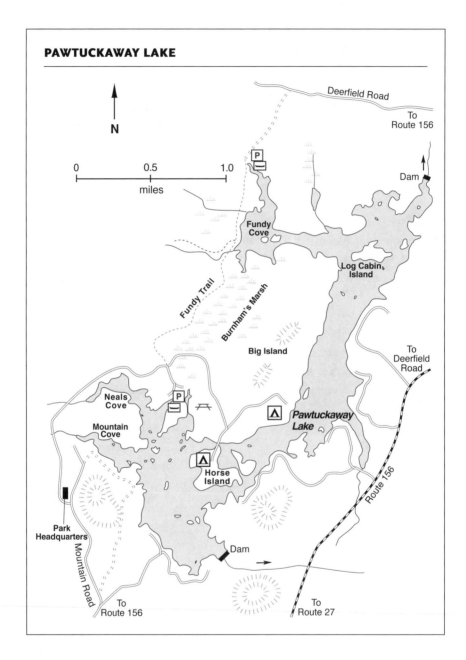

PAWTUCKAWAY LAKE

N

0   0.5   1.0
miles

Deerfield Road

To
Route 156

Dam

Fundy
Cove

Log Cabin
Island

Fundy Trail

Burnham's Marsh

Big Island

To
Deerfield
Road

Neals
Cove

Mountain
Cove

Pawtuckaway
Lake

Horse
Island

Route 156

Park
Headquarters

Mountain Road

Dam

To
Route 156

To
Route 27

wooded shoreline. The generally open understory provides easy access onto the shore for a picnic lunch. In mid- to late summer, a profusion of highbush blueberry growing along the shores may impede your progress. Most of the marshy inlets offer good birding habitat. We also saw lots of yellow bladderwort floating in the water, along with water celery, with its narrow leaves lying flat on the water's surface.

When paddling here, be careful of large rocks at or just below the surface. Out with his dog one day, Alex managed to hang himself up on a somewhat concave boulder that lurked an inch or two beneath the water's surface. He had quite a time getting off—fortunately, his dog was patient. While paddling here on another occasion in a group, we all managed to paint a few rocks.

At the lake's northeast tip, the town of Nottingham maintains a beach (unfortunately limited to residents) very near the north outlet dam (not to be confused with the south outlet dam). If you venture down to the south end, you can explore some gorgeous islands, but you will never feel very remote at the lake's southern end.

Numerous hiking trails course through the park, including the Fundy Trail, which extends from the main park road near the picnic area, along Burnham's Marsh, to the access at the lake's northern end. Farther west, trails take you over several small mountain peaks, along a unique boulder field of glacial erratics, and into Round Pond. Because of the park's popularity, we recommend that you visit before Memorial Day or after Labor Day.

CARNIVOROUS PLANTS: THE TABLE IS TURNED

Carnivorous plants thrive in New England's marshes, and their meat-eating adaptations make them one of nature's true wonders. Carnivory in plants apparently resulted from convergent evolution: the development of similar traits among unrelated species. Plant families on nearly every continent have some carnivorous species, with two common characteristics: they live in mineral-poor soils, supplementing soil nutrients with those from animals, and they use modified leaves to trap food.

Two capture strategies have evolved: active and passive. The Venus flytrap, which grows in sandy soils along the Carolina coast, uses an active capture strategy. A few others have adopted active strategies, including bladderworts (genus *Utricularia*), which form dense mats in shallow marshes. Bladderwort leaves consist of minute bladders that ingest and digest insect larvae and other organisms.

Passive capture strategies have taken two main paths. Pitcher plant—*Sarracenia purpurea*—collects rainwater in funnel-shaped leaves, and enzymes digest insects that fall into the leaves. Sundews (genus *Drosera*) form sticky rosettes that digest trapped insects with enzymes.

Although each plant—bladderwort, pitcher plant, and sundew—captures prey in a different way, they all have the same reason for doing so: in nutrient-poor marshes, absorbing minerals from insects and other prey gives them a selective advantage over other plants. Tea-colored bog water, laden with organic acids from decaying vegetation, washes out minerals. Although carbon dioxide and water remain plentiful, nitrogen, phosphorus, potassium, and other important elements get leached out or bound up in underlying layers of sphagnum and peat.

Bladderwort

Bladderwort grows in shallow waters or in shoreline muck. Look for small yellow or purple snapdragon-like flowers, leading on short stalks to carnivorous underwater bladders that form dense feathery mats, bearing hundreds of tiny (0.02- to 0.1-inch-long) bulbous traps that form the plant's leaves. The bladders have two concave sides and a trapdoor. When a small organism bumps into the door's guard hairs, the bladder's sides pop out and the door swings open, sucking in the hapless critter. This occurs in 0.002 second, followed by digestion by plant enzymes.

Mosquito larvae form the bulk of the bladderwort's diet, but the plant also ingests other larvae, rotifers, protozoans, and small crustaceans. With large prey, such as a tiny tadpole, the door closes around the organism and the plant digests only part of it. The next time the hairs get triggered, the plant ingests more of the organism, eventually sucking it all in.

Several species of bladderwort grow in New England; two species have purple flowers, and as many as ten species have yellow flowers. We usually notice these plants when we see their snapdragon-like flowers protruding a few inches above the water's surface.

Pitcher plant

The northern pitcher plant grows from British Columbia to Nova Scotia, southward through the Great Lakes region, down the eastern coastal plain, crossing the Florida panhandle to the Mississippi River. Its pitcher-shaped leaves, initially green in spring, turn purple in fall and return to green next spring. Flowering occurs in June and July, and single reddish flowers, borne on stout stalks, tower a foot above the pitcher cluster. The curved pitchers

Left: Funnel-shaped leaves of the northern pitcher plant trap insects and dissolve them with plant and bacterial enzymes, providing the plant with extra nutrients. Right: Tiny sundew leaves, modified into pads lined with sticky hairs, trap insects that are attracted by droplets that glisten in the sun.

recline, allowing rain to fall into the open hood. Stiff, downward-pointing hairs in the plant's throat keep insects from climbing back out, and the narrow funnel leaves little room for airborne escape. The upper pitcher walls sport a waxy coating, making for slippery footing. A combination of plant and bacterial enzymes degrade the unlucky insects, and their nutrients pass easily through the unwaxed surface of the lower pitcher.

Sundew

Sundew grows mainly in sphagnum bogs from Alaska to northern California, across the Canadian Rockies and plains, through the Great Lakes, north throughout Labrador, south to Chesapeake Bay, and down through the Appalachians. The same plant grows in Europe, and four species occur in New England, including the most common species, roundleaf sundew (*Drosera rotundifolia*).

Sundew averages about 3 inches across and 1 inch high, with leaves modified into flattened oval pads, covered with red, stalked glands. The smallest plants may measure only 1 inch across, making them easy to overlook. Longer glands secrete a sticky fluid, while shorter glands secrete digestive enzymes. Attracted to nectarlike secretions, insects become trapped and then digested by plant enzymes. The usually white flowers hover well above the plant's leaves, borne on slender stalks. To find sundew, look for tiny glistening drops on their traps. Look carefully on sphagnum mats for many reddish rosettes.

19 | Great Bay

You should see osprey, shorebirds, waterfowl, gulls, crabs, and whitetailed deer while paddling this large, shallow tidal estuary.

Location: Durham, Greenland, Newington, Newmarket, and Stratham, NH
Maps: *New Hampshire Atlas & Gazetteer,* Map 30: I2; USGS Newmarket, Portsmouth
Area: 4,500 acres
Time: All day
Habitat Type: Shallow estuary
Fish: Coho, chinook, Atlantic salmon; striped bass, bluefish, rainbow smelt
Information: Great Bay ecology, www.armofthesea.info; National Estuarine Research Reserve, www.greatbay.org; Squamscott River tidal chart, www.maineboats.com/tide-charts/nh
Camping: Pawtuckaway State Park, Hampton Beach State Park; see Appendix A, #5, #6
Take Note: Paddle Great Bay's smaller bodies of water under windy conditions, and check the tide table before paddling here.

GETTING THERE

Adams Point. Go north on Route 108 to Newmarket, cross the Lamprey River, turn right onto Bay Road, and go 3.9 miles to Adams Point and Jackson Lab. Look for wading birds on the other side of the road from the access. *GPS coordinates*: 43° 05.523′ N, 70° 51.90′ W.

Squamscott River. Access is off Route 108, just south of the bridge. *GPS coordinates*: 43° 2.352′ N, 70° 55.656′ W.

Depot Road. From Route 108, go 1.7 miles east on Route 33, and turn left onto Depot Road. Go 1.0 mile (2.7 miles), turn left at the T, and park across the tracks. *GPS coordinates*: 43° 3.276′ N, 70° 53.790′ W.

Newmarket/Lamprey River. Heading south, turn left off Route 108, just after crossing the bridge over the river. *GPS coordinates*: 43° 4.578′ N, 70° 55.506′ W.

WHAT YOU'LL SEE

Most of Great Bay, a large tidal estuary on the Squamscott and Lamprey rivers in southeastern New Hampshire, lies within Great Bay National Estuarine

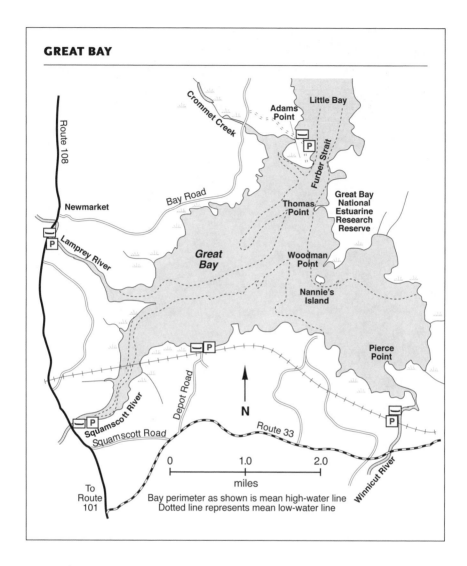

GREAT BAY

Route 108

Crommet Creek

Little Bay

Adams Point

P

Furber Strait

Bay Road

Newmarket

Great Bay National Estuarine Research Reserve

Thomas Point

Lamprey River

P

Great Bay

Woodman Point

Nannie's Island

Pierce Point

Depot Road

P

Squamscott River

N

P

Squamscott Road

Route 33

P

Winnicut River

To Route 101

0   1.0   2.0

miles

Bay perimeter as shown is mean high-water line
Dotted line represents mean low-water line

Research Reserve, which includes more than 4,000 acres of tidal waters and mud flats and some 48 miles of high-tide shoreline. Although located near Portsmouth, the bay has only sparse development, and few motorboats venture forth because of the bay's shallowness and variable water level.

The Great Bay tidal estuary—changing constantly, its shoreline migrating in and out twice daily with the tides—is quite unlike any other body of water in this book. At high tide, Great Bay swells to more than twice the low-tide size. While constant change makes it a great place to explore—one where you could spend a few days paddling—you need to take special precautions. With as much as a 9-foot difference between high and low tides, you could easily get

Canada geese and other waterfowl abound in Great Bay's waters.

stranded on mud flats as the tide goes out. Using the tide chart referenced above, time your visit to avoid paddling against strong tidal currents. Strong winds, common over the bay's great expanse, make paddling even more difficult.

Great Bay's large size provides dozens of places to explore. Among the best: Adams Point, Woodman Point, and Squamscott River inlet. To reach these from the Adams Point access, paddle south around the point that separates Great Bay from Little Bay. Because of the quite narrow channel, tidal currents can be very strong. If possible, launch from Adams Point into Great Bay as the tide comes in and return as it goes out. You can usually tell tide direction by looking at which way the boats moored at Adams Point face. The boats face upstream; thus, they face south when the tide goes out and north when the tide comes in. If you get caught fighting the tide, stay close to shore, where the current will be a lot weaker.

From Adams Point, you can paddle across Furber Strait to the Estuarine Research Reserve. Picturesque bluffs overlook the bay's eastern shore, with stands of large red pine above and rocky, seaweed-covered coves below.

Spectacular Woodman Point, at the reserve's southern tip, overlooks Nannie's Island, where common terns (a state-listed endangered species) nested as recently as 1980. Be careful of the particularly lush poison ivy at Woodman and Thomas points.

You can also explore the western shoreline southwest toward Newmarket. At high tide you can paddle into Crommet Creek, but avoid the exposed mud flats at low tide. In winter, bald eagles roost along this shore and across at the reserve. The shoreline and shallows south of Adams Point have the most productive oyster beds in New Hampshire and are often one of the only areas in the state not closed to oystering because of pollution.

The Squamscott River inlet into the bay provides another interesting area to explore. Except for the narrow Squamscott River channel, though, this entire south side of the bay consists of exposed mud flats during low tide.

At Great Bay and the surrounding salt marsh areas, you can expect to see a wide range of shorebirds (lesser yellowlegs, glossy ibis, snowy egret, American bittern, and green heron, to mention just a few), numerous species of ducks, cormorants, gulls, geese, and others. In the water, you should see horseshoe crabs, hermit crabs, oysters, and ribbed mussels. Depending on wind and water clarity, you can paddle over the shallows and watch for marine life hiding among the prolific eelgrass.

THE LOON: VOICE OF THE NORTHERN WILDERNESS

For us, no animal better symbolizes wilderness than the loon, whose haunting cry resonates through the night air on many northern lakes. The bird seems almost mystical, with its distinctive black-and-white plumage, daggerlike bill, and piercing red eyes. But like our remaining wilderness, the loon is threatened over much of its range. As recreational pressures increase, the loon gets pushed farther away. We who share its waters bear responsibility for protecting this wonderful bird.

The common loon, *Gavia immer,* a large diving bird that lives almost its entire life in water, visits land only to mate and to incubate eggs. Although adapted remarkably well to water, the loon has difficulty on land because its rearward leg position, which aids in swimming, prevents it from walking. Unlike most birds, the loon has solid bones, allowing it to dive to great depths. Its internal air sac controls how high it floats; by compressing this sac, a loon can submerge gradually, with barely a ripple, or swim with just its head above water.

Its heavy body and rearward legs make takeoff difficult. A loon may require a quarter-mile to build up enough speed to lift off, and it may have to circle a small lake several times to gain enough altitude to clear nearby hills. When migrating, a loon flies rapidly—up to 90 MPH—but cannot soar.

The loon generally mates for life and can live for 30 years. The female lays two eggs in early May, and both male and female incubate the moss-green eggs. It builds its nest close to shore—where a passing paddler can scare birds away and a motorboat wake can flood the nest with cold water. The loon most often nests on islands to hide the eggs from predators.

Loon chicks hatch covered in black down and usually enter the water a day after hatching. Chicks grow quickly on a diet of small fish and crustaceans; by two weeks of age, they reach half the adult size and can dive to relatively deep lake bottoms. Loon chicks remain dependent on their parents for about eight weeks and do not fly until 10 to 12 weeks of age. After leaving the nest, loons return to land after three or four years, when they reach breeding age. Young mature at sea, having followed their elders to saltwater wintering areas.

New Hampshire and Vermont loons have achieved only moderate nesting success in recent years. Surveys by the Loon Preservation Committee in 1991 showed 102 pairs nesting in New Hampshire, producing 85 surviving

The common loon, *Gavia immer*, requires relatively untrammeled waters to survive.

chicks. In 2000, with 150 nesting pairs, 128 chicks survived. In 2006 through 2008, only about 100 chicks survived each year, and Squam Lake loons suffered precipitous declines in numbers of adults and in surviving offspring.

Vermont Institute of Natural Science surveys showed only 15 pairs nesting in Vermont in 1991, producing 14 surviving young. In 1998, 30 chicks survived. By 2006, 58 nesting pairs resulted in 56 surviving chicks. Because of the fourfold increase in breeding success, Vermont removed the loon from its endangered species list in 2005.

Population recovery has proceeded slowly. Besides encroachment by humans and nest predation by raccoons and skunks, loons suffer mortality in many other ways. According to the Tufts University Wildlife Veterinary Clinic, chicks die primarily from collisions with personal watercraft and motorboats, and adults die primarily from ingestion of lead sinkers and jigs. As with other diving waterfowl, ingestion of lead sinkers and shotgun pellets poisons loons.

Because paddlers can easily disturb loons, watch for warning displays during nesting season, early May through mid-July. If a nest fails, loons may try up to two more times, although the later a chick hatches, the lower its chance of survival.

The loon has lived in the Northeast longer than any other bird—an estimated 60 million years. Let's make sure this wonderful species remains protected so that future generations may listen to its enchanting music on a still, moonlit night.

2 | CENTRAL NEW HAMPSHIRE

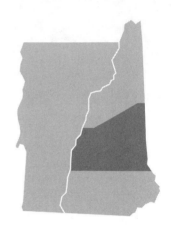

The central band across the state includes the Lakes Region, New Hampshire's premier summer recreation destination. Squam Lake, where Oscar-winning *On Golden Pond* was filmed, sees a lot of boat traffic on its 6,800 acres; numerous islands provide some protection from the wind as well as nesting sites for its large loon population. When the wind blows, visit the much smaller ponds near Squam Lake: Garland, White Oak, and Copps ponds and Manning and Wicwas lakes.

Central New Hampshire also provides other biologically rich areas to paddle, including The Bay on the Blackwater River, Danbury Bog, Campton Bog, and McDaniels Marsh. When we really want to view wildlife and study plants, we head to one of these four bodies of water. Wildlife abounds there, and you have a good chance of seeing beaver, otter, muskrat, mink, deer, and moose.

If you are looking for seclusion and don't mind a hike to the put-in, we recommend Mountain Pond in the White Mountain National Forest. Besides Mountain Pond, the Conway region offers four other paddling destinations, each with gorgeous views of the White Mountains' tall peaks.

In the central region's southeast corner, we enjoy paddling the Suncook and

Salmon Falls rivers, but if we had time to paddle just one southeast body of water, we would choose the Merrymeeting River because of its marshy character and the opportunity to see wildlife.

On the state's west side, Grafton Pond draws many visitors, and justifiably so. If you arrive and see a paking area full of cars, we would visit nearby McDaniels Marsh instead.

20 | McDaniels Marsh

McDaniels Marsh is a shallow, pristine marsh filled with aquatic plants and marshland birds and animals. Expect to see waterfowl and turtles, and you might see beaver, otter, and moose.

Location: Springfield, NH
Maps: *New Hampshire Atlas & Gazetteer,* Map 34: E3; USGS Enfield Center
Area: 513 acres
Time: Half a day
Habitat Type: Extensive pristine, shallow marshland
Fish: Pickerel, perch
Information: McDaniels Marsh Wildlife Management Area, www.wildlife.state.nh.us/Wildlife/WMAs/WMA_McDaniels_Marsh.htm
Camping: Mt. Sunapee State Park; see Appendix A, #7

GETTING THERE

From I-89, Exit 13, go 0.7 mile south on Route 10, and turn left onto Route 114. Go 4.8 miles (5.5 miles), and turn left onto George Hill Road. Go 2.2 miles (7.0 miles) to the access, at the junction with Bog Road. *GPS coordinates*: 43° 31.498′ N, 72° 4.763′ W.

WHAT YOU'LL SEE

Just a short distance north of popular Sunapee Lake, McDaniels Marsh offers an out-of-the-way, less-traveled treasure for the quietwater paddler. Beautiful, layered hillsides rise in the distance as you wend your way through islands toward the line of spruce and tamarack that marks the end of this deceptively long marsh. Pitcher plant grows in profusion on sphagnum-laden hummocks

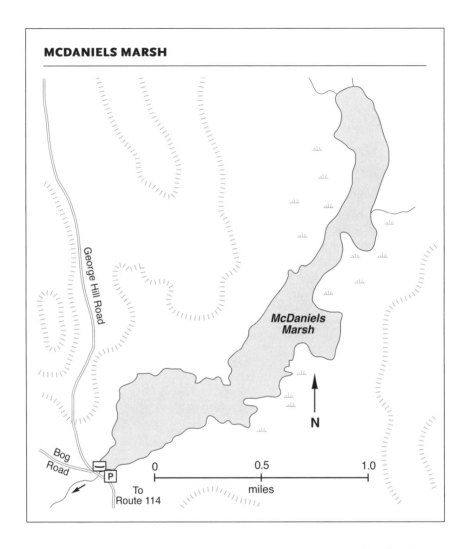

MCDANIELS MARSH

George Hill Road

McDaniels Marsh

N

Bog Road

P

To Route 114

0   0.5   1.0
miles

and floating islands. A small spillway raises the water level a few feet, barely submerging many stumps and granite boulders.

Paddling here in April, before aquatic vegetation emerged from dormancy, we easily reached the far corners of the marsh, teeming with bird life—especially wood ducks that had recently returned to the dozens of nesting boxes placed by the state. Hundreds upon hundreds of migrating tree swallows darted about, replenishing their energy stores from a dense hatch of emergent insects.

In August, vegetation covered perhaps 90 percent of the water surface, restricting paddling somewhat, but we found the experience just as enjoyable. Blooming pickerelweed bathed the marsh's northeastern end with a sea of

A shrubby shoreline and shallow waters provide ideal habitat for marshland species. Look for beaver, otter, and moose here.

lavender. Billowy white blooms of tawny cotton grass (*Eriophorum virginicum*), a member of the rush family (round stems), formed equally beautiful expanses of white. At this time of year, one has to work to find a passage to the northeast, but we found a relatively open, winding channel all the way to the far end (about two miles from the access). You also will see extensive areas of cattail and occasional arrowhead with its waxy white blooms. Floating-leaved and submergent plants also grow here in profusion: white and yellow pond lily, water shield, pondweed (*Potamogeton spp.*), bur-reed, water celery, and bladderwort.

Look for insectivorous pitcher plant and sundew on the thick sphagnum hummocks, along with the dominant leatherleaf, sweet gale, and steeplebush (*Spiraea*). You may also find rose pogonia orchids—we spotted a cluster of several dozen of the delicate pink flowers on one boggy hillock. Paddling through the shallow, universally ruddy brown, tannin-stained water, expect to stir up the mucky bottom, releasing strong-smelling marsh gas that results from incomplete decomposition of the abundant vegetation in this highly productive marsh.

Besides the usual mix of red maple, birch, white pine, balsam fir, and spruce, toward the northeast end tamarack dominates the boggy shore. Along with wood duck and tree swallow, we saw Canada goose, blue-winged teal, black duck, great blue heron, red-winged blackbird, kingfisher, osprey, yellow-rumped warbler, chickadee, phoebe, and cedar waxwing; we heard a winter wren singing from the dense underbrush. Painted turtles abound, along with beaver activity and quite a few abandoned lodges. We were surprised to see a painted turtle on a cool November afternoon. You also may be lucky enough to spot a moose or an otter, both frequently seen here.

21 | Grafton Pond

Clear, deep water and scenic hillsides make this gorgeous pond one of the premier paddling destinations in New Hampshire. It's common to see loon, osprey, great blue heron, beaver, otter, mink, and moose here.

Location: Grafton, NH
Maps: *New Hampshire Atlas & Gazetteer*, Map 34: C3; USGS Enfield Center
Area: 235 acres
Time: All day
Habitat Type: Deep lake with rocky islands and marshy inlets, forested hillsides
Fish: Smallmouth bass, pickerel
Information: Society for the Protection of New Hampshire Forests, www.spnhf.org
Camping: Mt. Sunapee State Park; see Appendix A, #7
Take Note: Gasoline motors prohibited

GETTING THERE
From Enfield Center, go 2.2 miles south on Route 4A, and turn left onto Bluejay Road. Go 0.9 mile (3.1 miles), and bear right at the fork onto Grafton Pond Road. Go 0.9 mile (4.0 miles), and turn right onto the access road. *GPS coordinates*: 43° 34.805′ N, 72° 2.741′ W.

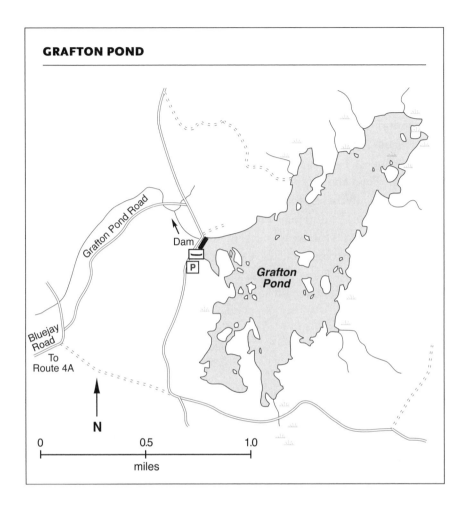

GRAFTON POND

Grafton Pond Road

Dam

P

Grafton Pond

Bluejay Road

To Route 4A

N

| 0 | 0.5 | 1.0 |

miles

WHAT YOU'LL SEE

Grafton Pond stands out as one of the finest paddling destinations in New Hampshire. The Society for the Protection of New Hampshire Forests, a very effective land preservation organization, protects a large portion of the surrounding land. A few houses perch along the western tip, but these do not detract too much from the lake's remoteness, because one can easily paddle out of view. Although small, the lake seems much larger, owing to the many deep inlets, hidden marshy areas, and rocky islands that provide ideal underwater habitat for the many smallmouth bass that inhabit the pond. One could spend a few days exploring all the nooks and crannies of this lake and hiking some of the surrounding old logging roads.

A natural lake, enlarged and deepened with a dam, Grafton Pond has a maximum depth of 66 feet with quite clear water. Along the generally rocky, heavily wooded shoreline, conifers dominate (balsam fir, red spruce, white pine, and hemlock), while farther from shore, red maple, white birch, and other hardwoods are more common. Granite outcroppings occur throughout most of the lake, some of which sport sizable mica crystals. (Watch out for granite boulders lurking just beneath the surface!) Birdwatchers may want to stay closer to the shallow, marshy areas. Islands and peninsulas jutting out into the lake provide wonderful grassy picnic sites.

Grafton Pond abounds with wildlife. Usually, a few loon pairs nest here. With many relatively safe islands for nesting (away from raccoons and other predators) and a plentiful food supply, Grafton affords a great spot for them. During a late-April visit, we also saw quite a few wood duck, osprey, and an assortment of more common lake and pond birds: black duck, mallard, great blue heron, kingfisher, and others. Quite a few beaver lodges occur along the northern shore, and one should keep an eye out for otter and mink.

Conifer-clad shores provide a scenic backdrop for paddling the crystal-clear waters of Grafton Pond.

22 | Clark Pond

This great paddling destination draws mostly fishermen and nesting loons. Its relatively remote location provides a good opportunity to see beaver.

Location: Canaan, NH
Maps: *New Hampshire Atlas & Gazetteer,* Map 38: I3; USGS Canaan
Area: 97 acres
Time: 2 hours
Habitat Type: Small, shallow pond with swampy inlet
Fish: Smallmouth bass, pickerel, yellow perch

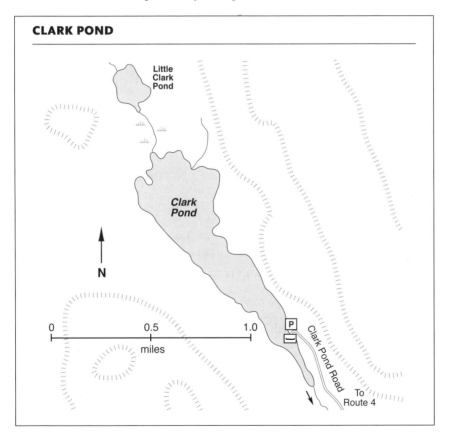

CLARK POND

GETTING THERE

From Route 4 in Canaan, go 3.4 miles north on Canaan Street/Switch Road, and turn right onto River Road. Go 2.0 miles (5.4 miles), and turn left onto Clark Pond Road. Go 1.3 miles (6.7 miles), and go right at the fork. Go 0.4 mile (7.1 miles) to the access. *GPS coordinates*: 43° 43.566′ N, 72° 3.408′ W.

WHAT YOU'LL SEE

Although Clark Pond gets a fair amount of traffic from anglers and has a few summer cottages along its shores, paddling on this long, narrow pond provides ample rewards. We most enjoyed the end farthest from the access, especially where the inlet from Little Clark Pond enters. You can paddle back in and portage over beaver dams. In early July, along with all of the typical bog plants, we found lots of rose pogonia orchid and cranberry in bloom.

The hillsides surrounding the pond harbor mostly deciduous trees, along with occasional tall white pine. Sweet gale grows thickly along the shores, particularly in swampy areas. We found lots of horsetail (*Equisetum*), pickerelweed, pondweed, water shield, bur-reed, sundew, narrow-leaved cattail, and fragrant waterlily at the northwest end. Two loons competed with the less successful anglers when we paddled here.

23 | The Bay/Blackwater River

This wide, marshy, slow-flowing river section offers a great opportunity to get some exercise for several hours without having to worry too much about wind. Expect to see plenty of waterfowl, and possibly beaver, here.

Location: Andover and Salisbury, NH
Maps: *New Hampshire Atlas & Gazetteer,* Map 35: I9; USGS Andover
Length: 5 miles one way
Time: 6 hours
Habitat Type: Shallow, marshy, slow-flowing river
Fish: Brook, brown, and rainbow trout

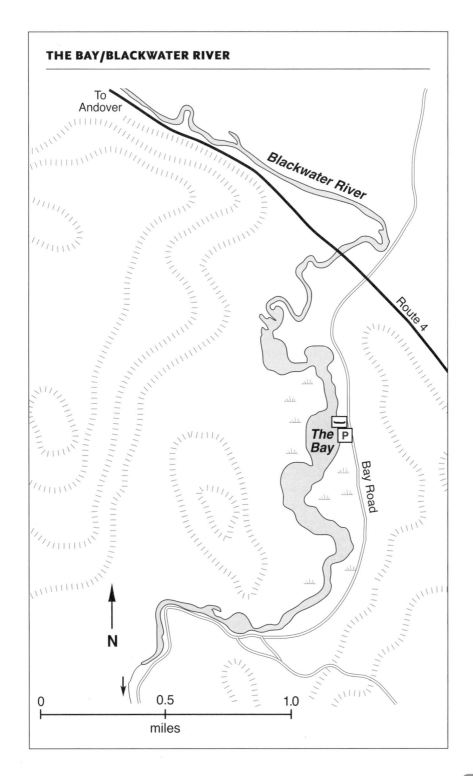

THE BAY/BLACKWATER RIVER

To Andover

Blackwater River

Route 4

The Bay

P

Bay Road

N

0   0.5   1.0

miles

GETTING THERE

From Route 11 in Andover, go 1.8 miles east on Route 4, and turn right onto easy-to-miss Bay Road. Go 0.7 mile (2.5 miles) to the access on the right. *GPS coordinates*: 43° 24.701′ N, 71° 46.587′ W.

WHAT YOU'LL SEE

This wide, marshy section of the Blackwater River harbors substantial amounts of wildlife. The mating calls of frogs and toads in spring create a primeval feeling at this wonderful place. Silver maple dots the shrubby shoreline, while pickerelweed and pondweed cover much of the water's surface. If you paddle upstream and go under the bridge, you will find some truly huge silver maple with bifurcated trunks. The winged samaras of the silver maple, the largest of the maple seedpods, serve as an important food source for squirrels and other wildlife.

Although a few houses occupy the shore, not much in the way of human presence impinges on this waterland, which provides an important breeding ground for mallard, black duck, and wood duck. If you paddle here in the early morning or evening, expect to see beaver swimming about.

Designed for ocean paddling, sea kayaks offer speed and ease of paddling and appear frequently on New England's lakes and ponds.

24 | Danbury Bog

Aquatic vegetation rules the surface of this extensive shallow marsh. In addition to the abundant waterfowl, you're likely to see great blue heron, turtles, deer, muskrat, and beaver here.

Location: Danbury, NH
Maps: *New Hampshire Atlas & Gazetteer,* Map 35: E8; USGS Andover, Danbury
Length: 2 miles one way
Time: 4 hours
Habitat Type: Shallow marsh
Fish: Pickerel, perch
Information: New Hampshire Fish and Game Department
www.wildlife.state.nh.us/Wildlife/WMAs/WMA_Danbury_Bog.htm

GETTING THERE

From Route 4 in Danbury, go 1.0 mile east on Route 104, and turn right onto Gould Hill Road. Go 0.3 mile (1.3 miles) to the access on the right. *GPS coordinates*: 43° 31.043′ N, 71° 50.480′ W.

We prefer to put in 1.0 mile (2.3 miles) farther along, where the road bisects the bog. *GPS coordinates*: 43° 30.155′ N, 71° 50.640′ W.

WHAT YOU'LL SEE

If you want to get away from the personal watercraft and water-skiers that frequent central New Hampshire's larger lakes, head to Danbury Bog Wildlife Management Area, where aquatic vegetation rules the water. Although picker-elweed and yellow pond lily dominate, expect to find water shield, pondweed, sedge, and dozens of other aquatic species growing in profusion, all cleverly designed to keep out boats with motors. This area does not see much traffic; during the two times we paddled here, we saw only one canoe and one rowboat.

With mist burning off the water as we paddled out early one morning, we listened to deer snort from the reeds as they sloshed off through the marsh. We had hoped to see moose, but neither time that we paddled here did we have any luck. We had to content ourselves with the deer, a profusion of painted

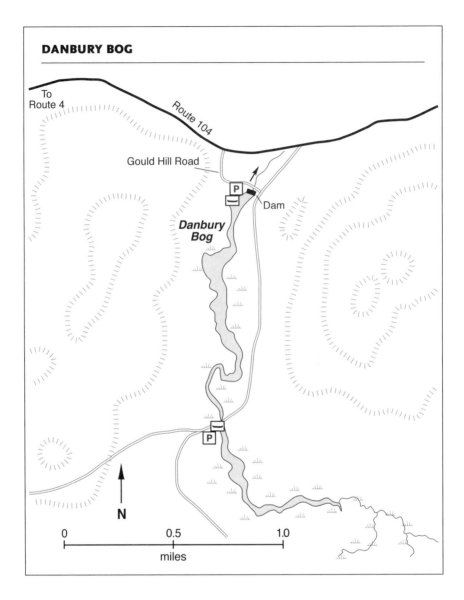

DANBURY BOG

To Route 4

Route 104

Gould Hill Road

P

Dam

Danbury Bog

P

N

0   0.5   1.0

miles

turtles, countless wood ducks, and myriad other wildlife and plant life. We saw black duck, blue-winged teal, great blue heron, and all of the usual marsh birds, including a bittern out in full view, goldfinch, and three swallow species.

This extraordinary, wonderful spot lies just north of Ragged Mountain, and you can paddle up into the foothills, portaging over a couple of beaver dams. We watched a beaver slam its broad tail on the water as it dove out of sight and saw muskrats harvest grass. Watch out for rocks poking up from the dark water

When the wind blows on the region's big lakes, paddle the more placid waters of Danbury Bog or other small ponds.

as you paddle through the limited open channel of this vast wetland. One could spend a great deal of time exploring this marsh, identifying the birds, mammals, and aquatic plants and the shrubs along the shoreline. We found the best wildlife viewing to be at dawn and in the late afternoon.

25 | Campton Bog

With the scenic White Mountains as a backdrop, this pristine bog offers one of the best opportunities in New Hampshire to see wildlife. Look for waterfowl, moose, otter, beaver, mink, muskrat, and deer here amid the huge variety of marshland plants.

Location: Campton, NH
Maps: *New Hampshire Atlas & Gazetteer,* Map 39: F11; USGS Plymouth
Length: 3 miles one way
Time: 4 hours
Habitat Type: Long, narrow, shallow bog
Fish: Brook trout
Camping: Lafayette Campground; see Appendix A, #15

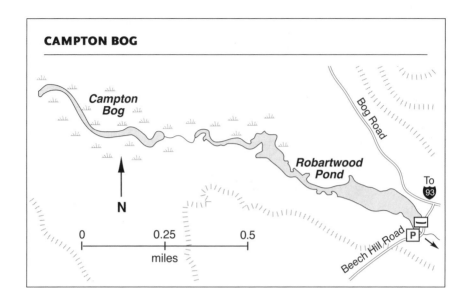

CAMPTON BOG

Campton Bog

Robartwood Pond

Bog Road

To 93

Beech Hill Road

P

N

| 0 | 0.25 | 0.5 |

miles

GETTING THERE

From I-93, Exit 27, go 2.3 miles west on Bog Road, and turn left onto Beech Hill Road. Go 0.1 mile (2.4 miles) to the access on the right. Do not block the fire hydrant. *GPS coordinates*: 43° 48.659′ N, 71° 42.222′ W.

WHAT YOU'LL SEE

This extraordinary pond, just off I-93, lies at the southern foot of the White Mountain National Forest. Peaks that rise more than 1,000 feet above the pond border it immediately to the north and west. Many channels, some kept open by beaver, wend their way back from the dam on this long, narrow pond. Near the back of the pond, we surprised a beaver paddling around in the middle of the day, a sure sign that this pond gets little boat traffic. A relatively high beaver dam on the west end supports a large expanse of water, also worth exploring.

Some black spruce and red maple have encroached on the boggy high ground crowded with shrubs. Look for round-leaved sundew on the sphagnum mats, and take note of the small leaves and flowers of the yellow pond lily. As we paddled the length of this weed-choked pond, our attention focused on the pondweed, water shield, fragrant waterlily, iris, sweet gale, and lots more. A bald eagle feeding along the shore surprised us as it took flight.

With a flock of cedar waxwings wheeling overhead, tree and barn swallows skimming the water's surface, and wood thrushes calling from the understory, we found ourselves reluctant to leave this aquatic wonderland. As we paddled back to the access, we wondered what was next—maybe a moose? Although the bog provides excellent moose habitat, we contented ourselves with wonderful scenery, myriad aquatic plants, a beaver that slapped the water with its tail as it dove out of sight, and the majestic bald eagle.

26 | Wicwas Lake

This popular fishing spot in New Hampshire's Lakes Region provides calmer water than nearby larger lakes. Expect to see loon, waterfowl, great blue heron, deer, muskrat, and possibly beaver.

Location: Meredith, NH
Maps: *New Hampshire Atlas & Gazetteer,* Map 35: B14; USGS Winnisquam Lake
Area: 328 acres
Time: 5 hours
Habitat Type: Lake with islands and inlets
Fish: Largemouth and smallmouth bass, crappie, perch, pickerel
Camping: White Lake State Park; see Appendix A, #8
Take Note: Personal watercraft prohibited

GETTING THERE
From I-93, Exit 23, go 4.8 miles east on Route 104, and turn right onto Meredith Center Road. Go 1.0 mile (5.8 miles), and turn right onto Chemung Road. Go 1.1 miles (6.9 miles) to the access on the right. *GPS coordinates*: 43° 36.287′ N, 71° 33.044′ W.

WHAT YOU'LL SEE
In spite of development around parts of the shoreline and some motor-boat traffic, Wicwas Lake still offers some of the best paddling in the Lakes Region. Lots of shoreline variation, a number of beautiful islands, several marshy inlets, and a reputation for excellent bass fishing make Wicwas an excellent choice, except on the busiest summer weekends. It offers enough room for a full day of relaxed exploring. We chose to include this lake over nearby Pemigewasset because Wicwas suffers from less road noise and sees fewer motorboats.

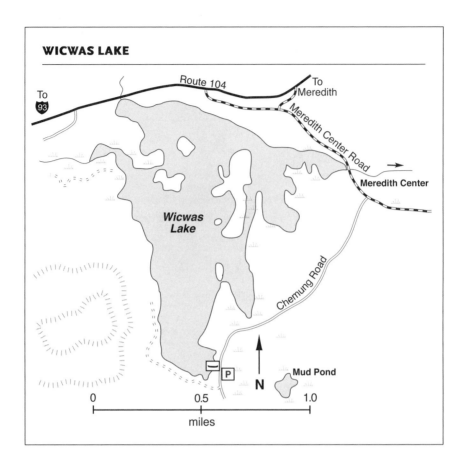

WICWAS LAKE

Route 104

To Meredith

To 93

Meredith Center Road

Meredith Center

Wicwas Lake

Chemung Road

P

N

Mud Pond

0   0.5   1.0

miles

White pine, hemlock, and various hardwood species cover the heavily wooded shores. Most development occurs along the lake's southern arm near the access, although the northern shore along Route 104 also has a few dozen houses. The eastern section, especially the deep inlet behind the large island, provides the most remote paddling. We could just barely paddle around the marshy eastern side of the island the two times that we paddled here, once in late May and once in late August in a high-water year. With a lot more pond vegetation or a slightly lower water level, that channel would not be navigable. On the other side of the island, a stand of tall red pine harbors a pleasant picnic spot on a large granite slab that extends into the lake.

Although we saw no bass anglers, we did see kingfishers and loons fishing. We know that smallmouth bass inhabit these waters because we saw a dead one, more than a foot long, by the access. Another notable sighting: the water celery, growing in some fairly deep water, had very long thin stems.

A paddler heads out from the Wicwas Lake access on a calm day. Look for loon and other waterfowl here.

27 | White Oak Pond

You can see loon and many marshland species, including the occasional beaver, while visiting this small, shallow pond.

Location: Holderness, NH
Maps: *New Hampshire Atlas & Gazetteer,* Map 39: I14; USGS Holderness
Area: 291 acres
Time: 3 hours
Habitat Type: Shallow pond
Fish: Pickerel, yellow perch
Camping: White Lake State Park; see Appendix A, #8
Take Note: Motors limited to 7.5 HP

GETTING THERE
From Route 113 in Holderness, go 1.8 miles east on Routes 3/25 to the access on the right. *GPS coordinates*: 43° 43.386′ N, W71° 33.555′ W.

From Meredith, go north on Routes 3/25 to the access on the left, 2.9 miles past the junction with Route 25B.

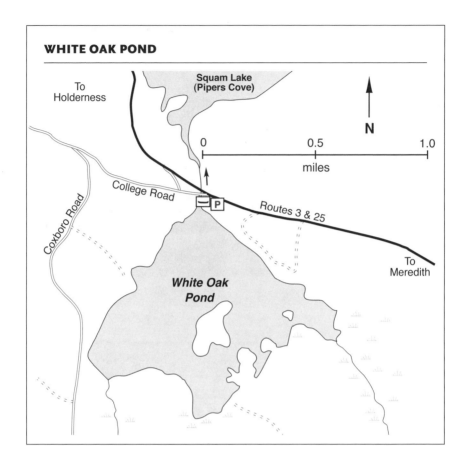

WHITE OAK POND

To Holderness

Squam Lake (Pipers Cove)

N

0   0.5   1.0
miles

College Road

Coxboro Road

Routes 3 & 25

P

White Oak Pond

To Meredith

WHAT YOU'LL SEE

Of the small Lakes Region ponds, White Oak remains one of our favorites. For starters, the state prohibits outboard motors larger than 7.5 HP. The few houses along the shore have small docks with canoes on racks, rather than huge docks jutting out into the lake with behemoth powerboats tied up waiting to be released. The lake seems tranquil and relaxed. On a Memorial Day weekend, we saw only one other boat, a solo canoe.

About a dozen unobtrusive houses dot the shoreline, primarily along the northeastern and western shores. Several privately owned islands, including a quite large one, provide extra shoreline to explore. The heavily wooded shoreline harbors white pine, red oak, red maple, and a few hemlock stands. After quite a bit of looking, we found a white oak, even though this area is pretty far north for white oak; in fact, the specimen we found was sickly. We also found a variety of ferns, with huge stands of royal and cinnamon ferns along the shore and dense carpets of various wood ferns farther up the banks.

At times of high water, one can paddle up the inlet creek on the pond's marshy eastern end, winding through cattails, old beaver lodges, mossy hummocks, and thick marsh—ideal habitat for all sorts of birds. We paddled about a half-mile up this inlet, surrounded by a peacefulness broken only by the singing of warblers, marsh wrens, and red-winged blackbirds. Out on the main lake, we watched a pair of loons from a distance.

28 | Squam Lake

The White Mountains form the backdrop for this large, gorgeous lake. Although it has some development, including on-site camping, and sees a lot of boat traffic, it retains a substantial loon population.

Location: Center Harbor, Holderness, Moultonborough, and Sandwich, NH
Maps: *New Hampshire Atlas & Gazetteer,* Maps 39: I14, 40: H1; USGS Center Harbor, Center Sandwich, Holderness, Squam Mountains
Area: 6,765 acres
Time: All day or longer
Habitat Type: Large, deep lake
Fish: Largemouth and smallmouth bass, landlocked salmon, lake and rainbow trout
Information: Squam Lakes Association, 603-968-7336, www.squamlakes.org; Squam Lakes Natural Science Center, 603-968-7194, www.nhnature.org
Camping: See description below
Take Note: Personal watercraft prohibited; always wear a PFD; expect motorboat traffic; paddle elsewhere under windy conditions

GETTING THERE
Belknap Woods, Dog Cove access. From Routes 3/25, go 0.9 mile east on Route 25B to the hard-to-see access to Dog Cove on the left. Park on either side of the road and carry your boat down a short trail to the water. *GPS coordinates:* 43° 42.173′ N, 71° 30.191′ W.

Piper Cove access. From Route 113 in Holderness, go 1.6 miles east on Routes 3/25 to the Squam Lake Association headquarters on Piper Cove. The parking fee in 2009 was $5. *GPS coordinates:* 43° 43.499′ N, 71° 33.75′ W.

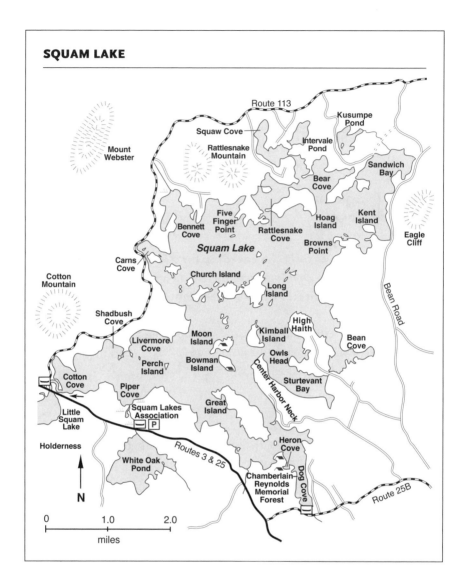

SQUAM LAKE

Route 113

Kusumpe Pond

Squaw Cove

Mount Webster

Rattlesnake Mountain

Intervale Pond

Sandwich Bay

Bear Cove

Five Finger Point

Hoag Island

Kent Island

Eagle Cliff

Bennett Cove

Rattlesnake Cove

Browns Point

Squam Lake

Carns Cove

Church Island

Long Island

Bean Road

Cotton Mountain

Shadbush Cove

High Haith

Moon Island

Kimball Island

Bean Cove

Livermore Cove

Owls Head

Perch Island

Bowman Island

Cotton Cove

Center Harbor Neck

Piper Cove

Sturtevant Bay

Little Squam Lake

Squam Lakes Association

Great Island

P

Holderness

Heron Cove

Routes 3 & 25

White Oak Pond

N

Chamberlain-Reynolds Memorial Forest

Dog Cove

Route 25B

0   1.0   2.0
miles

Alternate trail to the Rattlesnakes. From Routes 3/25 in Holderness, go 5.5 miles north on Route 113 to the parking area on the left. Cross the road, and walk 100 feet back toward Holderness. The hike up to West Rattlesnake lookout is about 1.0 mile and takes roughly half an hour.

WHAT YOU'LL SEE

Squam Lake, one of New Hampshire's real treasures, remains one of our favorite lakes for an extended visit. This large, highly varied lake boasts dozens of islands, deep coves, and marshy inlets to explore. One could easily paddle

A panoramic vista awaits you from the top of West Rattlesnake Mountain. The trail starts at Five Finger Point at the lake's northern end.

every day for a week and still not effectively explore the entirety of its 60-mile shoreline and all of the islands. Clean, crystal-clear water and sandy white beaches make for ideal swimming. Squam Lake, the setting for the film *On Golden Pond*, has its drawbacks, however. A fair amount of development crowds the shoreline and many of the islands. Although dreaded personal watercraft are banned, heavy motorboat traffic can make paddling unenjoyable, and even dangerous, in summer. If you decide to do a moonlight paddle, carry a bright flashlight to warn away oncoming motorboats.

Squam Lake also suffers from strong winds that can arise quickly and generate waves large enough to swamp an open boat. The wake from a big motorboat can amplify the wind-formed waves, compounding the problem. To reach some of the islands, including Moon and Bowman, you have to cross a mile or more of open water. Use great caution on Squam, and paddle elsewhere during adverse weather conditions.

In addition to the gorgeous setting and the myriad coves and shorelines to explore, Squam Lake boasts a huge loon population. Biologists and volunteers have recorded loon numbers since 1975, when 26 adult loons fledged six chicks. The population built slowly and reached 60 by 2000. By demarcating nest sites with pylons, providing artificial islands for nest sites, and making some coves off-limits to boats, naturalists may be able to assist the loons in sustaining this large population. Another positive step occurred when the New Hampshire Fish and Game Department banned lead sinkers, effective January 1, 2000, after an ingested lead sinker killed a bald eagle at Lake Umbagog; according to the Tufts University Wildlife Veterinary Clinic, lead poisoning causes more than 50 percent of loon mortality on its breeding grounds.

After a 50-year absence, bald eagles began nesting here in 2003 and fledged ten young by 2009. The Squam Lakes Natural Science Center (on Route 113, Holderness, a great place to visit, especially with children) and the New Hampshire Electric Cooperative have erected an osprey nest on a 60-foot pole to try to encourage osprey to nest here again.

Among the usual mixed hardwoods, white pine, red pine, and hemlock that lace the heavily wooded shores and islands, you will see a few unusual species, such as black gum (*Nyssa sylvatica*), whose leaves turn a brilliant crimson early in fall, and some huge, ancient specimens of more common trees. Beautiful stands of mountain laurel grace some islands and peninsulas. In the marshy coves, look for buttonbush, with its unusual round white flowers.

Because private citizens own most of the islands and surrounding land, you may want to concentrate your exploring in three primary areas with natural areas open to the public: Five Finger Point, Chamberlain-Reynolds Memorial Forest, and Moon and Bowman islands. Although just as beautiful as these public-use areas, the private areas—remarkably—remain largely free of No Trespassing signs. If we refrain from abusing private land, perhaps those shoreline trees can remain sign-free. Of course, we should not abuse public-access areas either.

On the lake's northern shore, the University of New Hampshire owns Five Finger Point, which offers deep coves, sandy beaches, marshy inlets, and forest trails to explore. From here, you can hike up the two steep knolls—the Rattlesnakes—that overlook the lake. The exposed rock outcropping on West Rattlesnake affords a superb view of the lake.

Rattlesnake and Squaw coves, to the east and north of Five Finger Point, enjoy protection from wind and represent the only parts of Squam Lake off-limits to water-skiing.

Picnicking is allowed on portions of Hoag Island; however, overnight camping and fires are prohibited.

The New England Forestry Foundation owns the 157-acre Chamberlain-Reynolds Memorial Forest, adjacent to Dog Cove and managed by the Squam Lakes Association. An extensive network of trails courses through this area, including a raised boardwalk through the swamp. The area, alive with birds, also supports some hemlock and pine more than 2 feet in diameter and more than 300 years old. A dock juts out on each side of nearby Heron Cove; a very nice, although heavily used, beach is located just around the peninsula from Heron Cove.

The Squam Lakes Association (www.squamlakes.org) maintains several camping areas on the lake: five near the southernmost tip of the lake in the Chamberlain-Reynolds Memorial Forest, two on Moon Island, and four on Bowman Island. These areas include both small sites (6-person) and group sites (12-person). The camping fee is per site, not per person, and reservations must be made in advance.

Heron Cove contains the most isolated campsite, situated on a point of land above the cove, nestled beneath tall hemlock and white pine, carpeted with soft pine needles and ringed with mountain laurel and blueberry bushes. It includes a composting toilet, a fire ring, a small dock, and room for several tents. Because of the surrounding marshy area, you can reach the campsite only by boat.

Moon and Bowman Islands support the most exciting camping spots for the serious paddler. The islands, purchased by the Squam Lakes Association in 1986 and 1994, harbor several tent sites. Short walks lead to a number of beautiful beaches—which Alex's daughters, ages 1 and 4, enjoyed for many hours during a four-day stay. Although paddling across open water can be hazardous, Moon and Bowman islands are wonderful places for kids.

If you plan to do much paddling here, buy a copy of the waterproof Squam Lake Chart, published by the Squam Lakes Association and available at a number of area stores, as well as through the association. The one-page map in this book lacks sufficient detail for a lake this size.

---

29 | Garland Pond

Set among scenic hillsides, Garland Pond offers protected waters to paddle. Look for water marigold among the many aquatic plants. This is a good location for wood duck, great blue heron, and muskrat, and you might see moose, beaver, and otter.

Location: Moultonborough, NH
Maps: *New Hampshire Atlas & Gazetteer,* Map 40: H4; USGS Center Harbor, Center Sandwich

Area: 120 acres

Time: 2 hours, more if you paddle the inlet stream

Habitat Type: Shallow, marshy pond with beaver-dammed inlet stream

Fish: Smallmouth bass, pickerel, yellow perch

Information: The Nature Conservancy, www.nature.org/newhampshire

Camping: White Lake State Park; see Appendix A, #8

Take Note: Gasoline motors prohibited

GETTING THERE

From Route 109 in Moultonborough, go 0.6 mile southeast on Route 25, and turn right on easy-to-miss Garland Pond Road. Go 0.1 mile (0.7 mile) to the sometimes swampy parking area on the right; carry your boat 100 feet to the water. *GPS coordinates*: 43° 44.963′ N, 71° 24.411′ W.

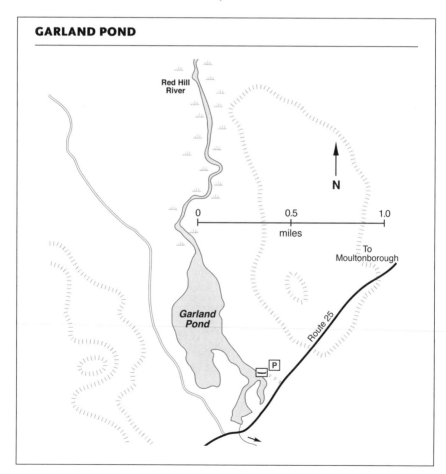

GARLAND POND

WHAT YOU'LL SEE

When the wind whips up waves on nearby Squam Lake, try Garland Pond instead. Because few people know about it, because no gasoline motors are allowed, and because The Nature Conservancy protects it, Garland Pond retains a wild, untrammeled feeling. Beautiful hillsides surround it, and the only house blends unobtrusively into the western hillside. Some road noise intrudes from Route 25, but that pretty much disappears as you paddle into the pond's northern reaches.

A diverse mix of deciduous trees dominates the hillsides and hovers over the shrubby shoreline. The usual pond vegetation, including rare water marigolds (*Megalodonta beckii*), provides ample places to hide for the many wood ducks that breed here. They scurried off into the brushy vegetation upon our approach. We watched a muskrat harvest yellow pond lily fronds as we listened to wood thrushes calling from the hillsides. To explore the area fully, you will have to portage over several beaver dams. A great blue heron rookery must be nearby, as we spotted many of these stately birds patrolling the marsh for fish, snakes, frogs, and more. As we listened to the yellowthroats calling from the sweet gale in the northern boggy area, a garter snake slithered into the water, and iridescent green damselflies with black wingtips lit on vegetation protruding from the water's surface.

30 | Copps Pond

Aquatic vegetation covers this small, shallow pond that harbors many frogs, turtles, and ducks.

Location: Tuftonboro, NH
Maps: *New Hampshire Atlas & Gazetteer,* Map 40: K7; USGS Melvin Village
Area: 180 acres
Time: 2 hours
Habitat Type: Small, shallow marsh pond
Fish: Pickerel, brook trout
Camping: White Lake State Park; see Appendix A, #8

GETTING THERE

From Route 25 in Moultonborough, go 8.4 miles south on Route 109, and turn left onto Route 109A. Go 0.2 mile (8.6 miles), and turn right onto the unmarked dirt access road. *GPS coordinates*: 43° 40.751′ N, 71° 16.985′ W.

WHAT YOU'LL SEE

In this region of New Hampshire, with many deep, clear lakes dotted with vacation homes, Copps Pond provides a pleasant alternative, especially on a windy day when you are looking for a more protected spot. With no boat ramp and huge mats of floating vegetation, you shouldn't have to contend with motorboats. A highway department building and storage sheds on the northern side, along Route 109A, represent the only development on the pond.

Really more of a marsh than an open body of water, Copps Pond—part of a wildlife management area—provides a great spot for birdwatching and plant identification. By mid-July, vegetation covers about 80 percent of this small pond's surface, with at least three different species of waterlily (water shield, fragrant waterlily, and yellow pond lily), pickerelweed, sedge, rush, and cattail. We also saw beautiful (and relatively rare) rose pogonia orchid and sundew on floating sphagnum mats. A number of wood duck nesting boxes surround the pond, which provides superb habitat for numerous species of waterfowl.

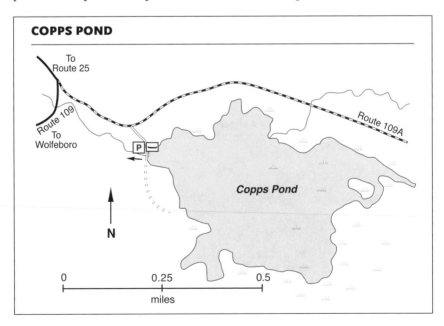

31 | Manning Lake

Scenic hillsides overlook this small, crystal-clear natural lake. Look for loons and possibly beaver and otter at this popular destination.

Location: Gilmanton, NH
Maps: *New Hampshire Atlas & Gazetteer,* Map 36: F5; USGS Gilmanton Iron Works
Area: 202 acres
Time: 3 hours
Habitat Type: Small, natural lake
Fish: Largemouth and smallmouth bass, pickerel, perch, brook trout
Take Note: Avoid on popular summer weekends

GETTING THERE

From Route 11 in Alton, go 5.9 miles west on Route 140, and turn right onto Crystal Lake Road. Go 3.1 miles (9.0 miles), and stay straight onto Guinea Ridge Road. Go 1.9 miles (10.9 miles), and turn right onto Manning Lake Road. Go 0.5 mile (11.4 miles) to the access on the right. *GPS coordinates:* 43° 28.990′ N, 71° 20.808′ W.

WHAT YOU'LL SEE

A few miles south of Lake Winnipesaukee, as the crow flies, Manning Lake (also known as Guinea Pond) stands out among places to paddle in central New Hampshire because of its crystal-clear water and the sandy bottom along much of the shoreline. The presence of numerous freshwater mussels provides evidence of the water's purity. Only a dozen or so houses dot the lake's shore, but you should expect to share the water with motorboats on busy summer weekends.

Nestled between Guinea Ridge to the south and the much taller Belknap Mountains to the north, Manning Lake enjoys a spectacular setting. Unlike the vast majority of lakes in Vermont and New Hampshire, Manning is totally natural. White pine, hemlock, red oak, basswood, red maple, highbush blueberry, and witch hazel—a fascinating low-growing tree that blooms in the late fall—grow along the shore. Large granite boulders dot some stretches of shore-

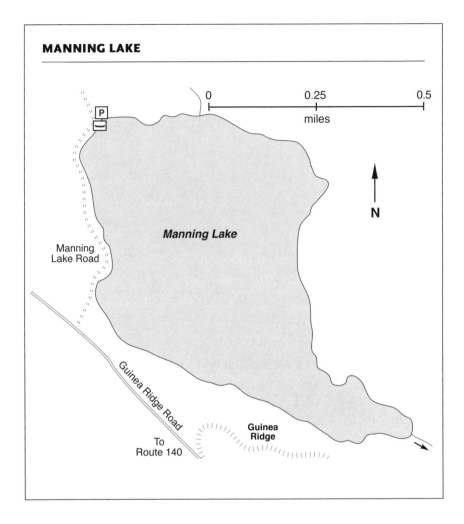

MANNING LAKE

Manning Lake

Manning Lake Road

Guinea Ridge Road

To Route 140

Guinea Ridge

0   0.25   0.5
miles

N

line, although vegetation comes right down to the water's edge around most of the shore. The sandy bottom drops off quite rapidly in some areas, reaching a maximum depth of 56 feet.

You can paddle leisurely around the perimeter of Manning Lake in a couple of hours. Of course, you should plan for a lot more time if you want to try a little bass fishing or enjoy some swimming. In the early morning or late evening, you should see a beaver or two, and perhaps an otter.

Scenic hillsides surround Manning Lake and its crystal-clear waters. Look for loon, beaver, and otter here.

32 | Suncook River

Protected inlets, bays, and islands abound on this impounded section of the Suncook River. It's a great place to study marshland plants.

Location: Barnstead, NH
Maps: *New Hampshire Atlas & Gazetteer,* Map 36: K7; USGS Pittsfield
Area: 672 acres
Time: 4 hours
Habitat Type: Shallow reservoir with bays and inlets
Fish: Largemouth and smallmouth bass, pickerel, white perch, rainbow trout
Camping: Bear Brook State Park, Pawtuckaway State Park; see Appendix A, #4, #5
Take Note: Stay away from the lower section on popular summer weekends.

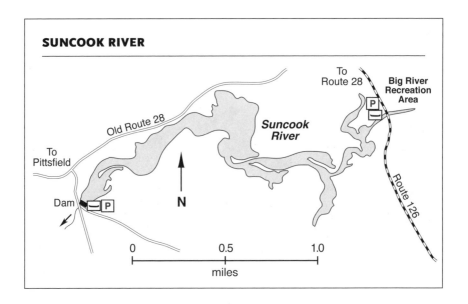

SUNCOOK RIVER

To Route 28

Big River Recreation Area

Old Route 28

Suncook River

To Pittsfield

Dam

N

Route 126

0   0.5   1.0

miles

GETTING THERE:

From Route 107 in Pittsfield, go 3.5 miles north on Route 28, and turn right onto Route 126. Go 0.6 mile (4.1 miles) to the Big River Recreation Area on the right, next to the police station. *GPS coordinates*: 43° 20.292′ N, 71° 15.592′ W.

WHAT YOU'LL SEE

The access is actually on Big Creek, which flows into the Suncook River. Plan to spend most of your time in the upper regions of the Suncook River (eastern end), including Big Creek, because once you paddle downstream to Old Route 28, houses line the shore and boat traffic picks up. Of course, if you want the exercise, you can paddle all the way down to the dam in Barnstead, which impounds this section of the Suncook, and back. We suggest that you avoid popular summer weekends. At any time in summer, we prefer the upper reach, with its many protected bays, inlets, and channels around islands.

This impoundment is one of the few we have paddled that includes large amounts of floating heart (*Nymphoides cordata*), a diminutive member of the gentian family. Its small heart-shaped leaves, about an inch across, are borne singly on long tendrils. Most aquatic plants are relegated to water shallower than about four feet; floating heart normally grows in much deeper water. Each stem can bear a few small white flowers in midsummer.

What struck us most about this area is the interesting mix of habitats: flowing and still water, protected bays and open water, mature forests and shrubby islands, marshes and deeper water. One could spend hours identifying the shrubs—alder, viburnum, elderberry, and so on—as well as both floating and emergent aquatic plants.

33 | Marsh Pond and Merrymeeting River

Contending with some road noise is worth it because of the myriad plants and animals on these bodies of water. Look for muskrat, beaver, and otter here, along with many other typical marshland species.

Location: Alton and New Durham, NH
Maps: *New Hampshire Atlas & Gazetteer,* Map 37: H9; USGS Alton
Area/Length: Marsh Pond, 389 acres; Merrymeeting River, 5 miles one way
Time: Marsh Pond, 3 hours; Merrymeeting River, 5 hours—longer if you paddle up Coffin Brook
Habitat Type: Shallow, marshy pond and river
Fish: Largemouth bass, pickerel
Information: Merrymeeting Marsh Wildlife Management Area, www.wildlife.state.nh.us/Wildlife/WMAs/WMA_Merrymeeting_Marsh.htm
Take Note: Gasoline motors restricted to 6 HP on Merrymeeting River

GETTING THERE

Western section. From Spaulding Turnpike, Exit 15, go northwest on Route 11. From the Old Route 11 crossing, go 1.6 miles north on Route 11 to the access on the left. *GPS coordinates*: 43°26.011′ N, 71°10.254′ W.

Marsh Pond. From the Old Route 11 crossing, go 1.2 miles, and turn right onto Depot Road. Go 0.3 mile (1.5 miles), and turn left onto Main Street. Go 0.6 mile (2.1 miles), and turn right onto Merrymeeting Lake Road. Go 1.5 miles (3.6 miles) to the access at the bridge. *GPS coordinates*: 43° 27.562′ N, 71° 10.626′ W.

WHAT YOU'LL SEE

The Merrymeeting Marsh Wildlife Management Area offers superb quietwater paddling. Busy Route 11 bisects the U-shaped section described here. We enjoyed paddling both sections, although the western part feels wilder— if you can ignore the Route 11 road noise. One could spend hours paddling

MARSH POND AND MERRYMEETING RIVER

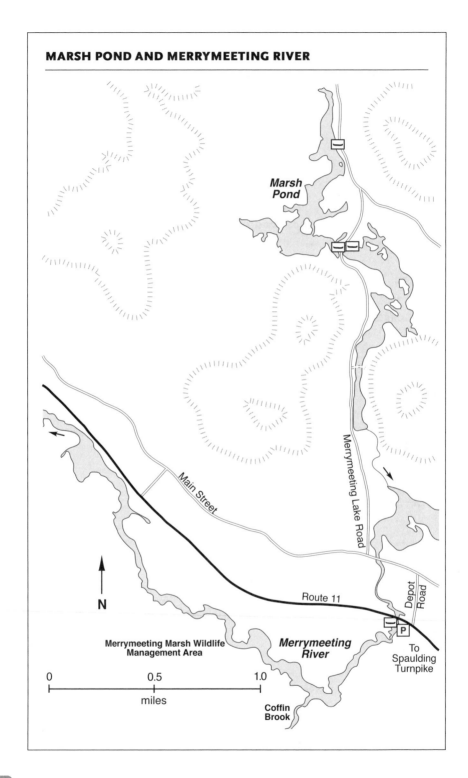

Marsh Pond

Merrymeeting Lake Road

Main Street

N

Route 11

Depot Road

P

Merrymeeting Marsh Wildlife Management Area

Merrymeeting River

To Spaulding Turnpike

0   0.5   1.0
miles

Coffin Brook

Beautiful swamp rose, *Rosa palustris*, grows along the shores of many New England marshes.

this waterway, absorbed in the marsh's biologically rich wonders.

The section west of Route 11 wends its way through seas of aquatic vegetation for more than 5 sinuous miles, by far the best section to paddle. You can escape much of the road noise by paddling up Coffin Brook, which takes off left about a half-mile from the access. Pickerelweed guards the narrow channel through the wide expanse of marsh. The shoreline, off in the distance, begins with low brush followed by white pine. All of the usual pond vegetation occurs here in profusion, along with the usual marsh birds, including loads of ducks. As we paddled back to the access with the sun setting over the marsh, a beaver slapped the water with its broad tail, as if to send us on our way so that the nighttime creatures could hold sway.

On the eastern side, deciduous trees and some scattered white pine form a backdrop, while narrow-leaved cattail, bulrush, pickerelweed, waterlily, sweet gale, sheep laurel, and many other shrubs populate the shoreline. Aquatic plants choke the water with vegetation. Watch for the typical marsh denizens, including beaver, muskrat, bullfrog, wood and black ducks, great blue heron, kingfisher, red-winged blackbird, song sparrow, yellow warbler, and eastern kingbird.

We found tree swallows nesting colonially in a martin house, apparently unaware that tree swallows do not nest colonially but instead chase other tree swallows away. To encourage bluebird nesting, people often put up nesting boxes in pairs. The more aggressive tree swallows occupy the first box and then chase away other tree swallows, leaving the companion box free for bluebirds, which the swallows ignore. Apparently, the tree swallows we saw had not heard of this theory. One hypothesis we formed to explain their atypical behavior was that the sheer volume of available insects in this productive marsh may overwhelm the swallows' aggressive territorial tendencies.

Development increases as you approach the southern end, so we prefer to paddle elsewhere and not go south of the small access bridge across the narrows. On the north side of Merrymeeting Lake Road, only a couple of houses impinge on the wild character of Marsh Pond; we prefer paddling here to paddling on the south side of the road. This extensive marsh boasts tons of aquatic vegetation and islands thick with tamarack.

34 | Salmon Falls River

Aquatic vegetation rules the surface of this 2-mile impounded section of the Salmon Falls River, which forms the lower border between New Hampshire and Maine. You will likely see lots of ducks and turtles, along with muskrat and possibly beaver.

Location: Milton, NH
Maps: *New Hampshire Atlas & Gazetteer,* Map 37: E14; USGS Great East Lake, ME/NH
Length: 2 miles one way
Time: 3 hours
Habitat Type: Small, marshy reservoir
Fish: Smallmouth bass

GETTING THERE

From Milton Mills, with the U.S. Post Office on the right, go 0.3 mile straight uphill, and turn right onto Hopper Road. Go 0.5 mile (0.8 mile) to the access, just over the bridge on the left. *GPS coordinates:* 43° 30.570´ N, 70° 57.246´ W.

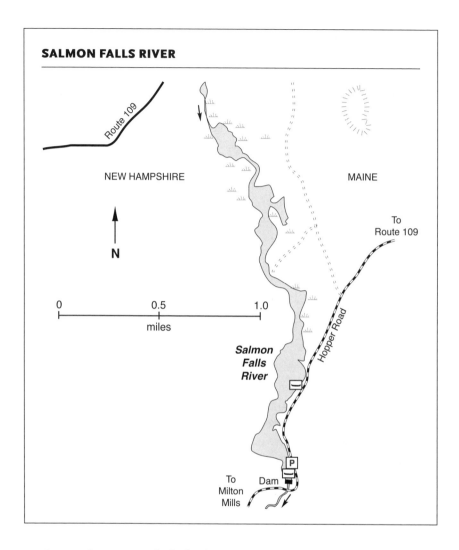

SALMON FALLS RIVER

NEW HAMPSHIRE

MAINE

N

To
Route 109

0   0.5   1.0
miles

Salmon
Falls
River

Hopper Road

Route 109

P

To   Dam
Milton
Mills

A second access avoids the backyards and submerged boulders; go 0.5 mile (1.3 miles) farther to the access on the left. *GPS coordinates:* 43° 30.954´ N, 70° 57.180´ W.

WHAT YOU'LL SEE

The Salmon Falls River forms the boundary between lower Maine and New Hampshire. Although a small stream for most of its considerable length, it widens to paddleable proportions north of a dam in Milton Mills.

Although this river section runs for only about two miles, it seems much longer. The channel meanders aimlessly through endless acres of aquatic vegetation, with some beautiful patches of floating heart, with its diminutive waterlily-like leaves. The huge amount of underwater structure supports healthy fish populations, with some huge smallmouth bass lurking under the lily pads.

If you enjoy exploring pond life among the lily pads, pickerelweed, arrowhead, sedge, and rush, paddle here. In places, vegetation masks the main channel; while what looks like a widened channel dead-ends, the real channel snakes through a dense stand of pickerelweed.

The last time we paddled here, we had to carry over a new beaver dam about a mile from the access. In addition to seeing a new beaver lodge, we saw muskrat, many ducks, kingfisher, hundreds of red-winged blackbirds, and many dragonflies and damselflies. In the upper reaches, lots of tamarack grow out of sphagnum hummocks.

The dam access has more parking, but if you put in at the upper site, you will avoid paddling through the backyards of two houses. Once you're past these, the evidence of human civilization is slight until you reach the upper stretch of this small reservoir. If you put in up above, you'll also avoid the barely submerged rocks that choke the lower section. Go slowly there.

35 | Cooks Pond and Cooks River

Set amid bear oak and pitch pine barrens, this trip offers a view of Mount Chocorua and the possibility of seeing moose and beaver.

Location: Madison, NH
Maps: *New Hampshire Atlas & Gazetteer,* Map 41: E9; USGS Ossipee Lake
Length: 1.5 miles one way
Time: 2 hours
Habitat Type: Tiny pond with short, marshy river section
Fish: Smallmouth bass, pickerel
Information: The Nature Conservancy,
www.nature.org/newhampshire
Camping: White Lake State Park; see Appendix A, #8

GETTING THERE
From Route 16 in West Ossipee, go 2.2 miles north on Route 41, and turn right onto East Shore Road. Go 1.2 miles (3.4 miles), and turn right onto Lead Mine

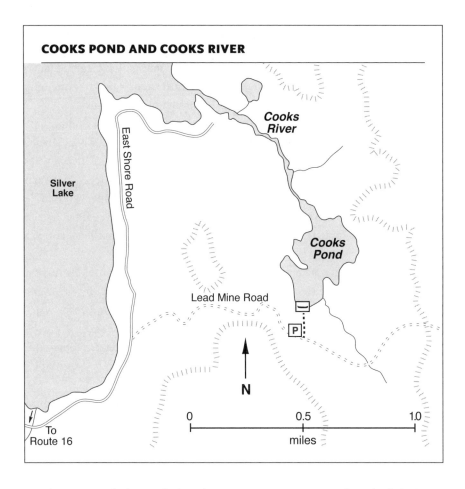

COOKS POND AND COOKS RIVER

Road. Go 0.6 mile (4.0 miles) to the easy-to-miss access trail on the left. Carry your boat 100 yards to the pond. *GPS coordinates*: 43° 51.265′ N, 71° 9.260′ W.

WHAT YOU'LL SEE

Driving up Route 41 toward Silver Lake, note the pitch pine along the road, particularly on the right (east) as you pass by the West Branch Pine Barrens, protected by The Nature Conservancy. The extensive stands of pine and shrubby, fern-clad understory bear a striking resemblance to the long-leaf pine forests of the rural south. As you drive down Lead Mine Road, you can see at road cuts the sand and gravel soil that supports this vegetation regime.

In 2008, The Nature Conservancy also acquired a 355-acre parcel that surrounds Cooks River and the north end of Cooks Pond. It includes 130 high-quality pitch pine barrens acres and extensive pine-oak forests.

Occasional fires maintain the dominant pitch pine (*Pinus rigida*)-bear/scrub oak (*Quercus ilicifolia*) plant community, but centuries of fire suppression and land development have caused this habitat to become globally rare. That is why The Nature Conservancy rated the Ossipee Pine Barrens—the last remaining in New Hampshire—second nationally of 80 key acquisition targets.

Paddling out from the access onto Cooks Pond, note that shoreline pine gives way to mostly deciduous trees on the hillsides. Dense stands of shrubs dominate the boggy shore; we noted quite a bit of sheep laurel. Three houses hover above the pond's shore, the only development in evidence between the road and Silver Lake, about a mile downstream. Don't expect to paddle too quickly down the winding channel through the pickerelweed; we had to negotiate a newly constructed beaver dam that raised the water level about a foot and a half.

Along the shallow waterway, a broad expanse of marsh provides habitat for everything from frogs to moose; we saw tracks of the latter in many places along the banks. Aquatic vegetation—pickerelweed, pondweed, water celery, and more—gives way to cattail, reed, and grass along the shore. Note the very short-needled black spruce, red maple, and dead trees on the sphagnum hummocks, along with pitcher plant and sundew. The few small sugar maples along the left shore must get pruned frequently by beaver.

Passing through the winding channel as you near Silver Lake, Mount Chocorua and surrounding peaks pop into view, making this a magical place to paddle.

36 | Chocorua Lake

Mount Chocorua forms the immediate backdrop for this small, shallow scenic lake. Although it's a popular recreation site and sits beside busy Route 16, motors are banned, making it a pleasant place to paddle.

Location: Tamworth, NH
Maps: *New Hampshire Atlas & Gazetteer,* Maps 40: C7, 41: C8; USGS Silver Lake
Area: 222 acres
Time: 3 hours

Habitat Type: Scenic, shallow lake with a couple of marshy inlets
Fish: Smallmouth bass, pickerel, perch, brook and brown trout
Information: Chocorua Lake Association, www.chocorualake.org/
Camping: White Lake State Park; see Appendix A, #8
Take Note: Motors prohibited

GETTING THERE

From Route 113 in Chocorua, go 2.1 miles north on Route 16, and turn left onto Old Route 16, one-way south to the access. Non-Tamworth residents must park within the first 0.1 mile. Another access exists at the picnic area at the south end. *GPS coordinates*: 43° 54.335′ N, 71° 13.964′ W.

WHAT YOU'LL SEE

Chocorua Lake, a pleasant spot for a morning or afternoon paddle, nestles beneath Mount Chocorua, one of New England's most picturesque and most photographed mountains. The 222-acre lake remains off-limits to motors, so you will only have to contend with road noise from Route 16, which runs along the lake's eastern side. At the southern end, you can paddle

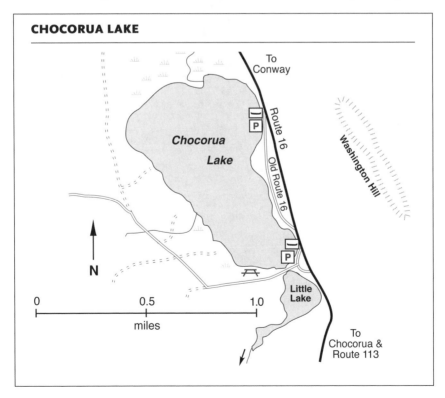

CHOCORUA LAKE

Chocorua Lake

To Conway

Route 16

Old Route 16

Washington Hill

N

0   0.5   1.0
miles

Little Lake

To Chocorua & Route 113

Nestled below scenic Mount Chocorua, 222-acre Chocorua Lake is off-limits to motorboats.

under a low bridge to get into adjoining Little Lake, smaller and more protected, but with more development.

Birdwatchers should explore the several marshy areas on Chocorua and
the more extensive marshy areas and two beaver lodges on Little Lake.
Conservation land, open to the public, covers the lake's eastern and northern
sides. You will find a great picnic area with big granite-slab tables and wooden
benches built into the large pine trees near the passage between the two lakes.
Huge white pine, red pine, and red oak add a wonderful backdrop to the lake's
eastern side. Brook trout fishing is supposed to be quite good at the lake's inlet
and outlet.

Beware of strong winds that descend from the mountains to the northwest, creating hazardous conditions. Watch for clouds building near Mount
Chocorua's craggy peak, possibly a sign of gale-strength winds to follow. The
second time here, we got drenched.

37 | Conway Lake

You will likely see loons, get a view of the White Mountains, and if you paddle in the early morning or evening, you may see moose and beaver.

Location: Conway and Eaton, NH
Maps: *New Hampshire Atlas & Gazetteer,* Map 41: A11; USGS Conway
Area: 1,298 acres
Time: All day
Habitat Type: Large, deep lake with numerous inlets and some marshy coves
Fish: Smallmouth bass, pickerel, landlocked salmon, rainbow trout
Camping: White Lake State Park; see Appendix A, #8
Take Note: Personal watercraft prohibited; avoid on windy days; always wear a PFD

GETTING THERE

Southern hand-carry access. From Route 16 in Conway, go 4.4 miles south on Route 153, and turn left onto Potter Road. Go 1.4 miles (5.8 miles) to the access. *GPS coordinates*: 43° 55.882′ N, 71° 3.649′ W.

Northern access. From Route 302 in Center Conway, go 0.7 mile south on Mill Street to the access on the right; parking is on the left. *GPS coordinates*: 43° 59.136′ N, 71° 3.133′ W.

WHAT YOU'LL SEE

This large lake, with its varied, lightly developed shoreline, marshy coves, and pine-covered islands, sits in a gorgeous backdrop just southeast of the White Mountains and offers excellent paddling. On a breezy day, particularly with wind from the south or west, one should paddle the southern end, which forks into two long and relatively narrow fingers. The smaller, southwestern finger remains undeveloped, and just a few houses impinge on the larger, more easterly inlet. Both provide marshy shelters for herons, ducks, beaver, and other wildlife.

We watched a deer drink at the water's edge and startled a great horned owl early one August morning at the southwestern tip. In the wider inlet, a pair of loons joined us, and judging from fresh tracks in the mud near the south end,

CONWAY LAKE

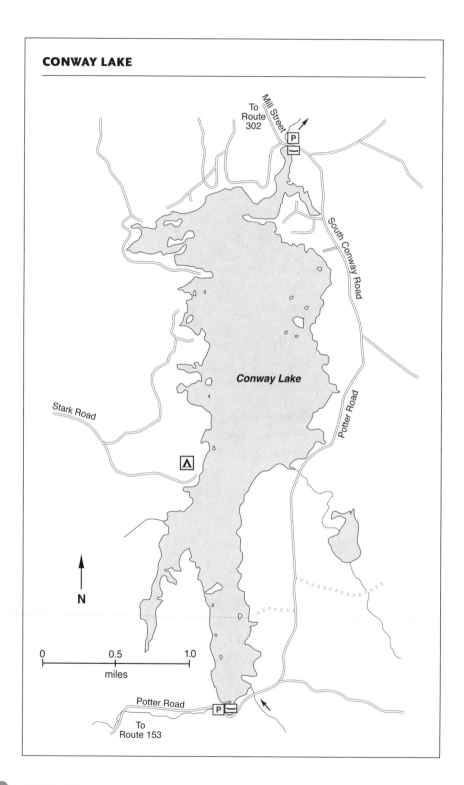

To
Route
302

Mill Street

South Conway Road

Conway Lake

Stark Road

Potter Road

N

0   0.5   1.0
miles

Potter Road

To
Route 153

A great horned owl eyes us warily as we paddle past its perch. These fierce aerial predators prowl the night for skunks, rabbits, and other prey.

we just missed seeing a moose. While paddling here on a windless June day, we photographed floating heart—one of the few aquatic plants that roots successfully in water deeper than 4 feet—water celery, and yellow pond lily. We also reveled in the beauty of the distant mountains.

The lake's western side most of the way up to the northern end has numerous deep, marshy coves to explore and very little development, except around the one road near the southern fork and at the northern end. Be aware that the quite wide northern half of the lake can suffer from strong winds that come up quickly. While some coves provide wind protection, you can reach them only by paddling out on the open lake.

For a pleasant walk, take the trail from the parking area at the northern access; signs describe several generations of water-powered mills that existed here. Near the ruins of the most recent mill building, you can still see metal hoops from the old wooden sluice, or penstock, scattered in the creek.

38 | Upper Kimball Pond

This small, marshy, isolated pond sees little traffic. Look here for moose and beaver. It's also a great spot for marshland birds.

Location: Chatham, NH
Maps: *New Hampshire Atlas & Gazetteer,* Map 45: H13; USGS North Conway East
Area: 136 acres
Time: 2 hours
Habitat Type: Small, marshy pond
Fish: Smallmouth bass, pickerel, perch
Camping: USFS Cold River Campground; see Appendix A
Take Note: Personal watercraft prohibited; motors limited to 10 HP

GETTING THERE

From River Road in North Conway, go 1.8 miles north on Route 16, and turn right onto Hurricane Mountain Road. Go 6.0 miles (7.8 miles) east on this scenic, steep, narrow, winding road, and turn left onto Green Hill Road. Go 2.0 miles (9.8 miles) to the access on the right. *GPS coordinates*: 44° 5.866′ N, 71° 0.410′ W.

From Route 302 in Fryeburg, Maine, go 2.1 miles west on Route 113, and turn left onto Green Hill Road. Go 5.4 miles (7.5 miles) to the access on the right.

WHAT YOU'LL SEE

Right next to the Maine border, in the southeastern corner of New Hampshire's White Mountains, lies Upper Kimball Pond, a small and narrow body of water that receives little traffic. A number of houses, set back from the water, impinge somewhat on the northern section, but the southern end and inlet, which winds through a boggy marsh rich in bird life and interesting flora, make the pond well worth paddling.

One can paddle into the inlet at least a half-mile through thick stands of pickerelweed, waterlily, sedge, reed, cattail, and floating mats of sphagnum, dotted with sundew, so named because of glistening secretions on its small reddish-green fronds that attract tiny insects to their doom. Cranberry, sweet

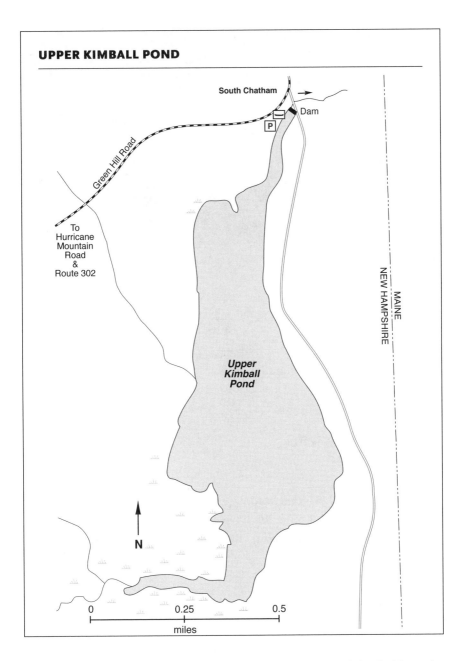

UPPER KIMBALL POND

South Chatham

Dam

P

Green Hill Road

To
Hurricane
Mountain
Road
&
Route 302

Upper
Kimball
Pond

MAINE

NEW HAMPSHIRE

N

| 0 | 0.25 | 0.5 |

miles

gale, various heaths, alder, and buttonbush have established footholds in the gradually filling fen. On solid ground along the shoreline, red maple and white pine dominate.

We paddled here in mid-August; even then the birds seemed to be every-where: tree and barn swallows danced over the water, red-winged blackbirds

Deer browse the foliage, and bees pollinate the spherical flowers of buttonbush, *Cephalanthus occidentalis.*

and cedar waxwings flitted among the pickerelweed blooms, sparrows hopped around old beaver lodges, and warblers dined on insects in the maple trees. On a July visit, we saw a flock of wild turkeys. Bring your binoculars and field guides for a great day of exploration!

39 | Mountain Pond

To get to this small pristine mountain lake in the White Mountains, you need to hike in 0.3 mile. We have seen loons here, and you might see beaver and moose. Camping is allowed around the lake.

Location: Chatham, NH
Maps: *New Hampshire Atlas & Gazetteer,* Map Map 45: E11; USGS Chatham
Area: 124 acres
Time: 3 hours, including hike to launch
Habitat Type: Small, forested, mountain lake with brushy shoreline
Fish: Brook trout
Information: White Mountain National Forest,
www.fs.fed.us/r9/forests/white_mountain/
Camping: Backcountry camping at USFS Mountain Pond Shelter and tentsite;
see Appendix A, White Mountain National Forest

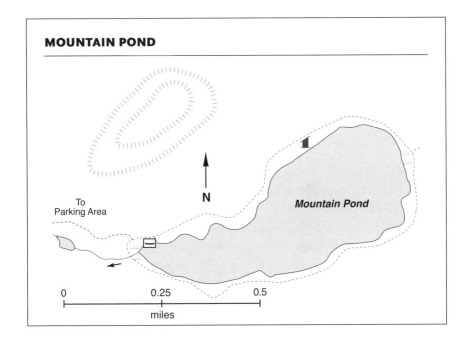

MOUNTAIN POND

To Parking Area

N

Mountain Pond

0   0.25   0.5

miles

GETTING THERE

From Route 16, go 1.8 miles north on Route 16A, and turn right onto Town Hall Road. Go 6.4 miles (8.2 miles), staying left at the fork, to the parking area on the right. The put-in is about 0.3 mile (about 15 minutes) along a wide, potentially soggy trail. At the loop trail, turn left, and go 100 yards; a trail to the right leads down to the put-in. The Adirondack shelter is another 0.4 mile along the loop trail. *GPS coordinates*: 44° 10.218′ N, 71° 5.286′ W.

WHAT YOU'LL SEE

Because of its remoteness, getting to Mountain Pond requires some effort, namely, a carry of about 0.3 mile to the pond. But if you appreciate out-of-the-way places—beautiful even on a drizzly, foggy day—your efforts will be amply rewarded. The pond, at an elevation of about 1,500 feet, nestles among the hills just over a dozen miles from Mount Washington, the Northeast's tallest mountain.

On the northern side of this totally natural pond, along the perimeter trail, an Adirondack lean-to shelter provides a haven for those looking for secluded lakeside camping, especially before Memorial Day and after Labor Day. You can also pitch a tent anywhere in this part of the White Mountain National Forest.

White pine, spruce, balsam fir, and white birch line the shores of Mountain Pond, along with a dense undergrowth of blueberry and other shrubs. Because of thick understory growth, few places allow you to pull the boat up and get out easily. Paddling around this small pond, you will find a beaver lodge and a small marshy area at the outlet on the western end, where you might see a great blue heron or a few ducks. Loons inhabit the pond, but we did not see young on our visits here. Be careful not to disturb nesting loons.

BLACK FLIES AND MOSQUITOES: SCOURGES OF THE NORTH

Anyone who has spent any time at all in the North Country knows these insects all too well. They can detract from outdoor fun in summer and can make most of June virtually off-limits to outdoor recreation in northern parts of the Northeast. Although it will not take away any of the itch, understanding these insects may help us accept them as part of the ecosystem we enjoy.

Black Flies

Black flies belong to the family *Simuliidae*, and most species of concern belong to the genus *Simulium*. Scientists have identified more than 1,500 species of black flies, including 300 in North America. Only 10 to 15 percent of black fly species suck blood from humans or domestic animals.

In parts of northern North America, black flies cause considerable livestock difficulties; mostly, they cause weight loss because cattle do not eat well when tormented by flies, but black flies can actually kill cattle. In parts of Alberta, mortality rates from black flies range from 1 to 4 percent. Researchers have collected as many as 10,000 feeding black flies from a single cow. Black fly problems in North America, however, pale compared to problems in Africa and Central America, where the aptly named species *Simulium damnosum* has infected an estimated 20 million people with onchocerciasis, or river blindness (a disease caused by roundworms transmitted by the fly).

Black flies begin their life cycle in streams and rivers. Females deposit eggs in the water, and emerging larvae attach to rocks, plants, and other surfaces. The larvae use two tiny, fanlike structures to sweep food particles into their mouths. Black fly larvae can become so dense that they form a slippery, mosslike mat. A several-hundred-foot stretch of a narrow stream can support more than a million larvae. In a river, the population can number in the multibillions per mile.

After a period of days or weeks, each larva builds a pupal case in which it metamorphoses into an adult black fly. When ready to emerge, it splits the case open and rides to the water's surface in a bubble of oxygen that had collected in the case.

Adult black flies have one primary goal: to make more black flies. Female black flies seek the nourishing blood meal that they need to lay eggs. Only females bite (actually puncture and suck); pacifist males sip nectar from flowers and may be important blueberry pollinators. Black flies rely heavily on eyesight to find prey, so they are active almost exclusively during the daylight—and at temperatures above 50° Fahrenheit. Some black flies fly more than 50 miles in search of blood meals.

No black fly species preys exclusively on humans. We are too new on the evolutionary chain to be a specific host to black flies, which arose during the Jurassic period 180 million years ago. An estimated 30 to 45 species in North America feed on humans. One species (*Simulium euryadminiculum*) feeds only on loons.

Mosquitoes

Another insect nemesis is the ubiquitous mosquito. Mosquitoes, members of the Culicidae family, number more than 3,400 species worldwide, including 170 in North America. Three-quarters of the mosquito species in the United States and Canada belong to three genera: *Aedes* (78 species), *Culex* (29 species), and *Anopheles* (16 species).

As with black flies, mosquito larvae live an aquatic life. Unlike black flies, most mosquitoes have adapted to still water. In any bog or salt marsh, you can find mosquito larvae wriggling about, eating algae and other organic matter that they filter out of the water with brushlike appendages. Larvae molt several times as they grow and develop into pupae. Both larvae and pupae breathe through air tubes at the water's surface.

Adult mosquitoes live short lives: females about a month, and males about a week. The high-pitched buzz comes from beating their wings at about 1,000 beats per second. Females generate a higher-pitched whine that helps males locate mates. You can recognize males with a hand lens; look for their bushier antennae, used to locate females.

Both sexes feed on plant nectar as their primary energy source, but females of most mosquito species also require a blood meal to fuel egg production. As with the black fly, a mosquito does not really bite. Rather, she

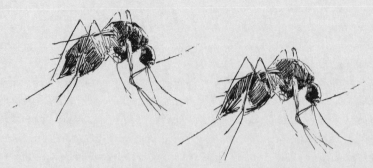

stabs through the victim's skin with six sharp stylets that form the proboscis center. Saliva flows into the puncture to keep the blood from coagulating. Most people have an allergic reaction to the saliva, comprising swelling and itching. Upon repeated exposure to bites, people gradually build immunity.

Although really just a nuisance in the Northeast, mosquitoes cause more deaths in the tropics than any other animal. They carry more than 100 different diseases, including malaria, yellow fever, encephalitis, filariasis, dengue, and West Nile virus. The most destructive of these, malaria, kills about 1 million people a year, mostly children, and as many as 200 million people carry the disease.

Southern latitudes have far greater mosquito-species diversity (tropical areas can harbor as many as 150 different species in a square mile), but the numbers of individuals generally increase farther north. In the Arctic, with fewer than a dozen species, adults can be so thick they literally blacken the skies. In one experiment, several rugged Canadian researchers bared their torsos, arms, and legs to Arctic mosquitoes and reported as many as 9,000 bites per minute! At this rate, an unprotected person could lose half of his or her blood in two hours.

So, you see, we really do not have it so bad in New Hampshire and Vermont. Most mosquitoes do not carry deadly disease (despite occasional cases of mosquito-borne encephalitis and West Nile virus), and even in the Connecticut Lakes region in June, we have found it rare to get more than a thousand bites a minute.

Black Fly and Mosquito Control

Humans have tried many different control strategies. For mosquito control, we drained thousands of square miles of salt marsh during the 1930s and 1940s by building long, straight drainage ditches—many still visible. As much as half of U.S. wetland area has been lost during the last 200 years—partly for mosquito control and partly for development and agriculture. Along with eliminating habitat, we have used thousands of tons of pesticides in the battle against mosquitoes. DDT remained the chemical of choice for decades because of its supposed safety—a claim that proved tragically untrue. Since DDT and other deadly chlorinated-hydrocarbon pesticides were banned in 1973, osprey, bald eagle, peregrine falcon, and other important bird species have begun to make a comeback in the Northeast.

Today, most attention focuses on biological control of these insects, relying on natural enemies: viruses, protozoa, bacteria, fungi, and parasites. A bacterium generally known as Bti (*Bacillus thuringiensis*, variety *israelensis*), discovered in 1977 in Negev Desert sand, has exhibited the most success-ful control. Gardeners use another variety of this bacterium for controlling cabbage loopers, corn borers, and other garden pests, and foresters use it for gypsy moth control. Bti produces protein crystals that react with other chemi-cals in the insects' stomachs, producing a poison that kills the larvae.

Although Bti currently enjoys high success rates, hidden problems could arise, just as with DDT, especially as bioengineers incorporate the Bti gene into plants. This widespread and indiscriminate spreading of the Bti protein could easily lead to pest resistance. Conservation biologists also worry that monarch butterflies, on their 1,000-plus-mile migrations to their Mexico wintering grounds, will suffer huge mortality rates from Bti-engineered corn.

Protecting Yourself from Biting Insects

To protect yourself from biting insects, you could stay out of the woods—buy a book on paddling and read it in the comfort of your home. This might be a good choice in June when clouds of black flies and mosquitoes could stick in your mind as the most memorable part of an outing. Largely because of biting insects, autumn and May—during that narrow window between ice-out and the black fly hatch—remain our favorite times for paddling the North Country. During all but the height of the black fly season in June, however, these insects should not spoil your trip. Out on the water where breezes often blow, paddlers can usually escape insects.

Proper clothing forms the most important line of defense. Dur-ing black fly season, wear long-sleeved, tight-knit shirts and pants with elastic cuffs, or tuck your pant legs into oversized socks. Black flies land on your clothing and search for openings, such as wrists, ankles, and necks. A mosquito-cloth headnet works well, but with a collared shirt, black flies will usually find a route in. Cotton gloves can help too.

Mosquitoes can penetrate soft clothing better than black flies can, so more rugged materials such work well for shirts and pants. Wearing two light shirts also works. Tight cuffs are not as important because mosquitoes usually fly directly to their dining table.

Insect repellents generally repel mosquitoes better than they repel black flies. Most repellents that North Country outdoorspeople swear by have DEET (N,N-diethyl meta-toluamide) as the primary active ingredient. Fortunately, one of our co-authors, a chemist, can actually pronounce this name. Unfortunately, he also knows enough about its chemical structure to be concerned about potential long-term toxicity to humans. Because DEET works by evaporating into the nearby air to clog insects' odor receptors, you have to keep slathering it on. We recommend clothing as the primary defensive strategy.

Some new, more natural repellents, such as Bite Blocker, Buggspray Vanilla, and Avon Skin-So-Soft Bug Guard Plus, may work for you. Eventually, natural-products chemists will find very effective, totally nontoxic alternatives. Applying a nontoxic skin softener sounds really great. We would be even more excited if it kept black flies away. Maybe it does provide ironclad protection for some people, but we remain unconvinced.

Is There Anything Good About Black Flies and Mosquitoes?

In reviewing all of the problems with black flies and mosquitoes, one wonders what might possibly be good about the little beasts. The answer lies in the role they play in aquatic ecosystems, where they provide a vital food source for a wide variety of animals. Many game fish rely on black fly and mosquito larvae for part of their diets. One study found that black fly larvae constitute as much as 25 percent of the brook trout diet. Even if black fly and mosquito larvae do not provide a direct food source for our favorite game fish and waterfowl, chances are pretty good that they form a vital part of the food chain upon which these animals rely. If we appreciate angling for brook trout, listening to the call of the loon, or watching the stately great blue heron, we should recognize that these species might not be here without black flies and mosquitoes.

3 | NORTHERN NEW HAMPSHIRE

Northern New Hampshire includes three separate regions: the middle Connecticut River region, the Lake Umbagog region, and the Connecticut Lakes region. The middle Connecticut consists of two river sections, Long Pond, and lakes Armington and Tarleton. Long Pond, a small, secluded body of water on the far west side of the White Mountain National Forest, is a great place to look for moose, mink, and otter. Armington, Tarleton, Comerford Reservoir, and the Woodsville/Wells section of the Connecticut River afford scenic views of the White Mountains to the east.

Although Lake Umbagog and nearby Pontook Reservoir/Androscoggin River are the only bodies of water that we include along the Maine border, they offer spectacular paddling opportunities. We have visited this area numerous times in summer and have never failed to see moose, loon, bald eagle, osprey, and beaver. Lake Umbagog does have some motorboat traffic, and its nearly 8-mile length can make for perilous paddling in windy conditions, but it is the premier paddling location for those seeking a multi-day experience.

The out-of-the-way Connecticut Lakes region, tucked up against the Canada border, represents a great opportunity for paddling in the heart of the northern boreal forest. Black-backed woodpeckers, crossbills, spruce grouse, and gray jays are among the unusual bird species found here, along with a large resident moose population. The two best places to look for moose are in Moose Pasture on East Inlet and along Route 3 between Second and Third Connecticut Lakes. We have also seen moose every time we have paddled here.

40 | Connecticut River— Northern Section and Comerford Reservoir

The two Connecticut River sections included here provide opportunities for lengthy paddles amid a backdrop of White Mountain peaks. Look for loons on Comerford Reservoir, and you might see a peregrine falcon on the lower part of the Woodsville/ Wells River section.

Location: Haverill, Lyman, and Monroe, NH; Barnet, Newbury, and Waterford, VT
Maps: *New Hampshire Atlas & Gazetteer,* Maps 42: H3, 46: J7; *Vermont Atlas & Gazetteer*, Maps 42: J5, 42: A6, 43: A9; USGS Barnet, VT, and Lower Waterford, NH
Length: Woodsville/Wells River, 10 miles (or more) one way; Comerford Reservoir, 6.5 miles one way
Time: Woodsville/Wells River, all day; Comerford Reservoir, 5 hours
Habitat Type: Large reservoirs
Fish: Largemouth and smallmouth bass, northern pike, pickerel, perch, walleye; brook, brown, and rainbow trout
Take Note: Avoid in windy conditions; personal watercraft limited to headway speed on Woodsville section

GETTING THERE
Woodsville, NH/Wells River, VT, section. From I-91, Exit 16 northbound, turn right onto Route 25. Go 0.5 mile, and turn left onto Route 5. Go 7.5 miles (8.0 miles), and turn right onto Newberry Crossing Road. Go 0.4 mile (8.4 miles) to the access on the left, just before Haverill Bridge. *GPS coordinates*: 44°4.021′ N, 72° 3.115′ W.

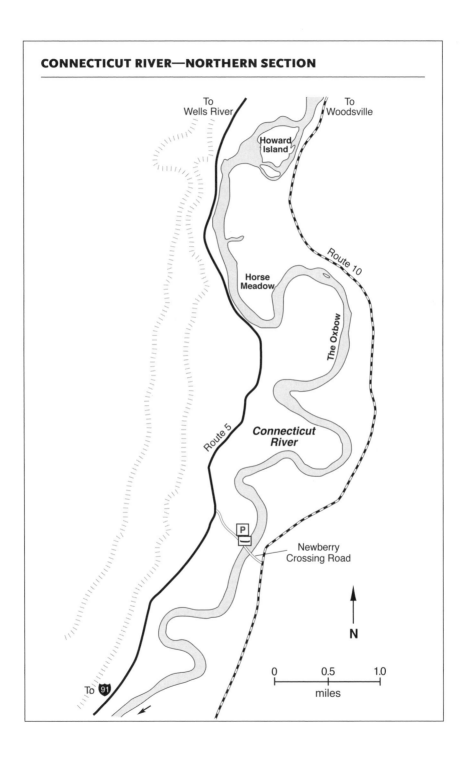

CONNECTICUT RIVER—NORTHERN SECTION

To Wells River

To Woodsville

Howard Island

Route 10

Horse Meadow

The Oxbow

Route 5

Connecticut River

P

Newberry Crossing Road

To 91

N

0   0.5   1.0
miles

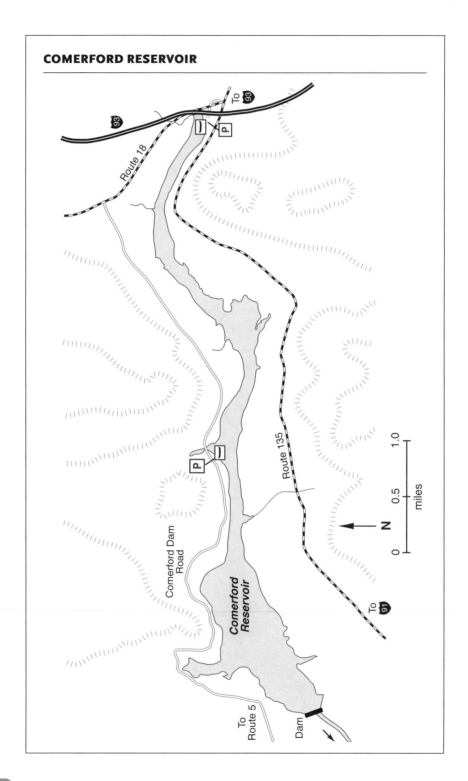

Comerford section, north end. From I-93, Exit 44, go 0.8 mile west on Route 18, and turn right into the parking area. Go under the bridge to the access. *GPS coordinates*: 44° 20.522′ N, 71° 53.341′ W.

Comerford section, Vermont side. From Route 5 in East Barnet, go 3.0 miles east on Comerford Dam Road to the access on the right. *GPS coordinates*: 44° 20.273′ N, 71° 59.665′ W.

WHAT YOU'LL SEE

Although adventuresome paddlers periodically traverse the Connecticut River's entire 410-mile length as it flows from the Canadian border in New Hampshire's Connecticut Lakes region to Long Island Sound, most of that paddle occurs on impoundments. Only a tiny fraction of total river miles consists of free-flowing water. We include two nice northern reaches of the river—the section below Woodsville/Wells River and Comerford Reservoir.

Woodsville, NH/Wells River, VT, section

From the access, you can paddle upstream for a few miles through rolling farm country. We saw cedar waxwing, black duck, kingfisher, lots of spotted sandpipers, and killdeer, as well as an osprey plying the waters for fish. Asters bloomed in profusion, and we paddled leisurely under the spreading canopy of ancient silver maple.

The real draw—and our primary reason for including this section—lies to the east: the string of White Mountain peaks providing a backdrop to this meandering section of the Connecticut. Traversed by the Appalachian Trail, the peaks reach to more than 4,000 feet—Kinsman Mountain at 4,358 feet; Mount Blue to the south at 4,529 feet; and way off in the distance Lafayette, Lincoln, and others in the Franconia Notch region that stretch to more than 5,000 feet. We found it hard to keep our eyes on the water amid such splendor. Paddling around The Oxbow affords views from several angles.

Paddling north, the current gradually picks up, blocking further progress. As you paddle back downstream, you get another look at the mountains. Those looking for exercise can continue paddling south for more than 40 miles, all the way down to the Wilder Dam. Many side channels, filled with birdlife, contain important wetland habitat.

Comerford Reservoir section

Some of the larger Connecticut River reservoirs, such as nearby Moore Reservoir, provide vast expanses of water that act as magnets for water-skiers, personal watercraft, and wind, none of which are compatible with quietwater

Andrew Hayes, son of one of the authors, paddles a sea kayak on the Connecticut River. These sleek craft are a joy to paddle.

paddling. We include smaller Comerford Reservoir because of its location in a relatively narrow gorge and its more streamlike character. In summer, winds generally blow either from the south or from the northwest; Comerford's generally northeast-to-southwest orientation provides a modicum of wind protection. A number of houses perch on the sides of the gorge, but trees cover the hillsides. Look for osprey, bald eagle, loon, and ducks here.

41 | Lake Armington and Lake Tarleton

The Appalachian Trail traverses nearby peaks near these small lakes. We have seen waterfowl, loon, great blue heron, and beaver here.

Location: Piermont and Warren, NH
Maps: *New Hampshire Atlas & Gazetteer*, Maps 38: A5, 42: K5; USGS Warren
Area: Lake Armington, 142 acres; Lake Tarleton, 315 acres
Time: Lake Armington, 2 hours; Lake Tarleton, 3 hours
Habitat Type: Small mountain lakes

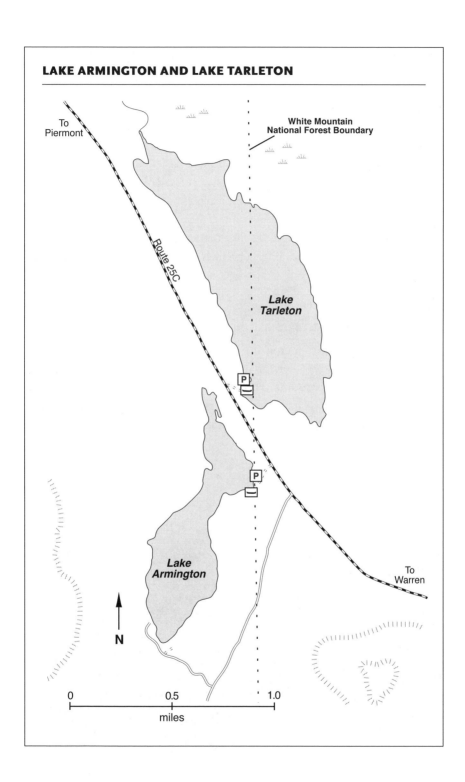

LAKE ARMINGTON AND LAKE TARLETON

To
Piermont

White Mountain
National Forest Boundary

Route 25C

Lake
Tarleton

P

P

Lake
Armington

N

To
Warren

0   0.5   1.0
miles

Fish: Smallmouth bass, pickerel, brown and rainbow trout; also lake trout in Tarleton

Information: Trust for Public Land, www.tpl.org

Take Note: Personal watercraft prohibited on Armington

GETTING THERE

From Routes 10 and 25 in Piermont, go 8.1 miles east on Route 25C to the Lake Tarleton access on the left. *GPS coordinates*: 43° 58.060′ N, 71° 57.816′ W. Go 0.3 mile (8.4 miles) to the Lake Armington access on the right. *GPS coordinates:* 43° 57.700′ N, 71° 57.757′ W.

From Warren, go west on Route 25C. Lake Armington access is on the left at the Piermont/Warren town line; Lake Tarleton access is 0.3 mile farther west on the right.

WHAT YOU'LL SEE

Although you will not paddle alone here, except perhaps in the off-season, the scenery makes Lake Tarleton and Lake Armington well worth a visit. The Appalachian Trail passes over the peaks just to the east, providing a scenic backdrop for both lakes. Although Lake Armington has some development along its shores, the farsighted efforts of the Trust for Public Land and the New Hampshire Charitable Trust have protected 5,300 acres surrounding Lake

The mountains to the east of Lake Tarleton offer many hiking possibilities, including on the Appalachian Trail.

Tarleton, with much of that added to the White Mountain National Forest.

Size marks the main difference between Lake Armington and Lake Tarleton. Armington's smaller size, coupled with having Piermont Mountain due west, makes it much less susceptible to wind. Although we prefer to paddle Armington because of its more intimate size and lack of personal watercraft, anglers may want to take advantage of the exceptional smallmouth bass and trout fishing on Tarleton.

The water's clarity and the rich and varied hillsides, with mixed stands of spruce, white pine, hemlock, and white birch, make these lakes particularly inviting. Colorful sheep laurel blooms in June, songbirds forage on elderberries in late summer, loons dive for fish, and cedar waxwings fly overhead. Beaver activity seemed greater on Lake Armington, and we saw more ducks with young—perhaps because of lighter boat traffic.

42 | Long Pond

Long Pond, a beautiful wilderness pond in the White Mountain National Forest, offers on-site primitive camping. Loons nest here, and it's an excellent location for otter, mink, beaver, and moose.

Location: Benton, NH
Maps: *New Hampshire Atlas & Gazetteer,* Map 42: I7; USGS East Haverhill
Area: 124 acres
Time: 3 hours
Habitat Type: Small mountain lake
Fish: Brook trout
Information: White Mountain National Forest, www.fs.fed.us/r9/forests/white_mountain/
Camping: On-site primitive camping; see Appendix A, #14
Take Note: $3 per day fee, or use an America the Beautiful pass

GETTING THERE
From I-93, Exit 32, go 12.4 miles west on Route 112, and turn left onto Route 116. Go 1.7 miles (14.1 miles), and turn left onto Long Pond Road. Go 2.4 miles (16.5 miles), and turn right onto the access road. *GPS coordinates:* 44° 3.579′ N, 71° 53.363′ W.

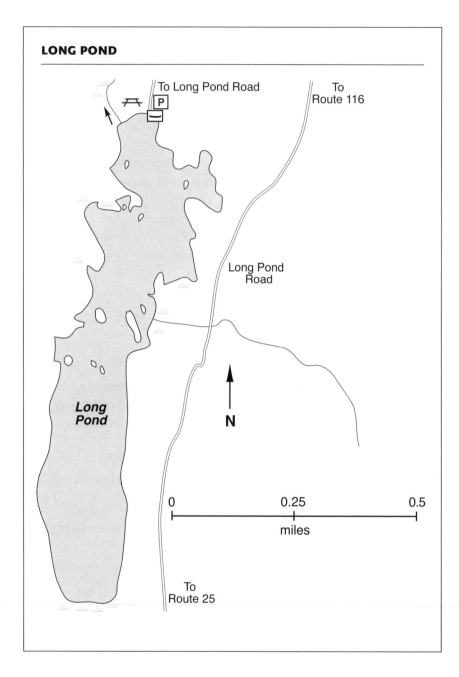

LONG POND

To Long Pond Road

To Route 116

P

Long Pond Road

N

Long Pond

0   0.25   0.5

miles

To Route 25

From I-91, Exit 17, go east on Route 302 through Woodsville, and turn right onto Route 112 east. Take a sharp right turn onto Route 116 south; continue as above.

From Route 25C in Warren, go 4.5 miles north on Route 25, and turn right onto High Street/Sanitorium Road. Go 1.0 mile (5.5 miles), and turn left onto Long Pond Road. Go 4.9 miles (10.4 miles), and turn left onto the access road.

WHAT YOU'LL SEE

Surrounded by the White Mountains and completely free from development, Long Pond remains one of our favorite bodies of water in the two-state region. Although relatively small, the pond feels much larger because of its long profile, highly varied shoreline, and several islands. One could sit for hours just absorbing the peacefulness and beauty.

The access and a small picnic area occur at the northern end. While Alex and his daughter had breakfast here on a crisp September morning (after camping at Russell Pond, a half-hour away), they watched an otter cavorting 50 yards from where they sat. Paddling around the pond, you will see a couple of beaver lodges. The best time to see beaver, otter, and mink is early in the morning.

The pond's northern half has a dozen or so islands to explore, and the marshy coves—particularly at the southern end—provide rich wildlife habitat. Tall trees dominate the shoreline; spires of balsam fir and spruce mix with occasional red maple and yellow and white birch. A dense growth of viburnum, alder, and other shrubs makes shore access quite difficult, but some rocky areas provide spots to disembark for a picnic lunch.

While you cannot camp on the islands in Long Pond, the national forest permits primitive camping in the surrounding area.

---

43 | Androscoggin River and Pontook Reservoir

Bald eagles nest here, and you may see osprey. Conifer-clad hillsides of the surrounding northern boreal forest harbor many moose, which often can be seen along the road or immersed in the reservoir or river.

Location: Dummer, NH
Maps: *New Hampshire Atlas & Gazetteer,* Map 50: K7; USGS Dummer Ponds, Tea Kettle Ridge; AMC Mahoosuc Map and Guide

Area/Length: Pontook Reservoir, 280 acres; Androscoggin River, 2 miles
Time: 5 hours for both sides
Habitat Type: Shallow, marshy pond west side; river reservoir east side
Fish: Pontook Reservoir—largemouth bass, pickerel; Androscoggin River—smallmouth bass, landlocked salmon; brook, brown, and rainbow trout
Camping: Coleman State Park, Mollidgewock State Park; see Appendix A, #9, #10

GETTING THERE

From Berlin, go north on Route 16 for about 19 miles along the Androscoggin River. From Route 110B in Milan, go 5.7 miles north on Route 16 to the access on the right. *GPS coordinates*: 44° 37.989′ N, 71° 14.959′ W.

WHAT YOU'LL SEE

Although Pontook Reservoir on the Androscoggin River spans Route 16, we heartily recommend this as a paddling destination. As you drive north along the Androscoggin from Berlin, note the boom piers in the water. The following comes from a plaque along the river:

> The small man-made islands in the river were used to secure a chain of boom logs, which divided the Androscoggin River during the colorful and dramatic annual log drives. When the Brown Paper Company and the International Paper Company shared the river to float their logs from the forests far upriver to the mills at Berlin, the logs were stamped on the ends with a marking hammer to identify their ownership, and they were sorted at a sorting gap further upriver. The log drives ended in 1963. The old piers continue to serve as a reminder of North Country heritage.

We watched three adult moose at the reservoir in June, two bulls with large racks and a cow. Myriad other wildlife typical of the northern forest appears here as well. We saw white-winged crossbill, white-throated sparrow, hermit and wood thrushes, a loon pair with two chicks, and an osprey

In spring 2000, a bald eagle pair built a nest here, and nesting has continued since then. New Hampshire fledged no eagles for many years, and then fledged its first in 1989. Reproductivity hovered between zero and two birds annually for fourteen years, with the exception of 2001, when six birds fledged. In 2003, fledging began to rise dramatically, and by 2008, 24 eagles had fledged, with three of those contributed by the Pontook pair. In all, 107 bald eagle chicks have fledged in the Granite State in the last twenty years.

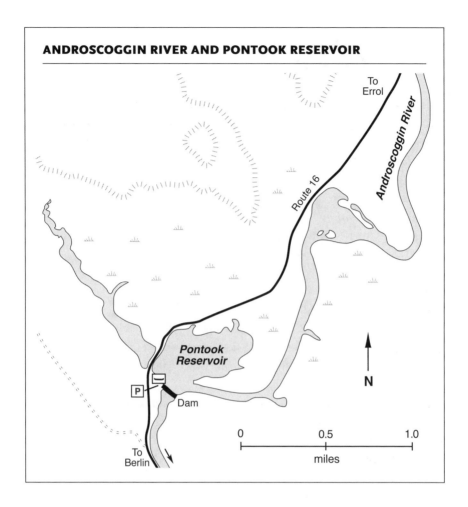

ANDROSCOGGIN RIVER AND PONTOOK RESERVOIR

On the river side of Route 16, we paddled about two miles upstream from the dam before we ran into current that helped us turn back. Beaver had pruned back the alder along the shore. Lichen-festooned balsam fir provided a solid visual wall between the reservoir and the forest, and we wondered if the lack of deciduous trees, except for the occasional red maple, resulted from long-term beaver activity.

On the west side of Route 16, a group of painted turtles sunned on a log, and we enjoyed the beauty of purple iris stands in bloom. Horsetail crowded the end of the shallow reservoir, and sweet gale and a few birches interrupted the balsam fir domination in this low-lying boggy environment. Paddling to the back of the pond not only puts distance between you and the lightly traveled road but also gets you into the heart of prime moose habitat.

44 | Lake Umbagog

This huge, shallow lake straddles the Maine–New Hampshire border. Bald eagle, osprey, and loon nest here, and the possibility of seeing a moose is high. Look also for otter, beaver, mink, black bear, and waterfowl.

Location: Errol, NH
Maps: *New Hampshire Atlas & Gazetteer,* Map 51: F12; *Maine Atlas & Gazetteer,* Maps 17, 18; USGS Umbagog Lake South, Umbagog Lake North; AMC Mahoosuc Map and Guide
Area: 7,850 acres
Time: Several days
Habitat Type: Large, shallow lake
Fish: Smallmouth bass, pickerel, northern pike, yellow perch, brook trout
Information: Umbagog Lake State Park, 603-482-7795; Lake Umbagog National Wildlife Refuge, www.fws.gov/northeast/lakeumbagog/
Camping: On-site; see Appendix A, #11
Take Note: Avoid paddling in open boats under windy conditions; you will share the water with motorboats

GETTING THERE

Northern access. From the Androscoggin River bridge in Errol, go 0.1 mile south on Route 26, and turn left onto North Mountain Road. Go 1.0 mile (1.1 miles) to the access. The main lake is about three miles upriver. *GPS coordinates*: 44° 47.236′ N, 71° 7.266′ W.

   Southern access. From the Androscoggin River bridge in Errol, go 7.0 miles south on Route 26 to the access on the left. *GPS coordinates*: 44° 42.137′ N, 71° 3.316′ W. Backcountry campers may launch from Umbagog Lake State Park, 0.1 mile east.

WHAT YOU'LL SEE

With the tremendous variety of wildlife and the number of ducks nesting here, we should not be surprised that Lake Umbagog has become one of the newest national wildlife refuges. Established in November 1992 with the federal government's purchase of the first tracts of land, the Lake Umbagog

LAKE UMBAGOG

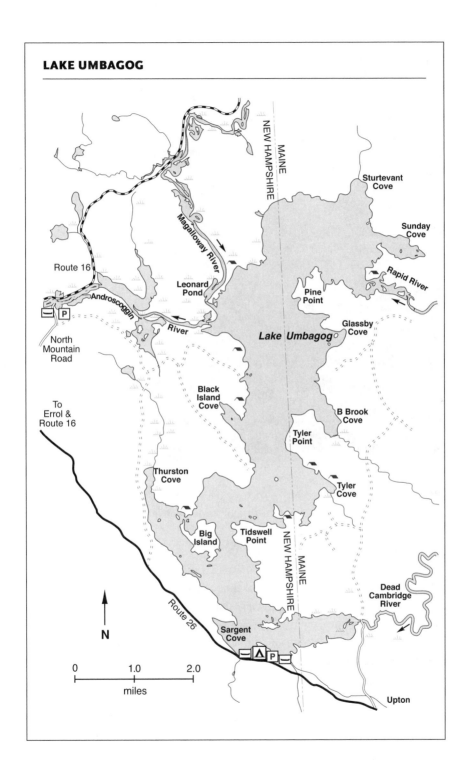

NEW HAMPSHIRE

MAINE

Sturtevant Cove

Sunday Cove

Magalloway River

Route 16

Leonard Pond

Pine Point

Rapid River

Androscoggin

P

River

Glassby Cove

Lake Umbagog

North Mountain Road

To Errol & Route 16

Black Island Cove

B Brook Cove

Tyler Point

Thurston Cove

Tyler Cove

Big Island

Tidswell Point

NEW HAMPSHIRE

MAINE

Dead Cambridge River

N

Route 26

Sargent Cove

0   1.0   2.0
miles

Upton

As day breaks over Big Island, near the lake's southern end, a fisherman tries his luck on Umbagog's productive waters.

National Wildlife Refuge has grown to 21,000 acres, but the U.S. Fish and Wildlife Service intends to obtain title or conservation easements that would increase the refuge by 48,000 acres.

Umbagog, pronounced "um-BAY-gog," straddles the Maine–New Hampshire border, covering more than 12 square miles. Oriented generally north-south, with a highly varied shoreline that extends for more than 40 miles plus dozens of islands, this magnificent lake exudes wildness. Readily accessible to the backcountry paddler, Lake Umbagog Campground manages 30 wilderness sites around the lake. A few private cottages and camps dot parts of the lake, and motorboat traffic has increased in recent years, but we expect very little future development. We should all encourage New Hampshire and Maine to restrict motorboat use for the protection of moose and nesting ducks, loons, and bald eagles.

A very shallow lake—Umbagog means "shallow water" in Abenaki—with average depths of only about fifteen feet, the many marshy areas provide ideal nesting habitat for such species as ring-necked, black, mallard, and wood ducks, and hooded and common mergansers. Wood ducks and hooded mergansers (our two common cavity nesters) use the approximately 100 nesting boxes around the lake.

Leonard Pond, the largest marshy area, near the northwestern corner of the lake, sports an extensive grassy marsh that has supported nesting bald eagles since 1989—no eagles nested in New Hampshire from 1949 to 1988—right where the Magalloway enters and the Androscoggin exits the lake. The last nest left in 1949 was in the same tree as the new nest in 1989.

The first chick of 1989 died, but biologists placed in the nest a chick from a captive pair; the eagles adopted the foster chick and raised it successfully. In some years since, the pair nested successfully, in others years, not. In spring of 1994 during nesting, the male died from lead sinker ingestion. (On January 1, 2000, New Hampshire banned the use of lead sinkers weighing 1 ounce or less to protect loons and other waterfowl.) The female abandoned the lone egg but found a new mate. In summer of 1997, nesting failed, but in 1998 the pair raised two young successfully; 1998 also saw the first nesting attempt by a second eagle pair in the state, this one at Spoonwood Pond in southern New Hampshire. In 1999, the Umbagog pair raised another pair successfully. In 2000, although the Umbagog hatchlings died, probably because of cold, wet weather, the year marked a new first: four pairs of eagles began nesting in New Hampshire. Besides the Umbagog and Spoonwood pairs that year, attempts were made on the Connecticut River near Hinsdale and at nearby Pontook Reservoir. By 2001, neither the female nor the male of the original pair were still alive. Other eagle pairs inhabited the nest with limited success for a few years, but in 2006 three young fledged from the Leonard Pond site.

This mirrors what has happened nationally in the lower 48 states: from a low of 417 pairs in 1963, the bald eagle population rebounded to 791 pairs in 1974; 1,188 pairs in 1981; 3,035 in 1990; 4,712 in 1995; and more than 6,000 in 2000. Because of the remarkable recovery of the population since the banning of DDT, which caused disastrous eggshell thinning, then-president Bill Clinton announced in 1995 that the bald eagle's status would change from endangered to threatened. In 2007, with more than 10,000 nesting pairs, the U.S. Fish and Wildlife Service removed the bald eagle from the endangered and threatened species list, capping an amazing comeback story.

Osprey, meanwhile, have had an even better time of it. In 1994, approximately 25 pairs nested in the vicinity of Umbagog, and they successfully reared 35 chicks. They continue to be common on Umbagog. Loons have had mixed success. A lot of loons summer on the lake—of 22 territorial pairs, 13 pairs actually nested, fledging a total of 11 chicks in 1994. However, in late July 1997, when we paddled here, biologists told us that few chicks had survived the late, cold spring. During May, June, and July, be particularly careful about nesting loons. Even a quiet paddler inadvertently getting too close to a nest can result in the adults abandoning it, and loons always nest very close to the water.

Our favorite places on Umbagog include Leonard Pond, the coves along the inlet of the Rapid River on the northeast, and the small coves and islands east of Tidswell Point. Big Island, purchased by the Society for the Protection of New Hampshire Forests in the 1980s, is also wonderful and includes six campsites. For camping with kids, sites on the north shore of Tyler Cove (numbers 21, 22, and 23) stand out because of the protected sandy swimming beach at the cove's end.

We also enjoy paddling the slow-flowing, meandering Androscoggin and Magalloway rivers. As you paddle toward Umbagog on either river, a number of marshy ponds both to the right and left await your exploration. Keep an eye out for moose, otter, and mink.

Moose abound. Look for them standing belly-deep in the Magalloway River, in ponds off to the left of the Androscoggin, or in any of the numerous coves on the lake. In the early morning light, in a cove just east of Tidswell Point, we watched three moose browsing by the water's edge. At the far southeastern end—the most developed part of the lake—we got our closest look at a moose not 200 yards from a cottage near the mouth of the Dead Cambridge River. We have also watched them swim across open water in the early morning, moving along at a brisk pace.

The varied vegetation around Umbagog includes conifers that predominate in most areas: balsam fir, spruce, northern white cedar, hemlock, and white pine. In other areas, deciduous trees—including yellow and paper birch, red maple, and an occasional red oak—predominate.

Potentially dangerous winds and waves can come up very quickly on this large lake, making open-boat paddling hazardous. Paddling around the lake during a two-day period in August, we got into heavy winds both afternoons, even though the water was like glass on each of those mornings. Wind blowing from the north or northwest across several miles of water can build up sizable waves!

Many fish inhabit the lake—as evidenced by the large osprey population. In mid-August we caught yellow perch, smallmouth bass, and lots of lake chub (a whitefish with large scales and a deeply forked tail) up to a few pounds. With the right bait, lures, or flies, one should not have too much trouble pulling a few tasty meals out of the lake.

45 | First Connecticut Lake and Lake Francis

These large, deep, remote lakes near the Canadian border are in the heart of moose country. Wildlife abounds, including waterfowl, loon, osprey, moose, otter, black bear, and mink.

Location: Clarksville and Pittsburg, NH
Maps: *New Hampshire Atlas & Gazetteer,* Maps 52: H5/F7, 53: F8; USGS Lake Francis, Magalloway Mountain, Pittsburg
Area: First Connecticut Lake, 2,807 acres; Lake Francis, 2,051 acres
Time: First Connecticut Lake, all day; Lake Francis, all day
Habitat Type: Large, deep lakes
Fish: Landlocked salmon, lake and rainbow trout; Lake Francis also pickerel, brown trout
Information: Town of Pittsburg, NH, www.pittsburg-nh.com
Camping: Mollidgewock State Park, Lake Francis State Park, Deer Mountain State Park; see Appendix A, #10, #12, #13
Take Note: Dangerous in windy conditions

GETTING THERE
Lake Francis. From Route 145 in Pittsburg, go 1.3 miles north on Route 3 to the access on the right. *GPS coordinates*: 45° 2.962′ N, 71° 21.852′ W.

To reach a more remote access, continue 5.1 miles (6.4 miles), and turn right onto River Road. Go 2.2 miles (8.6 miles) to the access, just beyond the Lake Francis State Park entrance. *GPS coordinates*: 45° 3.488′ N, 71° 18.180′ W.

First Connecticut Lake. From Route 145 in Pittsburg, go 6.8 miles north on Route 3 to the access on the right. *GPS coordinates*: 45° 5.432′ N, 71° 17.330′ W.

To reach a more remote access at the northeastern tip, continue 4.8 miles (11.6 miles), and turn right onto Magalloway Mountain Road. Go 1.1 miles (12.7 miles) to the timber bridge put-in. You'll encounter some light rapids for the first 200 feet downstream; you can paddle or line your boat back up easily. *GPS coordinates*: 45° 7.103′ N, 71° 12.534′ W.

WHAT YOU'LL SEE
First Connecticut Lake and Lake Francis, like the other Connecticut Lakes (see Trips 46 and 49), are jewels of northern New Hampshire. Although some

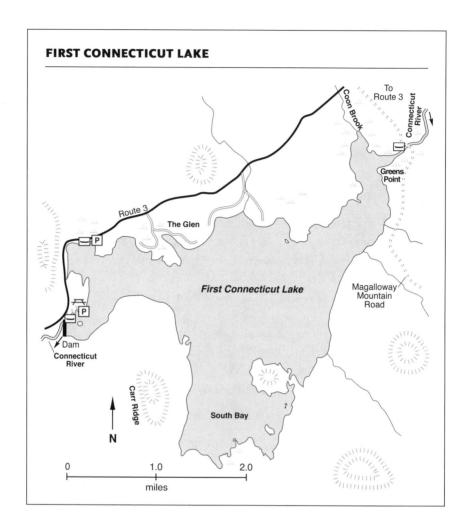

FIRST CONNECTICUT LAKE

To Route 3

Connecticut River

Coon Brook

Greens Point

Route 3

The Glen

First Connecticut Lake

Magalloway Mountain Road

Dam

Connecticut River

Carr Ridge

South Bay

N

| 0 | 1.0 | 2.0 |

miles

limited development has encroached on their shores, they still offer superb wilderness paddling. In the more remote inlets during all but the busiest seasons, moose and people may appear with about the same frequency. When we paddled here on a Fourth of July weekend, few boats plied these waters. For the angler, these lakes offer excellent lake trout and salmon fishing.

Be forewarned, though, that on these large lakes even a fairly gentle wind can generate sizable waves. Make it a rule to stick close to shore. When the wind blows, visit one of the smaller ponds instead (see Trips 47, 48, 49). Unexpected winds coming out of the southeast were so strong as Alex paddled down the northern shore of First Connecticut Lake that he found himself surfing on 2-foot waves in his small solo canoe. The front third of the boat rose right out of the water as large waves passed under. Exciting perhaps, but potentially

LAKE FRANCIS

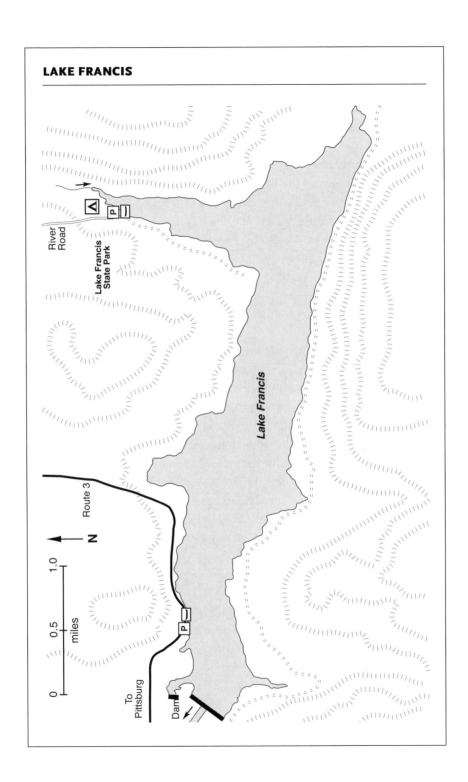

quite dangerous. Be careful!

When the weather forecast promises calm conditions, a huge amount of shoreline awaits exploration on either of these lakes. With an uncertain weather forecast, stick close to the access points, where you have better access to Route 3 and civilization.

First Connecticut Lake

This wild area is more secure thanks to the efforts of the Connecticut Lakes Headwaters Partnership. Conservation groups including the Trust for Public Land, The Nature Conservancy, the Society for the Protection of New Hampshire Forests, AMC, and others worked with state and congressional leaders to secure funding to protect 171,000 acres around the four Connecticut Headwaters lakes, which include First Connecticut Lake and Lake Francis. The final phase of this project was completed in 2003, with this acreage permanently protected from development and managed for recreation, wildlife habitat, and sustainable forestry.

The northern tip of First Connecticut Lake, including the Connecticut River and Coon Brook inlets, provides marshy habitat for moose, beaver, deer, and otter. You can paddle up Coon Brook a short distance through the marsh and alder thickets until rocks block your progress. You can really feel the remoteness on this part of the lake, surrounded by thickly wooded spruce-fir forests—the country of the pointed firs—listening to the eerie cry of the loon. On an early morning with mist rising from the lake, moose browsing on aquatic vegetation, and birds singing from the wooded shore, it feels like a different world.

The western arm of First Connecticut Lake, although not seeming quite as remote, is also very beautiful. You could spend a half-day just paddling around this end from the put-in near the dam, never even venturing onto the largest section of the lake.

Lake Francis

Lake Francis, particularly the eastern end, has a similar feel to that of First Connecticut Lake. We prefer the put-in near Lake Francis State Park because Route 3 travels close by the northern shore on the lake's west end, and traffic noise can be bothersome on busy weekends. The main part of Lake Francis, elongated in an east-west direction, can be treacherous when the wind blows from the west or northwest; under these conditions, paddle one of the smaller bodies of water in the region or stick to the protected west shore of the upper arm near the state park. We have paddled here under both dead-calm and substantial whitecap conditions.

46 | Second Connecticut Lake

Second Connecticut Lake is about half the size of First Connecticut and Lake Francis, making it somewhat less dangerous in windy conditions. Wildlife abounds, including waterfowl, loon, osprey, moose, otter, black bear, and mink.

Location: Pittsburg, NH
Maps: *New Hampshire Atlas & Gazetteer,* Map 53: D9; USGS Second Connecticut Lake
Area: 1,286 acres
Time: 6 hours
Habitat Type: Large, deep lake
Fish: Smelt, landlocked salmon, brook and lake trout
Information: Town of Pittsburg, NH, www.pittsburg-nh.com
Camping: Mollidgewock State Park, Lake Francis State Park, Deer Mountain State Park; see Appendix A, #10, #12, #13
Take Note: Dangerous in windy conditions; always wear a PFD

GETTING THERE

From Route 145 in Pittsburg, go 13.9 miles north on Route 3 to the access at the dam on the right. Or go 0.2 miles farther to the picnic area. *GPS coordinates:* 45° 8.545′ N, 71° 10.853′ W.

To reach a more remote access, continue for 3.2 miles (17.1 miles), and turn right onto East Inlet Road. Go 0.3 mile (17.4 miles) to the access at a timber bridge. *GPS coordinates:* 45° 10.905′ N, 71° 10.656′ W.

WHAT YOU'LL SEE

Second Connecticut Lake remains one of our favorite big lakes in Vermont and New Hampshire. Less than half as large as First Connecticut Lake, it suffers much less from development. Second Connecticut Lake, although more manageable for paddlers than First Connecticut Lake or Lake Francis, can still suffer from sizable wind-driven waves that arise quickly; if the winds blow, choose one of the nearby smaller bodies of water instead (see Trips 47, 48, 49).

The 11 miles of highly varied shoreline—with deep spruce-fir forests all around—offer almost endless opportunities for exploration. At dawn and dusk you may see moose grazing on pond vegetation in the various marshy inlets,

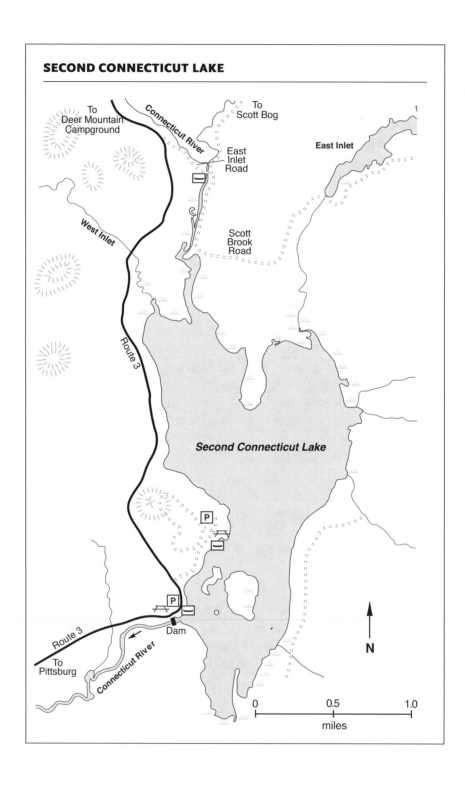

SECOND CONNECTICUT LAKE

To
Deer Mountain
Campground

Connecticut River

To
Scott Bog

East
Inlet
Road

East Inlet

West Inlet

Scott
Brook
Road

Route 3

Second Connecticut Lake

P

P

Dam

Route 3

To
Pittsburg

Connecticut River

N

0   0.5   1.0
miles

along with otter, mink, great blue heron, various ducks, and several pairs of loons. Fishing for lake trout and salmon can be excellent.

A great place to put in for a day of paddling is at the northern tip where the Connecticut River (still more of a creek here) passes beneath a timber bridge on a dirt road. Scott Creek joins the river just above the bridge. Paddle south on the gently flowing and gradually widening channel for about a mile until it opens into the main lake. This entire northern end of the lake, including the river and West Inlet, offers fantastic paddling: thick, grassy marshes full of inlets to explore and dark green spruce and fir trees rising in sharp spires behind them. The water is clean, although slightly reddish-brown from natural tannins. We especially liked the bent-over leaves of a slightly purplish water celery that graced the surface.

As we paddled down the river from the East Inlet Road access and neared the open lake on one trip, we spotted a bald eagle perched along the edge, and a bittern shot up from the shoreside grasses. White-throated sparrows called from the brush as we investigated the large patches of purple iris in bloom.

Paddling around the lake's eastern, undeveloped side, you will pass a number of other similar inlets, each with its own secrets to reveal. Among the rocky and marshy shoreline sections, you will also find a few sandy beaches. Two fairly large islands and one small one add interest to the lake's southern end. As with all islands on remote lakes, be careful not to disturb nesting loons.

47 | East Inlet

In the evening, moose wade belly-deep in the water of this long, narrow, dammed-up creek section. Also expect to see great blue heron, waterfowl, and possibly otter, beaver, and mink.

Location: Pittsburg, NH
Maps: *New Hampshire Atlas & Gazetteer,* Map 53: C9; USGS Second Connecticut Lake
Area: 60 acres
Time: 2 hours
Habitat Type: Small, marshy, shallow stream
Fish: Brook trout

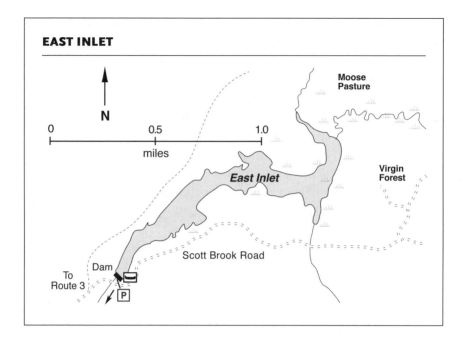

EAST INLET

Moose Pasture

Virgin Forest

East Inlet

Scott Brook Road

Dam

To Route 3

P

Information: Town of Pittsburg, NH, www.pittsburg-nh.com; The Nature Conservancy, www.nature.org/wherewework/northamerica/states/newhampshire/preserves/art6133.html

Camping: Mollidgewock State Park, Lake Francis State Park, Deer Mountain State Park; see Appendix A, #10, #12, #13

Take Note: Gasoline motors prohibited

GETTING THERE

East Inlet. From Route 145 in Pittsburg, go 17.1 miles north on Route 3, and turn right onto East Inlet Road. Go 0.3 mile (17.4 miles) to a T, and turn right onto Scott Brook Road. Go 1.6 miles (19.0 miles) to the access on the left. *GPS coordinates*: 45° 10.760′ N, 71° 9.671′ W.

  Virgin forest. Continue past the East Inlet dam for 2.5 miles, then take the left fork. From there, it is a rather difficult hike past the ruins of an old bridge. The old-growth forest will be on your left (west).

WHAT YOU'LL SEE

A moose grazed belly-deep on the far shore of East Inlet when we drove in on one trip; on another trip, a young bull moose cavorted in the shallows about a half-mile up on the left. In neither case did the moose seem overly concerned by our presence. Tree swallows skimmed the surface, and families of black and wood ducks scurried for protective cover among the reeds at water's edge. Several great blue herons fished the shallows, while trout dimpled the surface all around. Paddling next to the shore, we could study the remarkable pitcher plants in full bloom, their odd reddish flowers on straight stems bowing over as if looking at the sphagnum beneath.

East Inlet is within the Norton Pool and Moose Pasture Natural Area, preserved by The Nature Conservancy. Located in the northern tip of the state near the better-known Connecticut Lakes, East Inlet has to be one of the most beautiful bodies of water we have paddled. It is small—just 60 acres of open water in a long, sinewy channel set within several 100 acres of marsh—but truly wild and pristine. Water celery dominates the surface. Ancient, rotting stumps peer out from the brackish water, and huge fields of reed and sedge sway in the breeze. Farther away from the water on solid ground, deep green spires of spruce and fir make up the northern boreal forest. Paddling this extraordinary place sure beats fighting the waves on the larger lakes in this area.

We see moose frequently in the Connecticut Lakes region. Look for them in Moose Pasture on East Inlet.

At the far end of the open water and across the alder swamp is a section of virgin spruce-fir forest, one of the only remaining stands of such forest in New England. You can reach it by canoe and foot, but you will get your feet plenty wet. A better way to get there is by road. Paddling northeast from the dam, the wide channel continues for a mile or so, eventually turning to marsh as the inlet stream winds a serpentine pathway through a thick alder swamp. Tamarack joins the spruce and fir along the shores at this end. For more paddling room, go left through this marshy section, called Moose Pasture, where separating the real channel from an isolated oxbow is quite a challenge. With some diligence, and if you ignore the bugs, you can paddle quite a distance up the inlet stream.

Paddling here has an air of excitement to it, since you never know what might be around the next bend: beaver, a family of ducks, moose, and otter. The farther up this inlet you paddle, the smaller the channel becomes, with the ever-present alders reaching out into the creek from both sides. Eventually the alders completely block your passage.

48 | Scott Bog

Located in the northern boreal forest, this small, shallow bog is well off the beaten path. Expect to see beaver swimming about in the evening and great blue heron patrolling the shore. Moose are often seen in the pond's vicinity.

Location: Pittsburg, NH
Maps: *New Hampshire Atlas & Gazetteer,* Map 53: B9; USGS Second Connecticut Lake
Area: 100 acres
Time: 2 hours
Habitat Type: Shallow bog
Fish: Brook trout
Information: Town of Pittsburg, NH, www.pittsburg-nh.com
Camping: Mollidgewock State Park, Lake Francis State Park, Deer Mountain State Park; see Appendix A, #10, #12, #13
Take Note: Motors prohibited

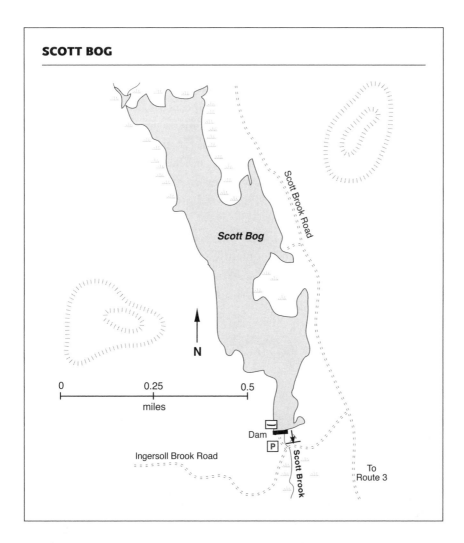

SCOTT BOG

Scott Bog

Scott Brook Road

Dam

P

Ingersoll Brook Road

Scott Brook

To Route 3

N

| 0 | 0.25 | 0.5 |
miles

GETTING THERE

From Route 145 in Pittsburg, go 17.1 miles north on Route 3, and turn right onto East Inlet Road. Go 0.3 mile (17.4 miles) to a T, and turn left onto Scott Brook Road. Go 2.5 miles (19.9 miles), staying left at the fork, and turn left onto Ingersoll Brook Road. Go 0.5 mile to the access on the right. *GPS coordinates:* 45° 12.585′ N, 71° 10.023′ W.

WHAT YOU'LL SEE

Way in the northern tip of New Hampshire, along with the well-known Connecticut Lakes, a few out-of-the-way bodies of water are highly worth exploring. On difficult-to-find Scott Bog, located between Second and Third Connecticut Lakes, you will not see too many other visitors—at least of the human variety. One privately owned cabin stands on the lake's east side, leased from the paper company that owns most of the surrounding land.

Spruce-fir forests surround Scott Bog, a beautiful, shallow northern fen, with floating sphagnum mats, yellow pond lily, water celery, pitcher plant, bur-reed, alder, and tamarack. The smells of the northern forest seeped into our senses here. A beaver dam clogs the northern end, along with many sun-whitened snags of old trees, left over from dam construction. When we paddled here the second time, in the evening, three beaver swam about, slapping the water with their tails.

If high winds keep you off the larger Connecticut Lakes, Scott Bog, just a short drive from Deer Mountain Campground, is a good alternative. The marshy shores, full of wildlife, make ideal moose habitat. In the early morning hours, moose may join you in Scott Bog and along the roads leading into the bog.

Pickerelweed greets paddlers on Scott Bog, amid a backdrop of conifers in the northern boreal forest.

49 | Third Connecticut Lake

The smallest of the Connecticut Lakes included in this book, this deep lake sits up against the Canadian border in the northern boreal forest.

Location: Pittsburg, NH
Maps: *New Hampshire Atlas & Gazetteer,* Map 53: A8; USGS Second Connecticut Lake
Area: 278 acres
Time: 3 hours
Habitat Type: Small, deep lake
Fish: Lake, brook, and rainbow trout
Information: Town of Pittsburg, NH, www.pittsburg-nh.com
Camping: Mollidgewock State Park, Lake Francis State Park, Deer Mountain State Park; see Appendix A, #10, #12, #13

GETTING THERE

From Route 145 in Pittsburg, go 21.3 miles north on Route 3 to the access on the left. Driving along Route 3, watch out for moose—and for cars stopped in the middle of the road as the occupants watch moose! *GPS coordinates*: 45° 14.357′ N, 71° 11.766′ W.

WHAT YOU'LL SEE

Third Connecticut Lake lies less than a mile from the Canadian border, near the northern tip of New Hampshire. Close to the headwaters of the Connecticut River (that distinction belongs to tiny Fourth Connecticut Lake), Third Connecticut nestles beautifully into the deep boreal forest of Coos County. With an entirely undeveloped shoreline, this 100-foot-deep lake provides good lake trout fishing. Rainbow and brook trout are also found here.

Unlike the larger and better-known First and Second Connecticut Lakes, Third Connecticut's gravel shoreline has little variety, with few inlets to explore. From the access on Route 3, you can scan nearly the entire lake perimeter. If motorboats cruise by, the remote feeling disappears easily. Nonetheless, visit Third Lake for fishing or for no other reason than to get out on the north-western shore and step across the Connecticut "River"—just a couple of feet

THIRD CONNECTICUT LAKE

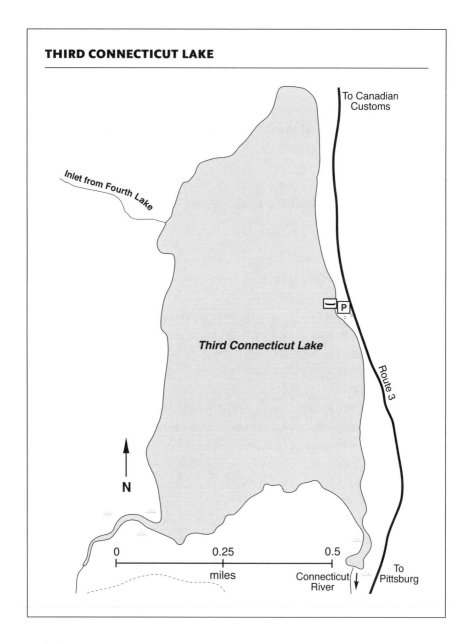

To Canadian Customs

Inlet from Fourth Lake

P

Third Connecticut Lake

Route 3

N

0   0.25   0.5
miles

Connecticut River

To Pittsburg

wide here—where it trickles into the lake. At the northern tip, you can also take advantage of a nice, sandy swimming beach.

If you want a real surprise, drive north on Route 3 from Third Connecticut Lake into Canada. As you cross the border, a sudden and dramatic change takes place. You leave the deep boreal wilderness forest of spruce and fir and enter into open farmland. You have to experience it to believe it.

At the U.S. Customs office, you can pick up a hiking map and walk to the so-called Fourth Connecticut Lake. The walk takes you along the U.S.-Canada border, then down to the little pond where the mighty Connecticut River (New England's longest and most important river) begins its 410-mile journey to Long Island Sound.

THE SNAPPING TURTLE: HIDDEN DWELLER OF THE POND

The snapping turtle (*Chelydra serpentina*)—New Hampshire and Vermont's most common species of turtle, even more common than the painted turtle—inhabits almost every beaver pond, millpond, lake, marsh, and slow-moving stream in the Northeast. Hundreds live in some bodies of water, but you would not know it. Even if you spend quite a bit of time paddling, you rarely see this large turtle. Unlike its sun-loving cousin, the painted turtle, the snapping turtle prefers pond-bottom depths and rarely basks in the sun.

You can easily recognize a snapping turtle, especially out of water. A long, spiny-ridged tail and very large head relative to body size give it away. The young has a distinct ridge on the top shell (carapace), although on a large adult, the shell may have worn smooth. On the underside, the small bottom shell (plastron) has a crosslike shape. Mature snapping turtles grow quite large, much larger than any other Northeast turtle. The carapace can reach a length of 20 inches (an overall length, nose to tail, of more than 3 feet), and a large turtle can weigh more than 60 pounds.

When paddling relatively clear, shallow water, we occasionally see a snapping turtle underwater or on a bank above a pond or slow-moving river—probably en route to a nearby body of water or, perhaps, a female out of water to lay a clutch of eggs. It may travel a great distance in search of a suitable nesting site—one marked individual traveled 16 kilometers round-trip. Our usual glimpse, though, is just the triangular nose sticking out of the water ahead as we paddle along.

Many people fear the snapping turtle—and we admit to having had a bit of concern when two large specimens chased each other just inches beneath our boat in a shallow pond—but it really poses no harm *as long as it remains in the water*. Even in the unlikely event that one bites a swimmer's toe, it quickly lets go, realizing that the quarry is more than it can handle. In the water, the shy snapper avoids human contact. Watch out for a snapping turtle on land, though. It lashes out with lightning speed when threatened. With its massive jaw muscles and razor-sharp beak, a large snapper exerts a force of more than 400 pounds per square inch—enough to sever a finger easily.

The snapping turtle has existed for at least 80 million years, and scientists believe it to be the oldest North American reptile. Like all turtles, its rib cage and vertebrae have evolved into a bony carapace and plastron. Although the carapace provides armored protection, the small plastron offers almost no protection to its underside, making it also vulnerable to leeches; it sometimes leaves the water to rid itself of these parasites.

Most turtles hibernate for long periods, but we sometimes see the relatively cold-resistant snapping turtle swimming beneath the ice, although in northern New England it typically hibernates in the bottom mud for at least a while during the dead of winter. When idle underwater, it does not need to surface for air. Special surfaces in its rear cloacal cavity extract oxygen from the water, much like gills. When active, though, it needs more oxygen and must surface for air—providing the quiet paddler an opportunity to catch a glimpse.

Omnivore and opportunist, the snapping turtle dines on a wide range of animals and plants, including fish, frogs, salamanders, occasional ducklings and loon chicks, dead animals, and aquatic plants. A snapper can kill anything its size or smaller, but it seems to prefer the easy meal. A superb sense of smell helps it to scavenge for dead animals. The snapping turtle literature recounts a story of a Native American who assisted in locating drowning victims, using a snapping turtle on a long leash. When released into the water, the turtle unerringly headed for the decomposing corpse and latched on to it with its strong jaws. Its handler then slowly reeled it in—corpse and all.

A mature female leaves the water in late spring or early summer to lay eggs. She digs a hole and typically deposits from 20 to 30 (rarely, up to 80) eggs the size of pingpong balls, then covers the hole. Some lay eggs in two or more holes; some dig several false holes to mislead predators, which take a heavy toll on snapping turtle clutches. The eggs usually hatch in fall, some 70 to 100 days after laying (depending on temperature), and the inch-long hatchlings make a beeline for the water—often as raccoons, birds, and other predators gobble them up.

As with many turtle species, nest temperature determines sex. Several studies found that at very cool or very warm temperatures, the embryos all developed into females, while intermediate temperatures produced males. In most nests, temperature varies with location of the egg, so both males and females develop.

CATHY JOHNSON

The snapping turtle population remains secure in the Northeast—unlike that of most other turtles. It seems to tolerate current levels of environmental pollution and lives in even highly polluted marshy areas in cities. Some regard snapper meat highly, resulting in heavy trapping in certain areas. We see fewer snappers crushed on roads, compared with more terrestrial turtles. If you come across a snapping turtle on land, avoid the temptation to deliver it to the nearest body of water—chances are pretty good that she knows where to head to lay her eggs and does not need assistance in this endeavor.

4 | SOUTHERN VERMONT

Although we include only eight bodies of water in southern Vermont, wonderful paddling opportunities abound. The two stretches of the Connecticut River offer hours of paddling, and birdwatchers report many rare species in the Herricks Cove area, which includes several other coves scattered along the river just above Bellows Falls. The area near Brattleboro offers more of a river experience, except in Retreat Meadows, where we often see beaver swimming about in the evening.

Somerset Reservoir harbors nesting loons and offers many miles of shoreline to explore, with Mount Snow as a backdrop. When winds whip 1,600-acre Somerset to a froth, we paddle the much quieter Grout and Branch ponds. You can camp at both, although Branch Pond provides a more wilderness feel. You might see moose in this area, and we often see beaver.

Sadawga Pond near the Massachusetts border offers an interesting paddling experience, with a large floating island a prominent feature. The island, an old piece of peatland bog, has not moved for several years, indicating that it may be taking permanent root.

Gale Meadows Pond and Lowell Lake, located close to each other on the eastern edge of the Green Mountain National Forest, provide similar paddling experiences. Shallow marshy ponds with scenic hillsides forming a backdrop, both are excellent locations to look for great blue heron, beaver, mink, muskrat, moose, and other wetland species.

50 | Sadawga Pond

A floating island, loosely tethered by roots to the pond's bottom, is a major feature of Sadawga Pond. Look for great blue heron and waterfowl among the rafts of aquatic vegetation.

Location: Whitingham, VT
Maps: *Vermont Atlas & Gazetteer,* Map 21: J14; USGS Jacksonville, Readsboro
Area: 194 acres
Time: 3 hours
Habitat Type: Small, marshy pond
Fish: Largemouth bass, pickerel, yellow perch
Camping: Woodford State Park, Molly Stark State Park; see Appendix A, #17, #18
Take Note: Personal watercraft prohibited

GETTING THERE
From Route 9 in Wilmington, go 8.8 miles south on Route 100, and turn left onto Sadawga Lake Road. Go 0.2 mile (9.0 miles), and turn right into the access. *GPS coordinates*: 42° 47.151´ N, 72° 52.589´ W.

WHAT YOU'LL SEE
Sadawga Pond, located just above the Massachusetts border in Whitingham, Vermont, has an unusual feature: a floating island. Sphagnum moss and other fen vegetation cover the sizable island—about 25 acres—which provides firm enough footing for some tamarack as tall as 20 feet. According to a 1952 article in *Vermont Life*, this is one of only two honest-to-goodness floating islands in the world (Switzerland has the other). While the article clearly exaggerated—floating mats of peat occur commonly in New England—Sadawga's floating island is probably the most dramatic you will see. Apparently, it formed in the

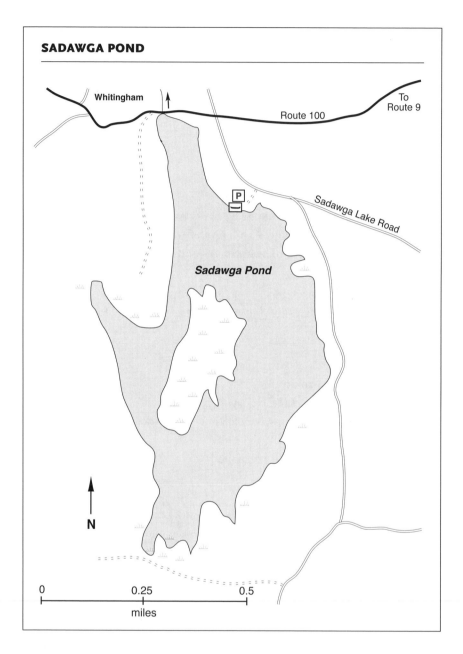

SADAWGA POND

Whitingham

Route 100

To
Route 9

P

Sadawga Lake Road

Sadawga Pond

N

0   0.25   0.5

miles

early 1800s when dams raised the small pond's water level. The original pond must have been a kettle hole that gradually closed in from the sides, with much of the pond edge floating (as in quaking bogs). When the water level rose, a root mass broke free and floated to the surface. Although the island—really several connected islands—does float, it does not sail around the lake like a raft. Roots now tether it to the ground beneath the pond. In shifting winds, the island pivots a little, usually the extent of its movement.

Sadawga's floating island has at times caused headaches for the lakeside residents on the northern and eastern shoreline. In 1926, a large section broke off in a storm and for several years floated around the pond, periodically lodging in front of cottages, disrupting access to the water. That continues to happen, although rarely. The main island appears to be solidly anchored to the bottom. Resist the temptation to land on the island. Your footsteps could damage the fragile fen ecosystem, and it would be dangerous if you fell through the cushiony mat into the deep water below.

In more recent years, Sadawga has been the subject of a mystery. Local residents found an overturned rowboat and believed its occupant had drowned. But they never found the body, despite extensive searches. Some have speculated that the disappearance was staged.

The name derives either from the Mohawk word *sadawga*, meaning "swiftly flowing water" or, according to local lore, from an old Indian by that name who stayed in the area long after his people left—the more likely explanation, given the stillness of the pond.

Except for the northern and eastern ends, Sadawga remains relatively undeveloped and the houses unobtrusive. Extensive marshy areas line the shore, and a few shallow inlets beg to be explored. As on the floating island, sweet gale, cranberry, various heaths, and diminutive sundew grow on tussocks of sphagnum moss on much of the fenlike shoreline.

We saw lots of wood ducks here, as well as a large congregation of Canada geese in mid-September. Farther away from the water, the heavily wooded land supports red maple, hemlock, and beech, along with a few large serviceberry trees, some with trunks as large as 8 inches in diameter.

51 | Somerset Reservoir

This large reservoir is home to Vermont's southernmost population of nesting loons. You should also look here for moose, black bear, mink, otter, and beaver.

Location: Somerset and Stratton, VT

Maps: *Vermont Atlas & Gazetteer,* Map 21: C13; USGS Mount Snow, Stratton Mountain
Area: 1,597 acres
Time: All day
Habitat Type: Large lake
Fish: Smallmouth bass, pickerel, yellow perch, brook trout
Camping: Woodford State Park, Molly Stark State Park; see Appendix A, #17, 18
Take Note: Personal watercraft, water-skiing prohibited; 10 MPH speed limit; waves can be treacherous under windy conditions

GETTING THERE

From Wilmington, go 6.0 miles west on Route 9, and turn right onto Somerset Road. Go about 9 miles to the access, staying right at the fork. *GPS coordinates:* 42° 58.398′ N, 72° 56.544′ W.

You can also reach the lake by portaging in 0.8 mile from the Grout Pond Recreation Area on marked trails.

WHAT YOU'LL SEE

Looking for some real exercise in beautiful surroundings? Try a day on Somerset Reservoir in southern Vermont. Rolling mountains—including Mount Snow, its northern face visible from most of the lake—bound this long, narrow lake on the upper reaches of the Deerfield River. Although surrounded by the Green Mountain National Forest, the reservoir and immediate shoreline were owned by New England Power Company, which sold its interest to Pacific Gas and Electric (PG&E), which sold to TransCanada. In May 2000, the Vermont Land Trust purchased development rights for 15,736 acres along the Deerfield Valley, including around Somerset.

An earlier change occurred in January 1996. A group of southern Vermont residents, led by co-author Alex Wilson, convinced the Vermont Natural Resources Board (formerly Water Resources Board) to ban personal watercraft and water-skiing and to restrict speeds to 10 MPH. Given the Natural Resources Board's propensity to allow high-impact uses on large bodies of water, we should all rejoice over this remarkable regulation.

The lake extends roughly 5 miles from the dam to the northernmost point, the East Branch of the Deerfield River inlet. Another arm extends farther to the east, fed by the Grout Pond outlet. A number of islands dot the lake's northern extension, including Streeter Island, maintained as a picnic area. To explore the

SOMERSET RESERVOIR

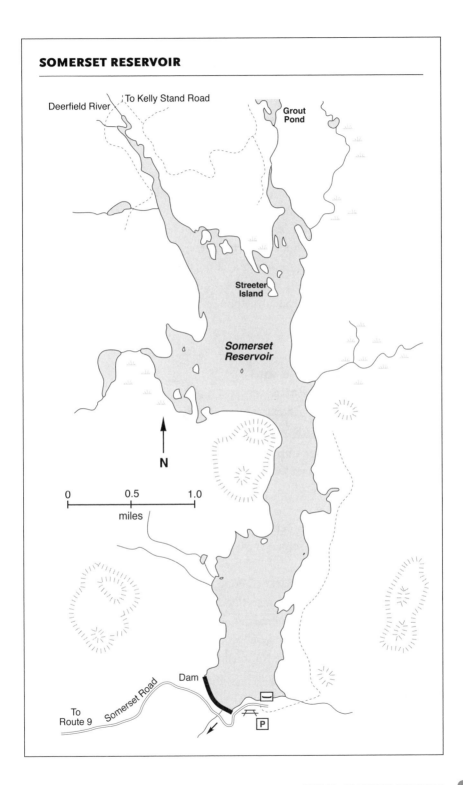

Deerfield River

To Kelly Stand Road

Grout Pond

Streeter Island

Somerset Reservoir

N

0   0.5   1.0
miles

Dam

To Route 9

Somerset Road

P

whole 16-mile perimeter requires a full day. If you tend to stop frequently to enjoy wildlife—we watched a mink drag a pumpkinseed sunfish almost as large as itself along the shore—you may have trouble getting all the way around in a day. The heavily wooded shoreline lends itself well to relaxed exploring and wildlife observation. The mixed deciduous and coniferous woods abound with warblers, woodpeckers, and other birds. Somerset is the southernmost Vermont lake with nesting loons.

TransCanada controls the reservoir level for hydropower generation (the water flows into the Searsburg Dam penstock, which you pass on the road in). Although it maintains the water level through loon nesting season (May through July), after July the level can drop significantly, making the reservoir less attractive. Note that winds can arise quickly on this long body of water—with surrounding mountains acting as a north-to-south funnel—generating serious whitecaps. On breezy days, stick to smaller bodies of water in the area, such as Grout, Branch, and Sadawga ponds.

52 | Grout Pond and Branch Pond

These small, remote ponds in the Green Mountain National Forest offer on-site primitive camping. This is a great place to enjoy a wilderness experience and to look for beaver, moose, and other animals.

Location: Stratton and Sunderland, VT
Maps: *Vermont Atlas & Gazetteer,* Maps 21: A13, 25: K11; USGS Stratton Mountain, Sunderland
Area: Grout Pond, 86 acres; Branch Pond, 43 acres
Time: Grout Pond, 2 hours; Branch Pond, 1 hour
Habitat Type: Small, shallow, marshy ponds
Fish: Smallmouth bass, pickerel, yellow perch
Information: Green Mountain National Forest, www.fs.fed.us/r9/forests/greenmountain/htm/greenmountain/g_home.htm
Camping: On-site camping; see Appendix A, Green Mountain National Forest
Take Note: Gasoline motors prohibited

GETTING THERE

Grout Pond. From Route 100 in West Wardsboro (14 miles north of Route 9; 9 miles south of Route 30), go 6.0 miles west on Kelly Stand Road/West Wardsboro–Arlington Road, and turn left onto the access road. Go 1.0 mile (7.0 miles) to Grout Pond. *GPS coordinates*: 43° 2.742′ N, 72° 57.132′ W.

   Branch Pond. From the Grout Pond turnoff, go 4.5 miles west on Kelly Stand Road, and turn right onto the access road. Go 2.5 miles (7.0 miles) to the end. Carry 0.3 mile to the pond, through deep spruce-fir woods full of trillium and other wildflowers. *GPS coordinates*: 43° 4.644′ N, 73° 1.050′ W.

WHAT YOU'LL SEE

These two small ponds, located within southern Vermont's Green Mountain National Forest, offer delightful paddling. The U.S. Forest Service allows primitive camping in most of the national forest, including around both of these ponds. A small, developed recreation area is situated close to the Grout Pond access. Numerous hiking trails crisscross the area, including one that extends around Grout Pond; one that leads to Somerset Reservoir's northern end; and our favorite, one that connects Branch Pond and Bourn Pond. The Appalachian Trail and the Long Trail also pass through the area.

Grout Pond

We return to this wonderful spot year after year. Although small, the pond offers plenty of space for a relaxed day of paddling, without the distraction of motorboats, personal watercraft, or water-skiers. Two shelters on the northeastern shore and a half-dozen tent sites with fireplaces and picnic tables lay scattered around the pond. You have to carry your boat about 50 yards from the parking area to the launching area.

   Grout Pond provides an ideal spot to acquaint young children with canoe camping. With a trail all the way around the lake and a quick paddle from even the farthest campsite, you can get to civilization quickly if you want. The primitive camping, however, provides a much different experience from public or private campgrounds with close-together campsites, RVs, TVs, satellite dishes, and the like. Kids will enjoy the sandy swimming beach at the northwestern access point, along with plenty of places to fish for yellow perch, sunfish, and bass. You can usually see beaver if you paddle the lake in the late evening or early morning—Alex's daughters got their first good look at these industrious animals here.

   We often come to Grout Pond in autumn for our last camping trip of the year. The pond, gorgeous in its full autumn regalia of reds and yellows, offers

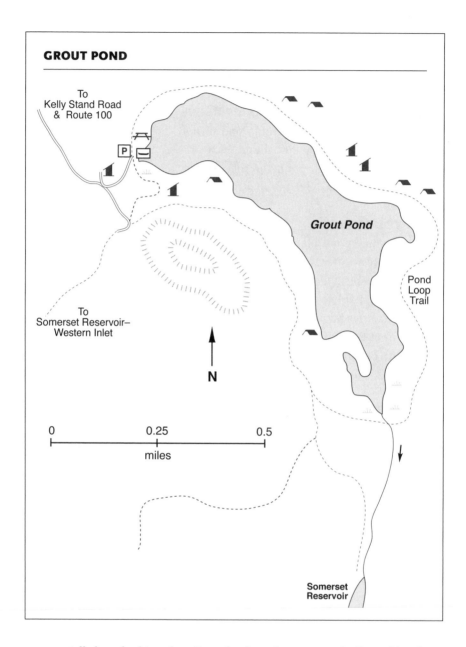

GROUT POND

To
Kelly Stand Road
& Route 100

P

To
Somerset Reservoir–
Western Inlet

Grout Pond

Pond
Loop
Trail

N

0	0.25	0.5

miles

Somerset
Reservoir

an especially breathtaking shoreline of red maples against a brilliant-blue, bug-free autumn sky.

Branch Pond

Branch Pond sits nestled high in the 15,680-acre Lye Brook Wilderness. Worthy of inclusion here for its pristine beauty and unusual vegetation, the pond offers

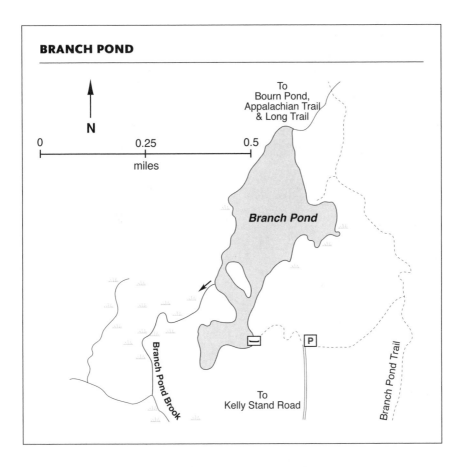

BRANCH POND

N

0   0.25   0.5

miles

To
Bourn Pond,
Appalachian Trail
& Long Trail

Branch Pond

P

Branch Pond Brook

To
Kelly Stand Road

Branch Pond Trail

a wonderful morning or afternoon of leisurely paddling. Look for moose here, along with the many unusual plants of a northern fen, including carnivorous sundews and pitcher plants, growing on tussocks of sphagnum moss. Along the shore you will see tamarack, a northern species and our only conifer to lose its needles in winter. The clear water and varied shoreline offer opportunities for some exploring, although lakeside vegetation restricts access somewhat. Be very careful walking on the sphagnum-moss tussocks; your footsteps can damage the fragile plants.

Several primitive campsites dot the shores of Branch Pond, and the U.S. Forest Service permits camping anywhere, for now, in this part of the Green Mountain National Forest. The fragile ecosystem around Branch Pond, however, needs careful treatment when camping.

Look for the reddish leaves of carnivorous pitcher plants, *Sarracenia purpurea*, on the sphagnum hummocks of Branch Pond.

53 | Gale Meadows Pond

Gale Meadows Pond is a small, shallow pond located within a wildlife management area, with views of Stratton Mountain. Prominent species include waterfowl, loon, beaver, mink, muskrat, moose, black bear, whitetailed deer, and coyote.

Location: Winhall, VT
Maps: *Vermont Atlas & Gazetteer,* Map 25: H14; USGS Londonderry, Peru
Area: 195 acres
Time: 4 hours
Habitat Type: Shallow, marshy pond
Fish: Largemouth bass, pickerel, yellow perch
Information: Gale Meadows Wildlife Management Area, www.vtfishandwildlife.com/wma_maps.cfm
Camping: Jamaica State Park, Emerald Lake State Park, Ball Mountain Dam State Park; see Appendix A, #20, #21, #40
Take Note: 5 MPH speed limit; personal watercraft prohibited

GETTING THERE

From Route 30 in Bondville, go 0.8 mile north on River Road, and take a left fork onto Gale Meadows Road. Go 0.9 mile (1.7 miles), and take a left fork. This road dead-ends at the access. *GPS coordinates*: 43° 10.086′ N, 72° 51.858′ W.

WHAT YOU'LL SEE

Located just north of Bondville, Gale Meadows Pond provides an ideal spot for a relaxed day of fishing, birdwatching, or simply exploring this wildlife management area. Marshes hug parts of the varied shoreline, particularly the southern end, where reed, sedge, alder, and cattail provide habitat for beaver; you will see lots of evidence of them. Large stands of fern—ostrich, sensitive, cinnamon, and royal—spill over the banks. At both the southern and northern ends, sun-whitened stumps left over from the pond's damming provide nesting holes for hundreds of tree swallows; several wood duck nesting boxes provide more nesting space. Aquatic vegetation and submerged logs may impede paddling in these parts.

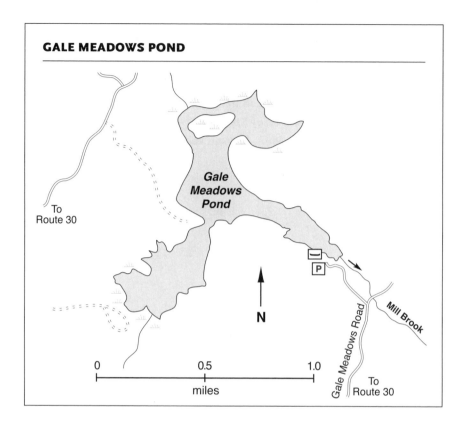

GALE MEADOWS POND

Gale
Meadows
Pond

To
Route 30

N

Gale Meadows Road

Mill Brook

P

To
Route 30

0   0.5   1.0

miles

The northern end seems much more fenlike, with tamarack and floating sphagnum islands. Except for the swampy areas, mixed conifer and deciduous trees line most of the heavily wooded shoreline. There is one farmhouse on the western shore, and another house sits back from the water at the southern tip, but there is no recent development. In the early 1960s, a group of area landowners protected the pond and surrounding area from development; the Vermont Department of Fish and Wildlife manages it. In late 1991, the Vermont Natural Resources Board established a 5 MPH speed limit on Gale Meadows Pond, which makes the pond excellent for quietwater paddling and fishing.

54 | Lowell Lake

Scenic hills form a backdrop for this small, marshy pond. Aquatic vegetation dominates the surface, and many beaver lodges dot the shoreline. We saw a bald eagle here, and you are likely to see great blue heron and many other marshland species.

Location: Londonderry, VT
Maps: *Vermont Atlas & Gazetteer,* Map 26: F3; USGS Londonderry
Area: 102 acres
Time: 2 hours
Habitat Type: Small, marshy lake
Fish: Largemouth bass, pickerel, yellow perch
Information: Lowell State Park, www.vtstateparks.com/htm/lowell.cfm
Camping: Jamaica State Park, Ball Mountain Dam State Park, Grafton/Mollie Beattie State Park; see Appendix A, #20, #40, #41
Take Note: Gasoline motors prohibited

GETTING THERE

From Route 100 north in Londonderry, go 3.0 miles east on Route 11, and turn left onto Lowell Lake Road. Go 0.7 mile (3.7 miles), and turn right at the T. Go 0.2 mile (3.9 miles) to the parking area. *GPS coordinates:* 43° 13.399′ N, 72° 45.915′ W.

WHAT YOU'LL SEE

Lowell Lake, a real gem in southern Vermont, covers about half of Lowell Lake State Park, created in 1981. The state substantially expanded and officially dedicated the park in 1996, when the Vermont Land Trust helped acquire an additional 154 acres from the White family. The park includes most of the shoreline and several islands.

Tall hills to the north and south provide a scenic backdrop to this shallow, weedy pond. Small islands make the pond seem larger, and some huge, tall trees lend a certain majesty. When we paddled here in late September, several other canoes and kayaks plied the waters, pushing through the thick surface vegetation of this productive water body. Hiking trails also course through the woods along the shoreline.

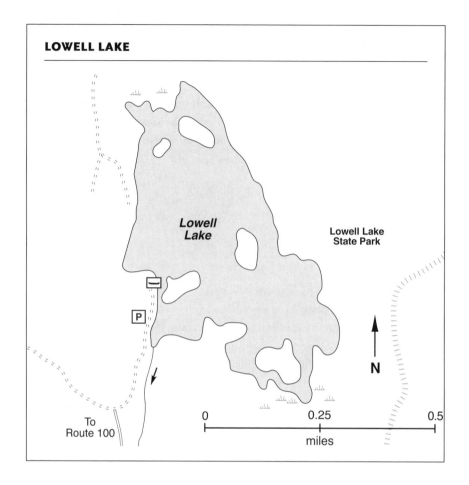

LOWELL LAKE

Lowell Lake

Lowell Lake
State Park

P

N

To
Route 100

0   0.25   0.5

miles

Water shield dominates the surface, although other marshland plants poke up here and there through thick subsurface vegetation, much of which consists of masses of bladderwort. Buttonbush, leatherleaf, and other shrubs line the shores. Make sure that you fully explore the marshland on the pond's north side, paddling in and out of the islands along the cattail swamp, through the fragrant waterlily and water shield. Many huge beaver lodges impressed us, although only a few were in use.

Toward dusk on a late-June visit, we watched an adult bald eagle survey its surroundings from a tall white pine at the lake's northern end. Later in the season, we paddled here on a warm, sunny day, and as we watched a gathering of Canada geese, they and the early turning red maple on the far shore told us that fall would come soon. We knew that we would be back to explore the pond as it awakens in spring.

55 | Herricks Cove, Retreat Meadows and Connecticut River—Southern Section

These sections along the Connecticut River provide scenic mountain views and opportunities to see osprey, bald eagle, waterfowl, and many other species. Herricks Cove and other nearby coves are noted birdwatching areas.

Location: Brattleboro, Rockingham, and Vernon, VT; Charlestown, Chesterfield, Hinsdale, and Walpole, NH
Maps: *Vermont Atlas & Gazetteer,* Maps 23: G7, 27: H10; *New Hampshire Atlas & Gazetteer*, Maps 18: E5, 25: F8; USGS Bellows Falls, Brattleboro
Length: Herricks Cove, 6 miles one way; Retreat Meadows, 7 miles one way
Time: Herricks Cove, all day; Retreat Meadows, 6 hours
Habitat Type: Marshy river inlets and large river
Fish: Largemouth and smallmouth bass, pickerel, northern pike, perch, walleye; brook, brown, and rainbow trout
Information: Vermont Canoe Touring Center, 802-257-5008
Camping: Fort Dummer State Park; see Appendix A, #19

GETTING THERE

Herricks Cove. From I-91, Exit 6 northbound, go 1.3 miles north on Route 5 to the picnic area access on the right. *GPS coordinates:* 43° 10.902′ N, 72° 26.665′ W.

From I-91, Exit 6 southbound, turn right onto Route 103, and go to the junction with Route 5. Turn left onto Route 5, and go 0.7 mile to the access on the right.

Retreat Meadows. From High Street in Brattleboro, go 0.9 mile north on Route 30 to the pull-off on the right. *GPS coordinates:* 42° 51.806′ N, 72° 34.023′ W.

You can also put in by the Marina Restaurant. From High Street, go 1.0 mile north on Putney Road/Route 5, and turn left at the Marina Restaurant sign. Park and launch at the far north end of the parking area. *GPS coordinates:* 42° 52.058′ N, 72° 33.415′ W.

WHAT YOU'LL SEE

It surprises many to learn that the vast majority of the Connecticut River's 410-mile length—from the Canadian border to Long Island Sound—backs up

HERRICKS COVE

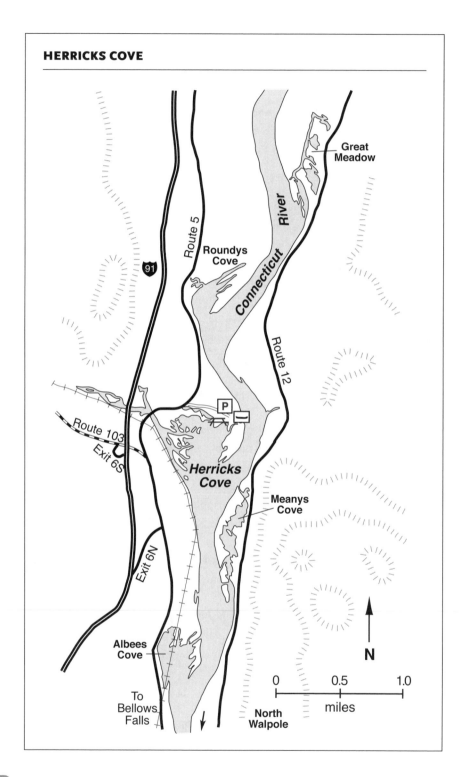

Great
Meadow

Connecticut River

Route 5

Roundys
Cove

Route 12

91

P

Route 103

Exit 6S

Herricks
Cove

Meanys
Cove

Exit 6N

Albees
Cove

To
Bellows
Falls

North
Walpole

N

0   0.5   1.0

miles

behind dams. Unfortunately, only a tiny fraction of the river consists of free-flowing water. The lower reaches of the Connecticut River offer fine paddling in the impoundments behind Bellows Falls and Vernon Dam.

Herricks Cove

Herricks Cove and several other marshy coves along the Connecticut River above Bellows Falls offer a very pleasant day of paddling through extraordinary marshes, favorite areas of birdwatchers, especially during spring and fall migration. Many rare species, including first records for the state, have shown up here.

From the access, you can explore the broad Williams River delta that forms this cove, or paddle either upriver or down to four other coves well worth visiting. On the cove's western edge, the current becomes quite noticeable and the bottom sandy—not bad for swimming on a hot day. You reach the Route 5 bridge about two-thirds of a mile from the cove's mouth and the much taller I-91 bridge several hundred yards farther. Paddling amid the many islands, we saw muskrat and lots of evidence of beaver. Songbirds filled the alder, dogwood, and willow, and an osprey wheeled overhead, searching for fish.

North of Herricks Cove, you will find Roundys Cove on the river's western shore and Great Meadow on the eastern shore. One could spend a great deal of time exploring here!

South of Herricks Cove, if you follow the western shore and look closely along the railroad bed, you will find extensive marble mine tailings and polished marble pieces that must have been dumped into the river at some point. We found some beautiful pieces—which provided ballast for Alex's ill-balanced solo canoe on a windy day. Samples ranged from pure-white to rich-green conglomerates, to pink and gray.

About 2 miles downriver, you reach Albees Cove on the western shore. We found, behind a beaver lodge, one very narrow, winding channel into the cove, probably impenetrable once vegetation grows up (we visited in mid-May). Just beyond this entrance, another, much wider channel allows access, and below the island the cove is fully accessible—although shallow water may limit access during low-water times. The adventurous might want to paddle under the very low concrete railroad bridge to the western section of Albees Cove. By mid-May, fragrant waterlily and assorted other aquatic vegetation grow thick. Depending on water depth and vegetation, you can paddle north until the marsh closes in.

On the New Hampshire side just south of Herricks Cove, you will find several entrances into Meanys Cove, really more of a channel through the cat-

RETREAT MEADOWS AND CONNECTICUT RIVER—SOUTHERN SECTION

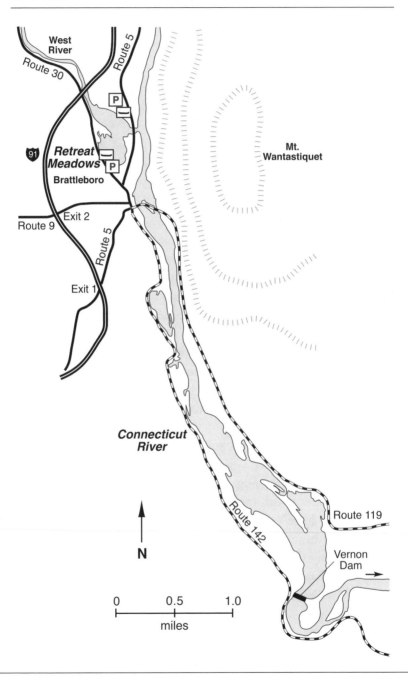

West River

Route 30

Route 5

P

91 *Retreat Meadows*

P

Brattleboro

Route 9

Exit 2

Route 5

Exit 1

Mt. Wantastiquet

Connecticut River

N

Route 142

Route 119

Vernon Dam

0   0.5   1.0
miles

Retreat Meadows is a great place to look for beaver and muskrat in the evening as they harvest tree branches and grasses.

tail swamp, thick with aquatic vegetation. We saw lots of fish amid the water-lily pads.

Retreat Meadows

Retreat Meadows, named for the Brattleboro Retreat, one of the oldest private mental hospitals in the United States (founded in the mid-1800s), offers a great place to spend a day of paddling within a stone's throw of downtown Brattleboro. Now largely transformed into a substance abuse and outpatient mental health facility, the Retreat's large residential buildings can be seen along the meadow's south shore.

The West River flows through Retreat Meadows before it intersects the Connecticut, offering a quiet place to paddle, especially when winds blow up and down the Connecticut. The marsh harbors the typical wetland bird species and some unusual visitors at times, such as the lesser black-backed gull. In the Retreat Meadows proper, look for muskrat and beaver (especially near dusk) as you explore the winding channels and islands of this extensive cattail marsh. In early spring we have often seen wood duck and hooded merganser here. You can paddle up the West River, passing under the I-91 bridge far above, until the current becomes too strong about a half-mile upstream.

You can sneak out onto the Connecticut to take in the beauty of Wantastiquet Mountain on the New Hampshire side and paddle downstream, away from the bustle of Brattleboro, exploring inlets, islands, and channels. On your way, just before entering the Connecticut, you pass the Vermont Canoe Touring Center (canoe and kayak rentals).

Bald eagles recently have nested in this area. Sometimes in winter, they perch out over the water just above and below the Vernon dam, fishing the waters kept open by Vermont Yankee Nuclear Power Plant's thermal pollution and scavenging fish killed by the water churning through the dam's turbines. We once watched a mature eagle dive-bomb two mergansers for about five minutes. Each time the mergansers tried to fly, the eagle swooped down on them; when they resurfaced after a dive, the relentless eagle dove on them again. Eventually, the mergansers flew upriver with the eagle in hot pursuit.

56 | Wallingford Pond

The White Rocks National Recreation Area of the Green Mountain National Forest contains this small, marshy wilderness pond. Look for loon, beaver, and moose here.

Location: Wallingford, VT
Maps: *Vermont Atlas & Gazetteer,* Map 29: K13; USGS Wallingford
Area: 86 acres
Time: 2 hours
Habitat Type: Small, shallow pond with 3 arms
Fish: Smallmouth bass, pickerel, yellow perch
Information: Green Mountain National Forest, www.fs.fed.us/r9/forests/greenmountain/htm/greenmountain/links/heritage/wallingford_pond.htm
Camping: On-site primitive camping; see Appendix A, Green Mountain National Forest
Take Note: Gasoline motors prohibited; 1-mile hike-in, road undriveable

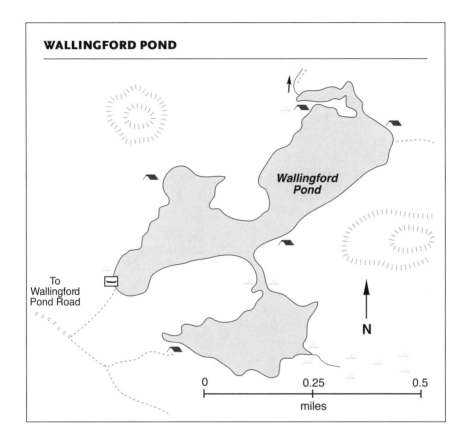

WALLINGFORD POND

Wallingford Pond

To
Wallingford
Pond Road

N

0   0.25   0.5

miles

GETTING THERE

From Route 7 in Wallingford, take Route 140 east. Turn right at the sign for White Rocks Picnic Area, but stay on the main gravel road instead of turning in to the picnic area. Go 2.0 miles, turn right onto Wallingford Pond Road, and go another 2.0 miles to the access road on the left. Park in a small turnout, just before the access road. It takes about 30 minutes—longer if you stop to rest— to hike the mile into the pond. There is a gradual climb, followed by a gradual drop to the pond; stay to the left at trail forks. *GPS coordinates*: 43° 24.678′ N, 72° 55.026′ W.

WHAT YOU'LL SEE

Situated completely within White Rocks Recreation Area of the Green Mountain National Forest, remote Wallingford Pond does not suffer from development. The pond seems much larger than its 86 acres, probably be- cause of its cloverleaf shape, which divides the pond into three segments. A variety of trees—balsam fir, spruce, red maple, white birch, and yellow birch—

populate the heavily wooded shoreline, along with thickly grown alder, making shore access difficult. Other sections of shoreline seem more boglike, with sphagnum tussocks, heath, and sundew. Several marshy areas, especially at the inlet near the southern end, provide nesting and feeding habitat for waterfowl and the occasional moose. Wallingford is one of a handful of southern lakes that supports nesting loons.

As you paddle into the southern arm of the pond, be careful of sharp rocks just below the surface in the connecting channel. Especially in late summer, with low water levels, be careful to avoid damaging your boat. Five or six unmaintained primitive sites around the pond provide places to camp.

THE BEAVER: RESIDENT WETLANDS ENGINEER

The beaver (*Castor canadensis*) is one of the most remarkable animals found in New England's lakes, ponds, and streams. Unlike most other animals, beaver actively modify their environment. The sole representative of the family *Castoridae*, this 30- to 100-pound rodent—largest in North America—descends directly from a bear-sized ancestor that lived a million years ago.

Quietwater paddlers frequently see beaver dams and lodges, especially on more remote lakes and ponds. This industrious mammal uses branches pruned from streamside trees or downed timber to construct dams and lodges. Beaver now work mostly under the cover of darkness, especially in areas heavily frequented by humans. In the wilds, however, many beaver work away in broad daylight. We mention in our descriptions where we have seen beaver abroad during the day.

Beaver build dams to raise a stream or pond's water level, providing the resident colony with access to trees growing farther away. The deeper water also allows beaver to cache branches underwater for winter retrieval, even when thick layers of ice cover their winter stores. They also dig small canals through marsh and meadow to transport branches from distant trees. Just as we find paddling easier than carrying a boat, beaver prefer swimming with a branch—taking advantage of water's buoyancy—to carrying it overland. They usually prune off leafy twigs to reduce drag.

Studies show that the sound of flowing water guides beaver in their dam-building—they jam sticks into the dam where they hear the gurgle of water. In one experiment, researchers played a tape of gurgling water; beaver responded by jamming sticks into locations that emanated sound, even though no

water actually flowed there. Beaver dams can be more than 10 feet high and hundreds of feet long. The largest dam ever recorded, near the present town of Berlin, New Hampshire, spanned 4,000 feet and created a lake with 40 lodges!

Beaver dams benefit many species, providing important habitat for waterfowl, fish, moose, muskrat, and other animals. Plus, the dams provide flood control, minimize erosion along stream banks, increase aquifer recharge, and improve water quality, both by allowing silt to settle out and by providing biological filtration through aquatic plants. We credit beaver with creating much of America's best farmland by damming watercourses, thus allowing nutrient-rich silt to accumulate over many years. As the ponds fill in, meadows form.

The beaver lodge includes an underwater entrance and usually two different platforms: a main floor about four inches above the water level and a sleeping shelf another two inches higher. Beaver may construct the lodge in a pond's center but more commonly site it on the edge. Before winter onset, beaver cover much of the lodge with mud—which they carry on their broad tails while swimming—that freezes to provide an almost impenetrable fortress. The river otter—the only predator that can get in—can swim through the underwater entrance. Beaver leave the peak more permeable for ventilation.

Near the lodge, in deep water, beaver store up a winter's worth of branches in an underwater food cache. They jam branches butt-first into the mud to keep them under the ice and then swim out under the ice to bring back branches to eat.

The beaver has adapted remarkably well to its aquatic lifestyle. It has two layers of fur: long silky guard hairs and a dense woolly underfur. By regularly grooming this fur with a special comblike split toenail and keeping it oiled, the beaver ensures that water seldom totally wets its skin. Special valves keep the beaver's nose and ears shut underwater, and special skin folds in the mouth enable it to gnaw underwater and carry branches in its teeth without getting water down its throat. Back feet have fully webbed toes to provide propulsion underwater, and the tail provides important rudder control, helping it swim in a straight line when dragging a large branch. Both the respiratory and circulatory systems have adapted to underwater swimming, enabling a beaver to stay underwater for up to fifteen minutes. Finally, as with other rodents, its teeth grow constantly and remain sharp through use.

Beaver generally mate for life and maintain an extended family structure. Young stay with their parents for two years, so both yearlings and the current year's kits live with the two parents in the lodge. Females usually bear two—sometimes three—kits between April and June. Born fully furred with eyes open, they can walk and swim almost immediately, although they rarely leave the lodge until at least a month of age. Yearlings and both parents bring food to the kits, as well as help with dam and lodge construction.

The demand for beaver pelts, more than any other factor, prompted the early European exploration of North America. Trappers nearly exterminated the beaver by the late 1800s, but last-minute legislative protection in the 1890s saved it from extinction. In New Hampshire, the state released six beaver in the late 1920s as part of a restocking program. Then began what certainly must be the most successful endangered species reintroduction program ever. By 1955, beaver had repopulated the entire state.

As you paddle along the shoreline of lakes or quiet rivers, keep an eye out for telltale beaver signs, including gnaw marks on trees, distinctive conical stumps of cut trees, canals leading off into the marsh, alder branches trimmed back along narrow passages, and well-worn paths leading away from the water's edge where beaver have dragged more distant branches to the water.

We see beaver most often in the late evening or early morning. Paddle quietly toward a beaver lodge around dusk. Wait patiently, and you will likely see the animals emerge for evening feeding and perhaps construction work on a dam or lodge.

5 | CENTRAL VERMONT

Most trips included here lie along the flat Champlain Valley. Wonderful marshy areas abound, especially along the Poultney River, Dead Creek, Otter Creek, Little Otter Creek, Winona Lake, Richville Pond, and the South Fork of East Creek. Waterfowl abound here too, but you can also see beaver, muskrat, otter, mink, bald eagle, and osprey. We also include the southernmost section of Lake Champlain where it nestles among scenic cliffs less than a mile apart. Watch out for wakes from large boats traversing the Champlain Canal.

Moving up into the Green Mountain National Forest's western edge, you will find Silver Lake—which requires a hike in, and you can camp along its shores—and Chittenden Reservoir and connected Lefferts Pond. These bodies of water sit amid a scenic backdrop of hills rising to the east.

On the state's east side, North Hartland Lake lies just south of the junction of I-89 and I-91. The Ottauquechee River flows down out of Quechee Gorge into the reservoir's north end. We have watched wild turkey on the hillsides and paddled along with otter here. Wrightsville Reservoir, a similar body of water, lies just north of Montpelier.

In the northeast section, set amid extensive Groton State Forest, three bodies of water attract nesting loons: Osmore, Kettle, and Peacham ponds. The similar, but larger Mollys Falls Pond lies just north of the state forest. Several state campgrounds populate the area. The last trip in this area is Symes ponds, an excellent area to look for moose among the pointed spires of the northern boreal forest.

57 | Lake Champlain— Southern End

The narrower southern end of Lake Champlain provides a wonderful paddling experience. You can explore many inlets and bays, observing the abundant plant life and wildlife.

Location: Addison, Benson, Bridport, Orwell, Shoreham, and West Haven, VT

Maps: *Vermont Atlas & Gazetteer,* Maps 28: E2, 32: G3; USGS Crown Point, Port Henry, Putnam, Ticonderoga, Whitehall, NY, and Benson, Bridport, Orwell, VT

Length: 35 miles one way, paddled south to north

Time: 4 days round-trip

Habitat Type: Large lake

Fish: Largemouth and smallmouth bass, pickerel, yellow perch, northern pike, landlocked salmon, walleye; brown, rainbow, and lake trout

Information: The Nature Conservancy, www.nature.org/wherewework/ northamerica/states/vermont/preserves/art7277.html; The Narrows Wildlife Management Area, www.vtfishandwildlife.com/wma_maps.cfm

Camping: Bomoseen State Park, Half Moon State Park; see Appendix A, #22, #23

Take Note: Dangerous in windy conditions and because of boat wakes

GETTING THERE

Use detailed road maps of the Vermont and New York sides to find accesses. We prefer the South Bay access in New York.

South Bay, New York. From Whitehall, go 2.8 miles north on Route 22, cross the bridge over South Bay, and take the second right. Go under the railroad trestle, and head left. *GPS coordinates*: 43° 34.452′ N, 73° 26.034′ W.

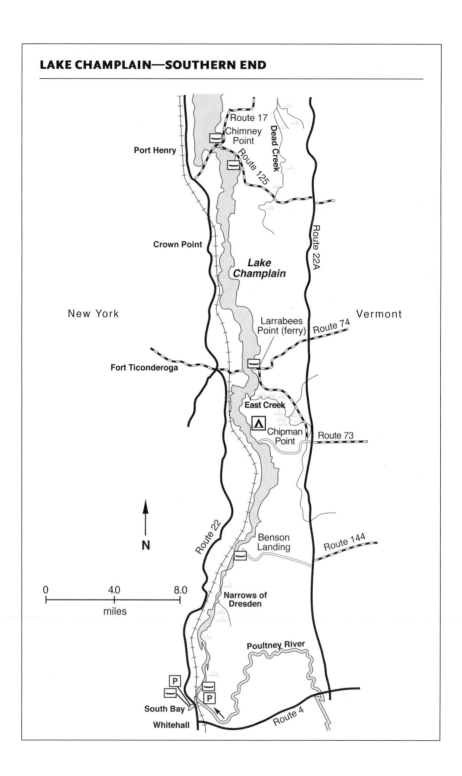

LAKE CHAMPLAIN—SOUTHERN END

Route 17
Chimney
Point

Port Henry

Route 125

Dead Creek

Crown Point

Lake
Champlain

Route 22A

New York

Vermont

Larrabees
Point (ferry)

Route 74

Fort Ticonderoga

East Creek

Chipman
Point

Route 73

N

Route 22

Benson
Landing

Route 144

0   4.0   8.0
miles

Narrows of
Dresden

Poultney River

P

P

South Bay

Whitehall

Route 4

Vermont. From Route 4 in Whitehall, go 0.5 mile north on Route 22, and turn right onto Saunders Street. Go 0.1 mile (0.6 mile), and turn left onto William Street. Go 0.7 mile (1.3 miles), and turn left onto Doig Street/Route 10. Go 0.6 mile (2.0 miles), turn left onto East Bay Road, and cross the Poultney River into Vermont. Turn left onto Galick Road, and go 1.8 miles (3.8 miles) to The Nature Conservancy's Helen W. Buckner Preserve at Bald Mountain. *GPS coordinates*: 43° 34.950´ N, 73° 25.272´ W.

WHAT YOU'LL SEE

Most of Lake Champlain is too large to tackle in an open boat, but the narrower southern end presents an enjoyable exception—although even here wind sometimes produces dangerous paddling conditions. Although the lake's narrowness seems comforting, watch for boat wakes. Large cabin cruisers pass through on the way from the Great Lakes to Florida, via the Champlain Canal, which extends south from the Poultney River. A 40-foot cabin cruiser, as we found out, creates a very large wake. In a lake only 100 or 200 yards wide, you will get the full impact, which can be a 3-foot wave—enough to swamp an open boat if you do not deal with it correctly. Point the boat into the approaching wave, or escape into a protected cove or behind an island when possible. We find ourselves constantly looking over our shoulders and planning an escape route.

The southern tip of Lake Champlain up to Benson Landing is relatively narrow. Silver maple and old willow line the marshy banks, extending their branches out over the murky water. A railroad follows the New York bank, but otherwise little development impinges on the water. Innumerable birds inhabit the banks and trees. Painted turtles slide into the water from partially submerged logs as you pass by. Numerous backwaters and inlets invite exploration. Filled with cattail, sedge, and arrowhead, these coves also contain, unfortunately, Eurasian milfoil and water chestnut, two introduced aquatic plants that choke out native vegetation. In some marshes along the lake, especially at the southern end near Nature Conservancy land, you will find wild rice.

Halfway up to Benson Landing, you pass through the Narrows of Dresden, a beautiful section of lake bounded by tall cliffs with cedar, hemlock, and white birch clinging to rock crevices and hanging down to the water's edge.

A nice 18-mile round-trip takes you to where the lake opens up, about a mile south of Benson Landing. If you continue north, big water, with mile-wide stretches, allows even moderate winds (10 to 15 knots) to generate big waves. We have experienced 1.5-foot-high waves that lapped over the bow of our

Inlet streams and hidden bays of Lake Champlain contain a wealth of plants and wildlife.

heavily laden canoe. Some fairly remote stretches of shoreline along here provide suitable camping spots, or you can continue north to the private campground at Chipman Point. There is a good access at Benson Landing and a smaller one 3 miles up, in Orwell.

East Creek, which flows into the lake across from Fort Ticonderoga, offers a fantastic side trip. You can paddle some four or five miles up this meandering brook (noted for its bass fishing) through cattail and sedge marshes and along deep deciduous woods and grassy dairy fields into the East Creek Wildlife Management Area. Shagbark hickory, white oak, and basswood, along with more typical Vermont trees, line the way. The variety of habitat found along East Creek provides excellent birdwatching. Unfortunately, you cannot paddle all the way to a road access—a large, beautiful falls dropping steeply over a sloping rock face blocks your way. Some of the largest silver maple we have seen grow along the North Branch. The one we had lunch under looked at least 24 feet in circumference!

Back out on Lake Champlain, a relatively short paddle takes you to Larrabees Point, where the ferry crosses; the access off Route 73, south of the ferry, makes a good access point for a trip to East Creek. From Larrabees Point north, the lake gradually widens; we recommend not going beyond the bridge at Chimney Point, another 14 miles above Larrabees Point, because the lake is too big to be enjoyed. (See Trips 67, 80, 81, and 82 for paddling locations farther north on Lake Champlain.)

The adventurous might want to try what we did on this section of the lake. We took a bicycle along in the canoe, and after two full days of paddling, John got the short straw, bicycled back to the car (Route 22 is a little more direct), and drove back to pick up the canoe and Alex, his well-rested canoeing partner.

A trip on Lake Champlain, even on the more manageable southern section, takes more planning than most other trips covered in this book. For more detailed information, use USGS topographic maps or the *Vermont Atlas & Gazetteer*.

---

58 | Poultney River

The river is surrounded by marshes filled with birds and mammals. Look for waterfowl, great blue heron, muskrat, beaver, otter, mink, and peregrine falcon.

Location: West Haven, VT
Maps: *Vermont Atlas & Gazetteer,* Map 28: D3; USGS Benson, Putnam, Thorn Hill, Whitehall, NY
Length: 8 miles one way

Time: 3 hours one way

Habitat Type: Shallow, muddy, meandering river

Fish: Northern pike, walleye, smallmouth bass, white and yellow perch

Information: The Nature Conservancy, www.nature.org/wherewework/
northamerica/states/vermont/; Ward Marsh Wildlife Management Area,
www.vtfishandwildlife.com/wma_maps.cfm

Camping: Bomoseen State Park, Half Moon State Park; see Appendix A,
#22, #23

Take Note: Access road along the river sometimes impassable because of
standing water

GETTING THERE

From Route 4, Exit 2, in Fair Haven, go 2.5 miles north on Route 22A, and turn
left onto Main Road. Go 3.3 miles (5.8 miles), and turn left onto Book Road.
Go 2.1 miles (7.9 miles), cross the bridge into New York, and turn right into
the access. *GPS coordinates*: 43° 37.432′ N, 073° 21.164′ W.

You can also cross back into Vermont, turn left onto Cogman Road, and go
1.1 miles (9.0 miles) to the Coggman Creek Culvert access. *GPS coordinates*:
43° 37.510′ N, 73° 22.240′ W.

WHAT YOU'LL SEE

The slow-flowing, meandering lower Poultney River runs muddy because of
silty soils. The Nature Conservancy has preserved much of the shoreline as
the Lower Poultney River Natural Area, comprising 251 acres in Vermont and
2,000 acres in New York, so no development occurs along the shores, although
a little-used road extends along the Vermont side for much of the distance.

The Ward Marsh Wildlife Management Area extends along a portion of the
Vermont side in this unique area; on this Vermont peninsula, you can look east
into New York. Just after rounding the southernmost bend, the Poultney River
joins the Champlain Canal, together forming Lake Champlain's southern end.
A large island in the lake, known as The Elbow, extends to the south toward
Whitehall, and farther to the northwest is the inlet into South Bay.

The Poultney River has the greatest diversity of freshwater mussels of
any river in the Northeast—12 species, with such colorful names as pink heel-
splitter, fragile papershell, fluted shell, giant floater, eastern lampmussel, and
pocketbook. Of the 300 species of freshwater mussels that once inhabited the
United States, roughly 10 percent are extinct and 50 percent are endangered.
Rare fish, including blackshin shiner, bridle shiner, channel darter, and eastern
sand darter, also inhabit the Poultney River.

POULTNEY RIVER

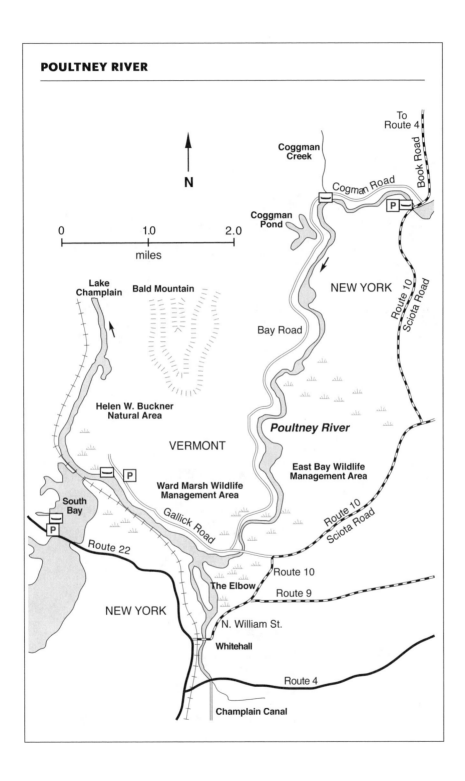

To
Route 4

Coggman
Creek

Coggman Road

Book Road

Coggman
Pond

P

NEW YORK

Route 10

Sciota Road

N

0   1.0   2.0
miles

Lake
Champlain

Bald Mountain

Bay Road

Helen W. Buckner
Natural Area

VERMONT

Poultney River

East Bay Wildlife
Management Area

P

South
Bay

P

Ward Marsh Wildlife
Management Area

Gallick Road

Route 10

Sciota Road

Route 22

Route 10

The Elbow

Route 9

NEW YORK

N. William St.

Whitehall

Route 4

Champlain Canal

The wife of co-author Alex Wilson takes a break, while her passenger patiently waits. Note the mountain bike for the return trip to retrieve the car.

While here, you can hike on Tim's Trail or the Susan Bacher Trail on The Nature Conservancy's Helen W. Buckner Natural Area at Bald Mountain. At more than 4,000 acres, this is the largest and most ecologically diverse Nature Conservancy preserve in Vermont. Bald Mountain and nearby Rattlesnake Ridge are the only places in Vermont with timber rattlesnakes and Vermont's only lizard, the five-lined skink. We had the good fortune to catch a glimpse of (and hear) a rattlesnake on the talus slope along Tim's Trail. We also saw peregrine falcons flying above Bald Mountain's cliffs, where they nest.

If you want to paddle just one-way, you can do what we did: bring a bicycle along in the canoe, and bike back to retrieve your car. Unless conditions are fairly dry, however, the dirt Bay Road that parallels much of the river may be too wet to bike easily.

59 | Bomoseen Lake, Loves Marsh, Glen Lake, and Half Moon Pond

The narrow, northern section of Bomoseen Lake is a great area to explore geology of exposed rocks. We have seen deer and osprey while paddling here, along with many marshland bird species.

Location: Castleton, Fair Haven, and Hubbardton, VT
Maps: *Vermont Atlas & Gazetteer,* Map 28: B7; USGS Bomoseen
Area: Bomoseen Lake, 2,360 acres; Loves Marsh, 62 acres; Glen Lake, 191 acres; Half Moon Pond, 23 acres
Time: Bomoseen Lake, 2 hours on the northern section; Loves Marsh, 1 hour; Glen Lake, 3 hours; Half Moon Pond, 1 hour
Habitat Type: Large lake and three small, marshy ponds
Fish: Bomoseen Lake—smallmouth and largemouth bass, yellow perch, northern pike, brook and brown trout; Loves Marsh—largemouth bass, northern pike; Glen Lake—smallmouth and largemouth bass, yellow perch, northern pike, rainbow trout; Half Moon Pond—largemouth bass, yellow perch, rainbow trout
Information: Loves Marsh Wildlife Management Area, www.vtfishandwildlife.com/wma_maps.cfm; State Parks, www.vtstateparks.com/htm/halfmoon.cfm; www.vtstateparks.com/htm/bomoseen.cfm
Camping: Bomoseen State Park, Half Moon State Park; see Appendix A, #22, #23

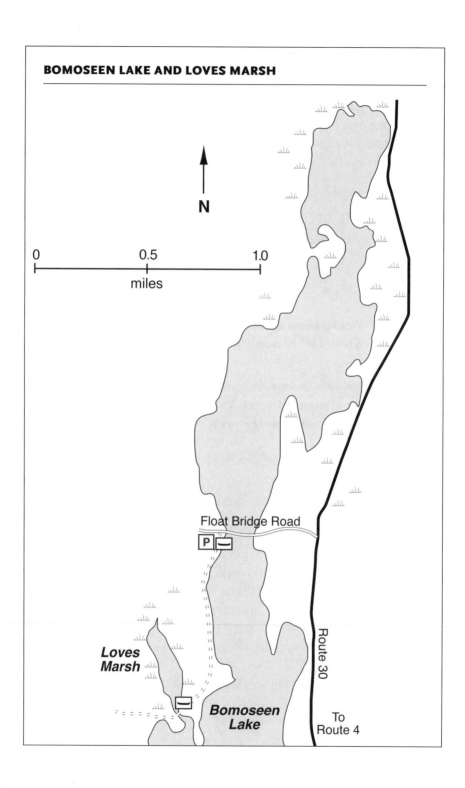

BOMOSEEN LAKE AND LOVES MARSH

N

0   0.5   1.0
miles

Float Bridge Road

P

Loves
Marsh

Bomoseen
Lake

Route 30

To
Route 4

GLEN LAKE AND HALF MOON POND

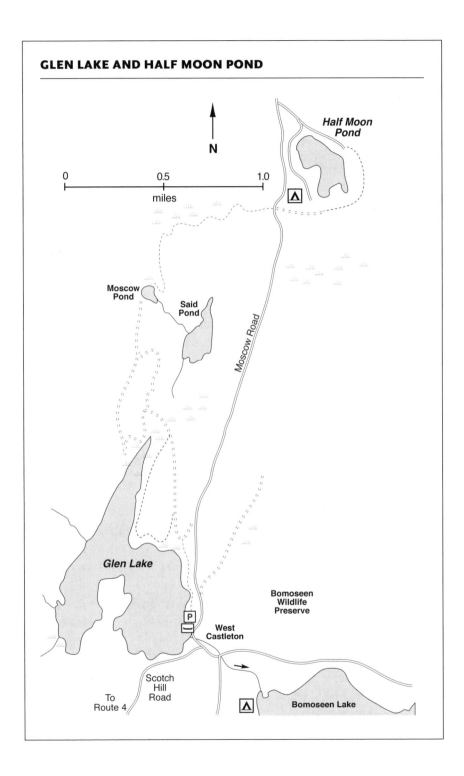

Take Note: Half Moon Pond, gasoline motors prohibited; Glen Lake, 5 MPH speed limit, personal watercraft prohibited

GETTING THERE

Bomoseen Lake. From Route 4, Exit 4, go 4.3 miles north on Route 30, and turn left onto Float Bridge Road. Cross the bridge, and turn immediately left to the access. *GPS coordinates*: 43° 40.620′ N, 73° 11.994′ W.

Loves Marsh. From Float Bridge Road, go 0.7 mile south to the access on the right.

Glen Lake. From Route 4, Exit 3, go 4.3 miles north on Scotch Hill Road to the access on the left. *GPS coordinates*: 43° 39.586′ N, 73° 13.942′ W.

Half Moon Pond. From Glen Lake, go 2.8 miles north on Moscow Road to the state park on the right. *GPS coordinates*: 43° 41.466′ N, 73° 13.188′ W.

WHAT YOU'LL SEE

Bomoseen Lake, Loves Marsh, Glen Lake, and Half Moon Pond nestle into the hills of western Vermont at the northern reaches of the Taconic Mountains. A number of nearby slate quarries still produce the slate shingles for which Vermont is known. You can get a feel for the area's sedimentary geology by exploring the exposed ledge and layered rock of the Glen Lake shoreline. Millions of years ago, clays that accumulated on the ocean floor compressed into shale. When the ocean floor uplifted to form the Taconic Mountains, heat and pressure metamorphosed the shale into much harder slate.

Bomoseen Lake

Bomoseen is a large, popular lake, the largest wholly within the state. Anyone looking for peace and quiet, except in the off-season, should avoid the main part of the lake. We include the far northern and least-traveled section here and adjacent Loves Marsh, and we probably would avoid the lake altogether on busy summer weekends.

Why do we include Bomoseen in a quietwater guide? For two reasons: First, because of enormous patches of fragrant waterlily, whose blossoms are the largest we have seen. We could not get over the size of these blossoms. We just paddled out into the middle and reveled in the splendor of these gorgeous plants. Second, because of the state parks and other protected lands, particularly to the west, where wildlife abounds. On a hot, busy Saturday in late June, we spied deer that had come down to the shore for a midday drink, saw several great blue herons stalking fish, and watched a wood duck feeding with its young.

From the access, go under the bridge; not as many boats motor into the shallow, Eurasian milfoil-choked north end. We prefer sticking mostly to the less-developed western shoreline. In addition to large patches of fragrant waterlily, and the invasive milfoil, expect to see a couple of species of pondweed, yellow pond lily, water shield, and lots of turtles and frogs. We saw one small patch of the invasive water chestnut, which we ripped up and carted off, but we would not be surprised to find in a few years that it had turned into a real problem, as it has elsewhere in the Northeast.

Loves Marsh

Part of a 100-acre wildlife management area, Loves Marsh contains an extensive cattail swamp that harbors a population of muskrat. You might also see beaver, otter, and mink in this small pond. A hardwood forest surrounds the pond on higher ground, back from the water's edge.

The marsh provides ideal waterfowl breeding areas for mallard and black duck. You will also probably see wood duck here. We have seen great blue heron and several other marsh birds here. Painted turtles climb out to sun on any available logs or beaten down cattails. Paddle here when you want to just sit in your boat and observe wildlife.

Glen Lake

Compared with the summertime frenzy on Bomoseen, paddling is quite pleasant on Glen Lake. A 5 MPH speed limit keeps large boats away, and the state forbids use of personal watercraft. This small lake has only minimal development, with three or four houses at the southern end near the dam and put-in point. The shoreline, mostly wild and heavily wooded (principally hemlock, white pine, red maple, and white birch), gives way to water that boasts excellent fishing—supposedly, somebody once pulled a 30-pound northern out of Glen Lake.

From the outlet, the Glen Lake Trail extends around the eastern shoreline on public land, rounds the northern tip of the lake, and then travels up to Moscow and Half Moon Ponds. Although not readily accessible by trail, Said Pond, southwest of Moscow Pond, might be found with a topographical map. Another trail, the Slate History Trail, takes you through what is left of the West Castleton Railroad and Slate Company. A self-guiding pamphlet describes the area's slate history. You can get this pamphlet and trail maps at Half Moon or Bomoseen state parks, just north and southeast, respectively, of Glen Lake.

A rocky outcrop at the Glen Lake access reminds us of the rich geological history of this area of Vermont, with its prominent slate quarries.

Half Moon Pond

We include small Half Moon Pond because it offers enjoyable paddling and harbors a very pleasant campground, with about 60 campsites and lean-tos around the pond. We found a beaver lodge at the northern end that you might want to check out in the evening or early morning. Half Moon State Park also rents canoes.

60 | East Creek, South Fork

These dammed-up sections of East Creek offer great opportunities to study aquatic plants. In summer there is little open water, and paddling is slow-going. Several species of waterfowl nest here.

Location: Orwell, VT
Maps: *Vermont Atlas & Gazetteer*, Map 32: I4; USGS Orwell
Area: 120 acres
Time: 3 hours
Habitat Type: Shallow, weed-choked, dammed-up stream
Fish: Largemouth bass
Information: East Creek Wildlife Management Area, www.vtfishandwildlife.com/wma_maps.cfm
Camping: Bomoseen State Park, Half Moon State Park; see Appendix A, #22, #23

GETTING THERE

From Route 73 in Orwell, go 0.6 mile south on Route 22A, and turn right onto Cook Road. Go 0.6 mile (1.2 miles) to the access on the left. *GPS coordinates:* 43° 48.120′ N, 73° 19.080′ W.

There is another access on Mount Independence Road. *GPS coordinates:* 43° 47.460′ N, 73° 18.906′ W.

WHAT YOU'LL SEE

The state has dammed the South Fork of East Creek in a few places, providing extraordinary waterfowl habitat in the low-lying farm country of the Champlain Valley. Farm runoff nutrifies the water, causing profuse aquatic plant growth that supports lots of fish and wildlife. However, this so-called nonpoint source pollution, so evident here, can have a profound effect on larger bodies of water, such as Lake Champlain, as it washes in from every little farm creek. Because the nutrifying source—primarily fertilizer—gets applied over such a wide area, keeping it out of bodies of water is a real challenge.

When we paddled here in early July, vegetation choked the water, leaving hardly any open. Do not expect to zip through this water. Instead, take a leisurely paddle, wending your way around the islands of thick vegetation: pondweed, bur-reed, narrow-leaved arrowhead, narrow-leaved cattail, bulrush, reed, sedge, duckweed, smartweed, and purple loosestrife, to name a few.

Note the white waterlily with the huge green leaves, some of which span nearly a foot. Fragrant waterlily (*Nymphaea odorata*) occurs as two subspecies: *odorata* and *tuberosa*. Most guidebooks list these as separate species, but taxonomists recently lumped them into one species. The more common subspecies, *odorata*, normally has much smaller leaves, with both the leaves and the flower sepals tinged with purple. The less common *tuberosa* subspecies has large green leaves and green sepals. A dwarf white waterlily (*Nymphaea leibergii*), critically imperiled in the Northeast, also exists. We have seen this rare plant in only a few bodies of water. The dwarf white waterlily used to be lumped with the pygmy waterlily (*N. tetragona*), of the Northwest, so this is an example of taxonomists splitting two populations into distinct species.

Many pairs of Canada geese raise their broods here, along with several other species of ducks. Grebes, dozens of tree swallows, red-winged blackbirds, and many other species also breed here.

The dense vegetation includes Eurasian milfoil and water chestnut. Note the warnings at the access about picking up "hitchhikers." This does not refer to the two-legged variety, but instead includes three serious aquatic pests: Eurasian milfoil, water chestnut, and zebra mussel. All three can easily hitch rides on boat trailers, in bilges, and even on canoe and kayak hulls, to be deposited later in the next waterway. Lake Champlain already suffers from infestation of these, and the worry is that they will get transported to every other body of water in the vicinity. We pulled up all of the water chestnut that we found, about a bushel, and tossed it out on the bank to rot.

Biologists worry that these three alien species, introduced from Europe and Asia to the East Coast by humans, will eventually infect most bodies of water in the East and Midwest. They arrived without their natural predators, established themselves easily, and now crowd out native species.

EAST CREEK, SOUTH FORK

To Orwell

Route 22A

East Creek South Fork

Mt. Independence Road

Cook Road

N

0   0.5   1.0

miles

61 | Richville Pond

Richville Pond and its covered railroad bridge are a real attraction. This shallow, dammed-up section of the Lemon Fair River brims with wildlife. Besides abundant waterfowl, expect to see great blue heron and whitetailed deer, and you might see beaver and otter.

Location: Shoreham, VT
Maps: *Vermont Atlas & Gazetteer,* Map 32: F5; USGS Orwell
Area: 124 acres
Time: 3 hours, more if you paddle the section east of the covered bridge
Habitat Type: Shallow, swampy, dammed-up river section

This historic timber-framed Shoreham covered railroad bridge is one of only two remaining in Vermont.

Fish: Largemouth bass, yellow perch, northern pike
Camping: Bomoseen State Park, Half Moon State Park, Branbury State Park; see Appendix A, #22, #23, #25
Take Note: 5 MPH speed limit, personal watercraft prohibited

GETTING THERE
Northern access. From Route 74 west in Shoreham, go 0.4 mile south on Route 22A, and turn left onto Richville Road. Go 2.5 miles (2.9 miles) to the access on the right, just after crossing the Lemon Fair River. *GPS coordinates*: 43° 52.398′ N, 73° 16.296′ W.

    Covered bridge access. Continue on Richville Road for 0.7 mile, turn right onto Shoreham Depot Road, and go 0.7 mile (1.4 miles) to the access on the right. *GPS coordinates*: 43° 51.582′ N, 73° 15.186′ W.

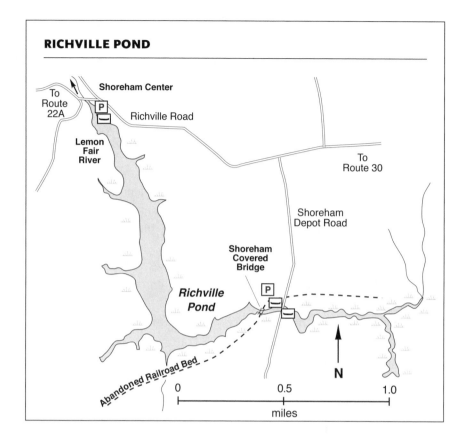

RICHVILLE POND

To Route 22A

Shoreham Center

Richville Road

Lemon Fair River

To Route 30

Shoreham Depot Road

Shoreham Covered Bridge

Richville Pond

Abandoned Railroad Bed

0   0.5   1.0

N

miles

WHAT YOU'LL SEE

Just to the east of Lake Champlain lies Richville Pond, another of those winding, marshy bodies of water absolutely brimming with wildlife (see Trips 60 and 66).

Richville Pond's northern reach, a widened section of the Lemon Fair River, rarely exceeds 100 yards in width. East of the covered bridge, the pond narrows to a winding creek; by the end of June weed growth may restrict passage along this section. About a half-mile east of the covered bridge the creek forks, and you can take either channel (the smaller north fork is a little difficult to find). The distance from the northern access to the covered bridge is a little less than two miles, and in spring you can paddle on the creek at least a mile past the bridge.

The entire marshy shore grows thick with cattail, sedge, bulrush, arrowhead, wild onion, and fragrant waterlily. Unfortunately, Eurasian milfoil, which first appeared here in 1988, has choked out some native vegetation. More recently, water chestnut has also shown up here.

Paddling along through rich, rolling farmland and patchy stands of mixed hardwoods and white pine, songbirds make this birdwatcher's paradise come alive. We watched a whitetailed doe grazing in reeds as high as her back and listened to a symphony of songbirds all along the pond. Fishing is supposed to be excellent.

The origin of the name *Lemon Fair* has generated quite a bit of disagreement over the years. Some say it is a corruption of *lamentable affair*. In 1824, Zedock Thompson recorded the story of an old woman who came across the stream and said it was truly a lamentable affair. Others attribute the lamentable affair to an Indian massacre or a drowning. Another says it is a pronunciation of the French *les monts verts* ("the green mountains"), or most likely, according to Esther Swift in *Vermont Place Names*, it comes from the French name for the river, *Limon Faire*.

The 108-foot-long Shoreham bridge, which crosses the pond where it narrows toward the eastern end, represents one of only two covered railroad bridges remaining in Vermont. The tall, stately, well-maintained Howe truss bridge, built in 1897 but not used since 1951, holds a lot of interest for those interested in heavy-timber construction.

62 | Otter Creek

This slow-flowing section of Otter Creek passes through northern white cedar swamps on its long journey to Lake Champlain. You might see beaver, otter, mink, and moose on your journey.

Location: Cornwall, Leicester, Middlebury, Salisbury, Sudbury, and Whiting, VT

Maps: *Vermont Atlas & Gazetteer,* Maps 32: D7; 33: H8, USGS Brandon, Cornwall, East Middlebury, Sudbury

Length: 15 miles one way

Time: All day, but shorter trips possible

Habitat Type: Slow-flowing river through swamps

Fish: Largemouth and smallmouth bass, pickerel, northern pike

Information: The Nature Conservancy, www.nature.org/wherewework/ northamerica/states/vermont/; Cornwall Swamp Wildlife Management Area, www.vtfishandwildlife.com/wma_maps.cfm

Camping: Bomoseen State Park, Half Moon State Park, Branbury State Park; see Appendix A, #22, #23, #25

GETTING THERE

From Route 7 in Middlebury, go 2.6 miles south on Creek Road to the access at the T with Three Mile Bridge Road. *GPS coordinates*: 43° 58.188′ N, 73° 9.396′ W. Use the *Vermont Atlas & Gazetteer* to locate other access points where roads cross the river.

WHAT YOU'LL SEE

Otter Creek and the Battenkill River originate side by side on the slopes of the southern Green Mountains in Bennington County. From there the Battenkill, a famous trout stream, flows west into New York, while Otter Creek flows northward through a whole litany of towns: Dorset, Danby, Peru, Mount Tabor, Wallingford, Clarendon, Rutland, Pittsford, Brandon—the list seems to go on endlessly—Sudbury, Leicester, Whiting, Salisbury, Cornwall, Middlebury, Weybridge, New Haven, Addison, Waltham, Panton, and Vergennes before flowing into Lake Champlain at Ferrisburg. Does any other Vermont river flow through more towns?

For much of its northward journey, Otter Creek flows through broad floodplains taken over by sometimes impenetrable marshes. Silver maple lines the bank as the creek meanders through open farm country. The river flows through the 15,000-acre northern white cedar swamps in Cornwall and Whiting. The Nature Conservancy, which calls this "the largest and most biologically diverse swamp complex in New England," has protected miles of riverbank and more than 2,000 acres of bottomland.

We include much of the middle section here, between Brandon and Middlebury—the section that flows through Cornwall and Whiting swamps. Beaver activity and floods cause logjams that can require short portages. We have paddled sections of Otter Creek in both directions, although during periods of high water you will need to make a one-way trip. We recommend paddling upstream from the Three Mile Bridge Road access through the Cornwall Swamp, followed by a leisurely paddle back to your vehicle.

Even though much of the river traverses open farm country, the generally wooded shores harbor lots of wildlife, including wood duck, Canada goose, flicker, crow, white-throated sparrow, downy woodpecker, yellow-bellied sapsucker, large numbers of grackles, and lots more.

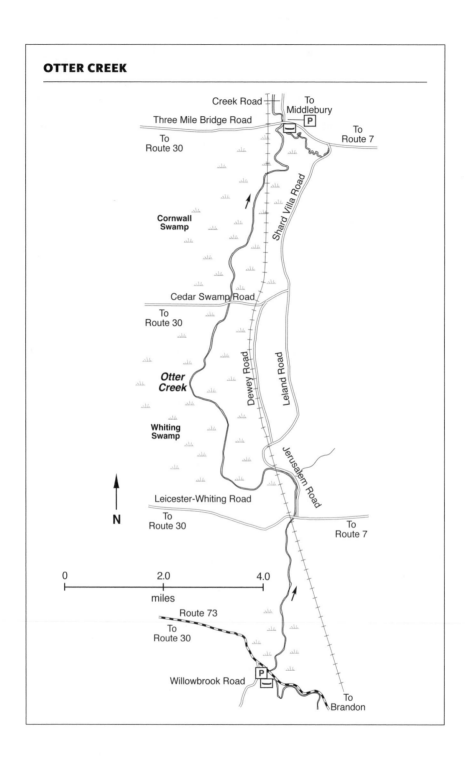

OTTER CREEK

Creek Road
To Middlebury
Three Mile Bridge Road
To Route 30
To Route 7
Shard Villa Road
Cornwall Swamp
Cedar Swamp Road
To Route 30
Dewey Road
Leland Road
Otter Creek
Whiting Swamp
Jerusalem Road
N
Leicester-Whiting Road
To Route 30
To Route 7

0   2.0   4.0
miles

Route 73
To Route 30
Willowbrook Road
To Brandon

A great blue heron rests between feeding forays. This monarch of the marsh eats fish, snakes, amphibians, crustaceans, young birds, and turtles.

63 | Silver Lake

This remote mountain lake in a scenic setting is reached by a 0.6-mile hike, and there is primitive camping on-site under towering hemlocks. This is a great area to combine with hikes on various trails within the Green Mountain National Forest.

Location: Leicester, VT
Maps: *Vermont Atlas & Gazetteer,* Map 33: E10; USGS East Middlebury
Area: 103 acres
Time: 2 hours, plus hike-in time
Habitat Type: Small mountain lake
Fish: Yellow perch, brown and rainbow trout
Information: Silver Lake and Moosalamoo Hiking Trails, Rutland Ranger District, 802-786-3851
Camping: Branbury State Park; see Appendix A, #25

GETTING THERE

East side. From the junction of Routes 53 and 73 north of Brandon, go 1.7 miles east on Route 73, and turn left onto Forest Road 32—follow carefully, as FR32 jogs left after 0.6 mile (2.3 miles). Go 2.4 miles (4.1 miles), and turn left off Carlisle Hill Road onto Silver Lake Road. Go 2.2 miles (6.3 miles) to the access. The carry is 0.6 mile, most of it gently downhill. At the lake's Loop Trail, campsites are a few hundred yards to the right. *GPS coordinates*: 43° 53.556′ N, 73° 01. 530′W.

West side. From Route 73, go 5.3 miles north on Route 53 to the parking area on the right. The trail is 1.5 miles, mostly steeply uphill, past the Falls of Lana, leading to the north end by the dam/picnic area; campsites are to the left on the east shore. *GPS coordinates*: 43° 54.096′N, 73° 01.530′W.

WHAT YOU'LL SEE

Silver Lake appeals to the hardy paddler who prefers less-traveled areas and does not mind a fairly long portage. This small lake has a fairly regular shoreline with few coves or marshy areas to explore, but camping under tall hemlocks and gazing across the lake on a quiet autumn morning more than makes up for the lake's limitations.

Fifteen campsites dot the Silver Lake Recreational Area. Two wells with hand pumps provide fresh water, and outhouses are located in both the picnic and camping areas. You can camp here year-round for free, but the water pump handles get removed before risk of freeze-up. Most campsites hover near shore; a few really stunning sites nestle beneath towering hemlocks on a thick bed of needles, surrounded by huge rock outcroppings.

Besides the Silver Lake Loop Trail, a number of good trails exist in this part of Green Mountain National Forest. If you did not hike in via the Falls of Lana, be sure to check it out. General Wool camped here with his troops in 1850, and his party decided such an attractive place needed a better name than Sucker Brook Falls, so they named it Falls of Lana after their leader—*lana* is Spanish for "wool." Other hiking trails in the vicinity of Silver Lake include the Leicester Hollow, Chandler Ridge, and Goshen trails.

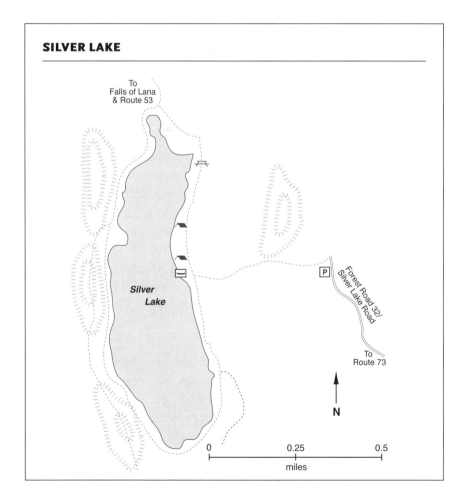

SILVER LAKE

To
Falls of Lana
& Route 53

Silver
Lake

P

Forest Road 32/
Silver Lake Road

To
Route 73

N

0   0.25   0.5
miles

64 | Chittenden Reservoir and Lefferts Pond

These two bodies of water are nestled below peaks of the Green Mountain National Forest. Loons nest here, and moose occur in good numbers. Look also for bald eagle, beaver, otter, muskrat, and mink.

Location: Chittenden, VT
Maps: *Vermont Atlas & Gazetteer,* Map 33: K13; USGS Chittenden
Area: Chittenden Reservoir, 750 acres; Lefferts Pond, 55 acres
Time: Chittenden Reservoir, 5 hours; Lefferts Pond, 1 hour
Habitat Type: Large reservoir and small, marshy pond
Fish: Chittenden Reservoir—walleye, yellow perch, landlocked salmon, brook, brown, and rainbow trout
Camping: Gifford Woods State Park; see Appendix A, #26
Take Note: Lefferts Pond—gasoline motors prohibited; Chittenden Pond— 5 MPH speed limit, personal watercraft and water-skiing prohibited

GETTING THERE
From Route 4 in Mendon, go north on Meadow Lake Drive to East Pittsford. At the T, turn right onto Chittenden Road. Where Mountain Top Road bears left, go straight onto Dam Road. Go 1.1 miles, and bear right onto Wildcat Road. Go 1.0 mile (2.1 miles), and turn left onto the Chittenden access road. The parking area is another 0.5 mile (2.6 miles). Chittenden is on the left; 200 hundred feet straight ahead is the northern cove of Lefferts Pond. *GPS coordinates:* 43° 43.188′ N, 72° 54.336′ W.

You can also reach Lefferts Pond from Wildcat Road; the carry-in access is on the left as the road passes the pond. *GPS coordinates:* 43° 42.816′ N, 72° 54.138′ W.

WHAT YOU'LL SEE
Chittenden Reservoir and Lefferts Pond nestle into the beautiful Green Mountains of central Vermont. The surrounding mountains—some of Vermont's tallest, stretching to more than 3,000 feet—provide a wild and remote feeling. Along the shores hardwoods predominate, including several species of birch and maple, although stands of hemlock, spruce, and balsam fir intersperse. On a peak autumn day, this area can be stunning. Plan for a little hiking in addition to paddling. A great trail starts at Lefferts Pond and extends

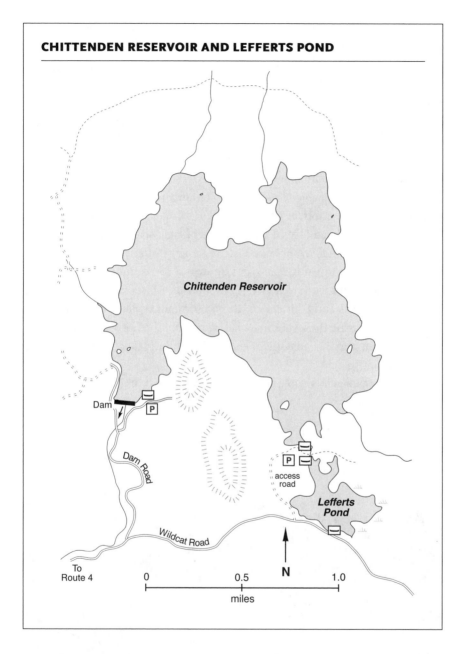

around Chittenden Reservoir. Moss-covered boulders, thick banks of fern, bubbling brooks, and lots of wildlife provide for great hiking. We saw numerous moose tracks during our visits. The famous Long Trail, which traverses Vermont from Massachusetts to Canada, also runs close by.

You might have some modest difficulty finding Chittenden Reservoir, but your effort will be rewarded. Exploring the numerous inlets and bays around the lake's perimeter could provide a full day of paddling. Central Vermont Public Service Corporation (CVPS), before it deeded over the surrounding land to the national forest, limited motorboats to 15 HP and banned personal watercraft and water-skiing. Although for a short time the Vermont Natural Resources Board allowed high-speed boating, it reversed itself and reimposed the former limits. Consequently, Chittenden has rejoined the other two bodies of water of greater than 500 acres that restrict high-speed boating: Green River Reservoir in northern Vermont and Somerset Reservoir in southern Vermont.

Wind can pose a problem because of Chittenden's large size. On a breezy day, stick close to the coves, or paddle on Lefferts Pond. Small and very shallow, Lefferts Pond, a real gem, teems with aquatic plants and wildlife. On an April morning not long after ice-out, we watched a river otter pull a 6- or 7-inch fish up on a rock and eat it. You can also expect to see muskrat and lots of waterfowl, including wood ducks, which often nest in boxes that CVPS put up on both Lefferts and Chittenden. Beaver sometimes dam up the outlet of Lefferts Pond, raising the level somewhat. A pair of loons also frequently nests on Chittenden, making this one of only a handful of lakes in Vermont that support nesting loons.

A wildlife management area surrounds Lefferts Pond, and the state does not

Although aquatic vegetation covers scenic Lefferts Pond by midsummer, we still enjoyed paddling here in the shadow of the Green Mountains.

permit gasoline-powered boats. Because of the shallow depth, aquatic vegetation restricts paddling during much of the season, particularly on the south end. When we paddled here midsummer, water shield, with lesser amounts of pondweed, covered more than 90 percent of the surface. A thick stand of horsetail covers some of the southern border. Even so, paddling and wildlife viewing were wonderful.

65 | North Hartland Lake

North Hartland Lake is a reservoir at the end of Quechee Gorge. Steep, forested hillsides enclose this long body of water. We have seen great blue heron, beaver, and wild turkey here.

Location: Hartford and Hartland, VT
Maps: *Vermont Atlas & Gazetteer,* Map 31: D12; USGS Hartland, VT/NH; USGS North Hartland, NH; USGS Quechee, VT
Area: 215 acres
Time: 3 hours
Habitat Type: Long, narrow reservoir with steep, forested hillsides
Fish: Largemouth bass, yellow perch, rainbow trout
Information: Army Corps of Engineers, www.nae.usace.army.mil/recreati/ nhl/nhlhome.htm; Quechee Gorge State Park, www.vtstateparks.com/htm/ quechee.cfm
Camping: Quechee Gorge State Park; see Appendix A, #24
Take Note: Entrance fee $2; hours 8 A.M.–8 P.M.; personal watercraft prohibited

GETTING THERE
From I-91, Exit 11 northbound, go 4.0 miles south on Route 5, and turn right onto Clay Hill Road. Go 1.1 miles (5.1 miles), and turn right onto the lake access road. *GPS coordinates:* 43° 36.327′ N, 72° 21.926′ W.

WHAT YOU'LL SEE
North Hartland Lake, a long, narrow reservoir, reaches back up to Quechee Gorge, with its 165-foot walls carved out by the Ottauquechee River. Surrounded by layered hillsides, this scenic area offers great paddling, hiking

(from the state park), camping, and fishing. Although you will not have to share the water with personal watercraft, you may find some high-speed boating on busy summer weekends.

In mid-May, the brushy shorelines appeared quite natural—with diverse shrubs close to shore and stately white pine standing guard from the hillsides. But the water level in the reservoir, particularly in early spring, can vary greatly, reaching 100 feet higher than the natural summer level. We wonder what the beaver do when water climbs well up the wooded hillsides.

Bird life abounds: We heard some very noisy great blue herons calling from the pines and wondered if a small rookery is located here. If so, it would be unusual; they usually nest in dead trees in marshes. Dozens of spotted sandpipers patrolled the shores, bobbing their tails incessantly whenever they alighted. And we surprised a flock of turkeys on the hillside. These magnificent game birds, standing more than 3 feet tall, once inhabited most forested parts

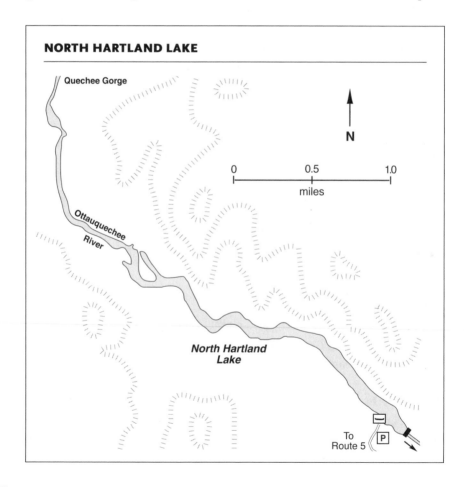

NORTH HARTLAND LAKE

Quechee Gorge

N

0   0.5   1.0

miles

Ottauquechee River

North Hartland Lake

To Route 5   P

of eastern North America, foraging on acorns, chestnuts, beechnuts, seeds, and insects. With the clearing of forests, loss of the American chestnut to chestnut blight, and unregulated hunting, the wild turkey disappeared over most of its range. Recently reintroduced in many areas, turkeys once again range over large tracts of Vermont and New Hampshire.

66 | Dead Creek

For anyone interested in marsh ecology, Dead Creek is an extraordinary resource. With 16 miles of waterway to paddle, you could spend more than a day paddling here among the waterfowl, osprey, great blue heron, muskrat, mink, otter, beaver, and possibly bald eagle. In the fall, huge flocks of snow geese pass through here.

Location: Addison and Panton, VT
Maps: *Vermont Atlas & Gazetteer,* Map 38: H4; USGS Port Henry, Westport, NY
Area: 753 acres from Otter Creek through the Dead Creek Wildlife Management Area
Time: All day
Habitat Type: Marshy, dammed-up creek sections
Fish: Largemouth and smallmouth bass, northern pike, yellow perch
Information: Dead Creek Wildlife Management Area, www.vtfishandwildlife.com/wma_maps.cfm
Camping: Button Bay State Park; D.A.R. State Park; see Appendix A, #27, #28

GETTING THERE
There are six access points.
   Northern section. From the stoplight in Vergennes, go 0.5 mile south on Route 22A, and turn right onto Panton/Sand Road. Go 3.2 miles (3.7 miles) to the access on the left. *GPS coordinates*: 44° 8.999′ N, 73° 19.164′ W.
   Middle Section, east side. From the stoplight in Vergennes, go 2.9 miles south on Route 22A, and turn right onto West Road. Go 2.5 miles (5.4 miles) to the access. *GPS coordinates*: 44° 7.493′ N, 73° 19.761′ W.
   West side. From Panton, go south on Jersey Street; after 0.6 mile, continue

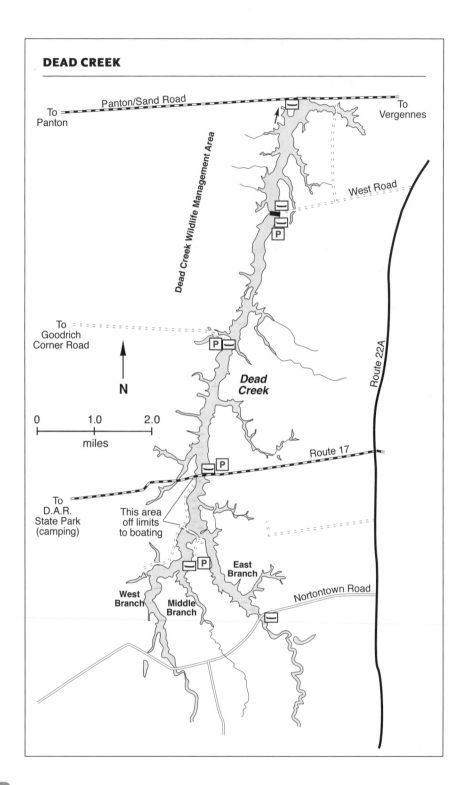

DEAD CREEK

To Panton

Panton/Sand Road

To Vergennes

Dead Creek Wildlife Management Area

West Road

P

To Goodrich Corner Road

N

0   1.0   2.0
miles

Dead Creek

P

Route 22A

Route 17

To D.A.R. State Park (camping)

This area off limits to boating

P

East Branch

West Branch

Middle Branch

Nortontown Road

The shallow waters of Dead Creek, set amid Champlain Valley's rolling farmland, provide a waterfowl haven. Also look for mink, beaver, otter, and muskrat here.

straight on Jersey Street. Go 2.0 miles (2.6 miles), and turn left onto the access road. *GPS coordinates*: 44° 6.610′ N, 73° 20.357′ W.

Route 17. From the stoplight in Vergennes, go 6.2 miles south on Route 22A, and turn right onto Route 17. Go 2.1 miles (8.3 miles) to the access on the right. *GPS coordinates*: 44° 5.113′ N, 73° 20.710′ W.

Southern section, west branch. From the Route 17 access above, go 0.1 mile west on Route 17, and turn left onto the access road. Go about 0.6 mile (0.7 mile), and take the left fork across a small wooden bridge. *GPS coordinates:* 44° 4.394′ N, 73° 20.876′ W.

East branch. From the stoplight in Vergennes, go 7.9 miles south on Route 22A, and turn right onto Nortontown Road. Go 1.4 miles (9.3 miles) to the access on the left; park on the right. *GPS coordinates:* 44° 3.544′ N, 73° 19.854′ W.

WHAT YOU'LL SEE

Flowing into Otter Creek a few miles from Lake Champlain, just west of Vergennes, several dammed sections of Dead Creek form a wonderful, spidery lake and marsh, with no development along the water. The most fertile farming country in Vermont surrounds the area.

Dead Creek seems somehow out of place in Vermont as it winds through rolling farmland, with silos visible across open fields of corn, and green pastures filled with grazing dairy cows. Except for the occasional stand of white pine, most of the trees along the banks consist of more southern varieties, the most common being white oak and shagbark hickory; Vermont's Champlain Valley represents one of the northernmost extensions of their range.

The murky brown water—the result of farmland nutrification and rooting carp—meanders slowly along on a nearly imperceptible north-flowing current. The shallow stretches, thick with cattail, provide ideal habitat for various wading birds, nesting geese, herons, and ducks. We saw an immature bald eagle perched on a dead snag, along with an adult osprey, red-tailed hawks, and other raptors. We also saw several delicate and colorful northern water snakes (nonpoisonous) swimming through the water with their heads sticking up to look around. Expect to see muskrat here; we saw a mink on our last trip here. During fall migration, this is one of the best places in New England to see snow geese.

Dead Creek provides a wonderful spot to lose yourself for a day or two. Leave behind the worries of society, and listen to the melodious song of the marsh wren. Some of that peace and quiet disappears for a few weeks each fall, however, during waterfowl-hunting season.

---

67 | Little Otter Creek

Large numbers of marshland species—including several pairs of nesting osprey—inhabit these waters. Reptiles and amphibians are abundant, and you may encounter beaver, mink, muskrat, otter, and whitetailed deer.

Location: Ferrisburg, VT
Maps: *Vermont Atlas & Gazetteer,* Map 38: E5; USGS Westport, NY
Area: 735 acres
Time: 5 hours
Habitat Type: Shallow, marshy Lake Champlain estuary
Fish: Largemouth and smallmouth bass, northern pike, yellow perch, walleye; brook, brown, and rainbow trout
Information: Little Otter Creek Wildlife Management Area, www.vtfishandwildlife.com/wma_maps.cfm

Camping: Button Bay State Park, Mt. Philo State Park; see Appendix A, #27, #29

GETTING THERE

From Route 22A in Vergennes, go 0.5 mile north on Route 7, and turn left onto Tuppers Crossing. Go 0.4 mile (0.9 mile), and turn right onto Botsford Road/Hawkins Road. Go 2.8 miles (3.7 miles) to the access on the right. *GPS coordinates*: 44° 13.590′ N, 73° 16.654′ W.

WHAT YOU'LL SEE

We can only describe Little Otter Creek Wildlife Management Area as spectacular. When paddling here, we spend most of our time paddling the area south of Hawkins Road because motorboats have no access there. The culverts under the road do not have enough headroom, so after paddling just a short distance to the right (south) from the access, we carry our boats up over the road and into the southern section.

You can paddle back up this south arm quite a distance; at a sharp right bend, it enters a very shallow wooded marsh with silver maple canopy. You will likely see lots of beaver activity and many black ducks here. Unfortunately, we also saw Eurasian milfoil and water chestnut invasion. This area may not be paddleable at low-water levels.

Given the profusion of wood duck nesting boxes, we expected to see wood duck—but we never could have imagined how many we would see in this expansive marsh when we paddled here in late August. One flock of more than 100 settled in to roost in the rushes right next to our boats, against the gorgeous backdrop of the setting sun. As they alighted, their un-duck-like cries magnified the feeling of primordial abundance. We also saw many black ducks and many other typical marsh birds, including several adult osprey and a couple of unoccupied nests in various locations within the 1,400 acres of the wildlife management area.

We paddled over and among the myriad types of aquatic vegetation, particularly the white waterlilies. (See Trip 60 for a discussion of waterlily species.) Interestingly, after they have finished blooming, the flowers of fragrant waterlily get pulled underwater by a coiling action of the stems. This protects the seed head and permits the seeds to ripen over a period of three or four weeks. After the seeds ripen, the seed head, or aril, breaks free and floats to the surface. Here it gradually decomposes and releases its seeds to sink into the pond bottom.

We paddled the rest of the Little Otter Creek Wildlife Management Area, including Lewis Creek, returning to the access after sunset, having seen

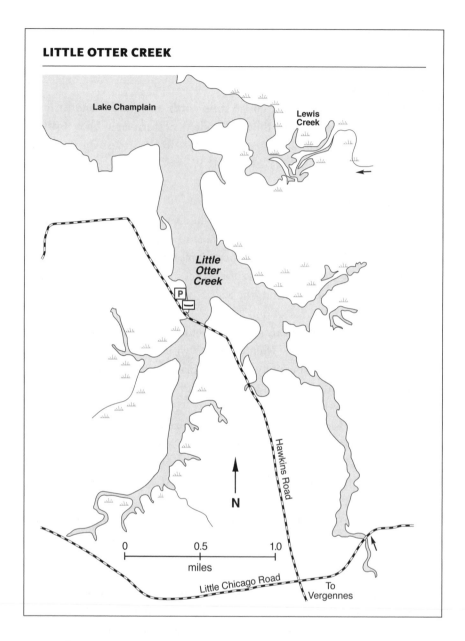

LITTLE OTTER CREEK

Lake Champlain

Lewis Creek

Little Otter Creek

Hawkins Road

N

0   0.5   1.0
miles

Little Chicago Road

To Vergennes

extraordinary plants, birds, and scenery. Paddle here when the winds come up on Lake Champlain; the south branch, in particular, affords protection from the wind. In late August, not only are you likely to see wood ducks, but much of the aquatic vegetation will be in bloom—from buttonbush to water smartweed, from floating heart to pondweed, and from fragrant waterlily to yellow pond lily.

68 | Winona Lake (Bristol Pond)

Scenic hillsides provide the eastern view while paddling this small, marshy pond. This is a great place to study aquatic plants. You will likely see great blue heron and osprey here and possibly beaver.

Location: Bristol, VT
Maps: *Vermont Atlas & Gazetteer,* Map 39: G9; USGS Bristol
Area: 234 acres
Time: 3 hours
Habitat Type: Marshy pond
Fish: Largemouth bass, yellow perch, pickerel, northern pike
Camping: Button Bay State Park, Mt. Philo State Park; see Appendix A, #27, #29
Take Note: Personal watercraft prohibited

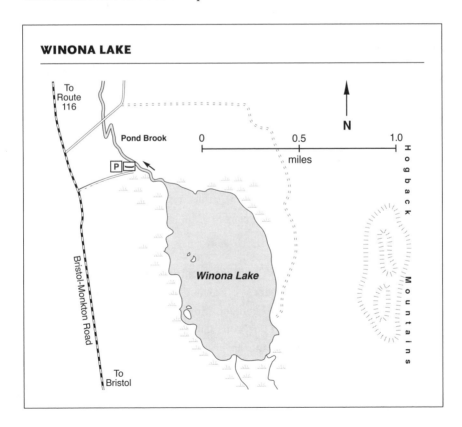

WINONA LAKE

To Route 116

Pond Brook

P

0   0.5   1.0
miles

N

Hogback Mountains

Bristol-Monkton Road

Winona Lake

To Bristol

Winona Lake is a great place to study aquatic plants, including the beautiful flowers of fragrant waterlily, *Nymphaea odorata*.

GETTING THERE

From Main Street in Bristol, go 3.7 miles north on North Street/Monkton Road to the access on the right. *GPS coordinates*: 44° 10.916′ N, 73° 6.008′ W.

From Route 116 in Hinesburg, go 5.3 miles south on Silver Street, and veer left onto Bristol-Monkton Road. Go 5.2 miles (10.5 miles) to the access on the left.

WHAT YOU'LL SEE

Winona Lake, also called Bristol Pond, represents another relatively unknown place, a real treat to stumble across. Located about 40 minutes south of Burlington and nestled beneath Hogback Mountains rising from the eastern shore, the 234-acre lake enjoys a gorgeous setting. The access on gently north-flowing Pond Brook provides a panoramic view of the lake to the south. As you paddle in, you see absolutely no development on the lake—only a few farms to the south—although a half-dozen camps hide among thick stands of trees on the eastern side.

Dense stands of swamp loosestrife (*Decodon verticillatus*)—not to be confused with invasive purple loosestrife (*Lythrum salicaria*), which has choked wetlands in recent years—dominate the marshy shoreline. Look for long, pointed, willowlike leaves in whorls of three growing out of arched, whitish stems and, in late summer, showy reddish-purple flowers growing out of the leaf axils. The loosestrife, cattail, arrowhead, various heaths, and boggy soils make shore access next to impossible.

You can explore a few coves and islands on the western side, but during high water, dozens more coves and inlets become accessible. Feathery tamaracks grow along the shore here and there, but most of the vegetation consists of shrubs. We found a large beaver lodge encrusted with jewelweed, swamp loosestrife, and swamp rose. Hemlock, white pine, white birch, and red and sugar maples grow farther from the water and along the wooded eastern shore. Marshland and water birds include wood duck and merganser, but most keep to the more protected marshy pools north and south of the main lake.

69 | Wrightsville Reservoir

You can paddle to a scenic waterfall on this tiny reservoir by traveling a long inlet stream. We have seen otter here, and you might see beaver.

Location: East Montpelier, Middlesex, and Montpelier, VT
Maps: *Vermont Atlas & Gazetteer,* Map 40: B7; USGS Montpelier
Area: 89 acres
Time: 3 hours
Habitat Type: Small reservoir with long inlet stream
Fish: Largemouth bass, yellow perch, brown trout
Camping: Elmore State Park; see Appendix A, #30
Take Note: Personal watercraft prohibited, 2 MPH speed limit north of the narrows

GETTING THERE
From Route 2 in Montpelier, go 4.7 miles north on Route 12 to the access on the right. *GPS coordinates*: 44° 19.384′ N, 72° 34.656′ W.

WHAT YOU'LL SEE

This reservoir seems larger than its 89 acres because you can paddle the inlet stream for quite a distance, up to a scenic waterfall by an island covered with stones worn smooth by cascading water. Embedded mica causes the stones to shimmer in the sun. For us, paddling up to the waterfall gave us an opportunity not only to have lunch but also to see a river otter in the upper reaches. Although the reservoir may not look interesting from the access, paddling up to the falls is well worth the effort. The clear water of the inlet stream, the North Branch of the Winooski River, provides habitat for numerous animals and plants. North of the access, including the entire inflow stream, motorboats are limited to 2 MPH. (At our best as paddlers, we can exceed this speed limit by a factor of three!)

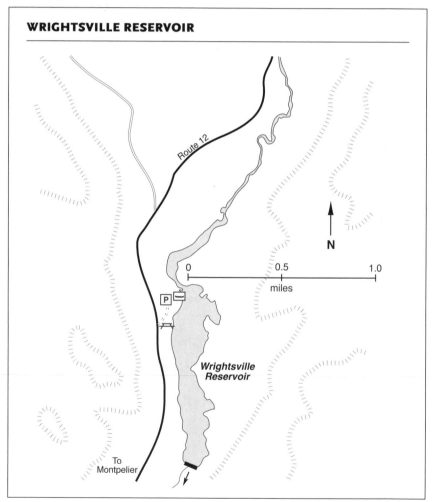

WRIGHTSVILLE RESERVOIR

A scenic waterfall on the Winooski River North Branch marks the beginning of Wrightsville Reservoir. Look for river otter here.

When we paddled here at the end of May, large patches of bunchberry (*Cornus canadensis*), in the dogwood family, bloomed under a canopy of white pine, white and yellow birch, and other species that line the shores. Red-winged blackbirds sang to mark their territories in the marshy areas, while ovenbirds, black-throated green warblers, and song sparrows called from the wooded areas. We also saw five large beaver lodges and lots of cuttings stored in the water. The best time to see the resident beaver is early morning or just before closing at dusk.

70 | Kettle Pond and Osmore Pond

On-site camping is allowed around these two small, marshy ponds in Groton State Forest. These are great spots to see loon and beaver, and you might see otter and moose.

Location: Groton, Marshfield, and Peacham, VT
Maps: *Vermont Atlas & Gazetteer,* Map 41: B14; USGS Marshfield
Area: Kettle Pond, 104 acres; Osmore Pond, 48 acres

Time: Kettle Pond, 2 hours; Osmore Pond, 1 hour
Habitat Type: Small, marshy ponds
Fish: Kettle Pond—yellow perch, rainbow trout; Osmore Pond—brook trout
Information: Groton State Forest map, www.vtfpr.org/lands/groton/map.pdf
Camping: New Discovery State Park (register here for Kettle and Osmore ponds primitive sites), Stillwater State Park, Ricker Pond State Park, Big Deer State Park; see Appendix A, #31, #32, #33, #34
Take Note: Osmore Pond—gasoline motors prohibited; Kettle Pond—5 MPH speed limit, personal watercraft prohibited

GETTING THERE

Kettle Pond. From Route I-91, Exit 17 southbound, go 8.5 miles west on Route 302, and turn right onto VT 232. Go 7.1 miles (15.6 miles) to the access on the left. Carry your boat 0.3 mile to the water. *GPS coordinates*: 44° 17.681′ N, 72° 18.268′ W.

Osmore Pond. Go another 2.2 miles (17.8 miles), and turn right into New Discovery State Park. Follow signs to Osmore Pond Picnic Area. Carry your boat 50 yards to the water. *GPS coordinates*: 44° 19.313′ N, 72° 17.339′ W.

WHAT YOU'LL SEE

Kettle and Osmore ponds nestle among the hillsides of Groton State Forest. While water remains the main attraction here, hiking trails travel among the peaks and skirt the edges of Peacham Bog, one of only two or three raised bogs

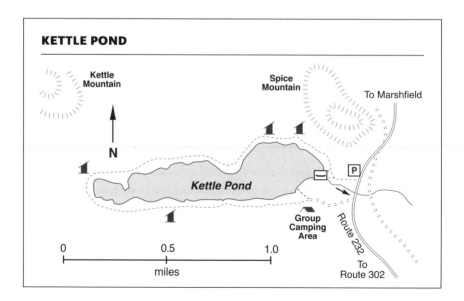

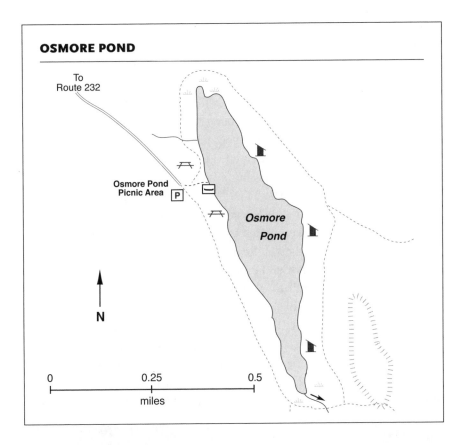

OSMORE POND

To
Route 232

Osmore Pond
Picnic Area

P

N

Osmore

Pond

0   0.25   0.5

miles

in Vermont. If you visit the bog, expect to see rhodora, leatherleaf, Labrador tea, sphagnum, black spruce, tamarack, and many more typical bog plants.

Kettle Pond

From an ecological standpoint, Kettle Pond is the most interesting body of water in Groton State Forest. Loons often nest here, and the shoreline— especially the western end—harbors a rich assortment of bog plants, including pitcher plant, sweet gale, various members of the heath family, sphagnum, and sundew. Although a group camping area exists on the east end, set back from the water, the pond has a very remote feel to it. We saw beaver and signs of otter. A hiking trail extends around the pond.

Along with the group camping area, available to organizations by reservation only, there are five primitive camping lean-tos and one tent site around the pond. We camped here in the mid-1980s and were disappointed on more recent visits to see the area quite littered with trash. (The litter bag we always carry filled right up on one visit.)

Osmore Pond

Nestled beneath several low mountains, small and shallow Osmore Pond is a beauty. Spruce, fir, yellow birch, and sugar maple cover the heavily wooded hills and rocky shoreline. Small, marshy areas occur at both ends. A shoreline trail extends all the way around the pond, although going might be slow during berry season—we found the pond to be a veritable treasure trove of raspberries, blueberries, shadbush, currants, and gooseberries. When we camped here in late July, a solitary loon serenaded us late into the evening.

The pond offers primitive camping, with four lean-tos on the eastern side. The lean-tos sit quite far apart, and each has a well-designed fireplace and a nearby outhouse. On the pond's western side, groups sometimes use a large picnic shelter well into the night, but by avoiding popular summer weekends, you should find peace and quiet. Register for primitive camping on Osmore Pond at the New Discovery Campground.

Although few people realize it, Vermont permits primitive camping on many state lands, including most of Groton State Forest. Small groups do not require a permit. Except at designated sites, you must camp at least a quarter-mile from everything (roads, streams, lakes). If you prefer a family campground, Groton State Forest has Stillwater, Big Deer, Ricker, and New Discovery. New Discovery is closest to Osmore and Kettle ponds, although it is not on the water. Both Stillwater and Ricker campgrounds are on the water; Ricker is much quieter.

Hobblebush, *Viburnum lantanoides*, is a common understory shrub. Large sterile flowers attract insect pollinators to small fertile flowers in the center.

71 | Peacham Pond

Although Peacham Pond suffers from some development, it sits in a gorgeous postcard-like setting. Because of motorboat traffic, we avoid paddling here on summer weekends. This is one of the few Vermont lakes where loons breed successfully.

Location: Peacham, VT
Maps: *Vermont Atlas & Gazetteer,* Map 41: A14; USGS Marshfield
Area: 331 acres
Time: 4 hours
Habitat Type: Scenic mountain pond but with some development
Fish: Yellow perch, brown trout
Information: Groton State Forest map, www.vtfpr.org/lands/groton/map.pdf
Camping: New Discovery State Park, Stillwater State Park, Ricker Pond State Park, Big Deer State Park; see Appendix A, #31, #32, #33, #34
Take Note: Personal watercraft allowed

GETTING THERE
From New Discovery State Park (see Trip 70), go 1.5 miles north on VT 232, and turn right onto Peacham Pond Road. Go 0.6 (2.1 miles) to the access. *GPS coordinates*: 44° 20.014′ N, 72° 15.928′ W.

From Montpelier, go northeast on Route 2. From the junction with Route 14 north, go 11.3 miles east on Route 2, and turn right onto Route 232. Go 3.0 miles (14.3 miles), and turn left onto Peacham Pond Road.

WHAT YOU'LL SEE
Situated on the northern edge of Groton State Forest and nestled beneath the rolling mountains of north-central Vermont, Peacham Pond enjoys a gorgeous setting such as those seen on postcards. In the autumn, nothing beats drifting lazily, just absorbing the beauty: deep reds and yellows of shoreline vegetation contrasting with the rich blue of the pond and sky. Even the moderate development at the western and eastern ends seems somehow all right, although on a warm summer afternoon, the motorboat, personal watercraft, and water-skiing traffic can be a bit much. We recommend paddling elsewhere on summer weekends.

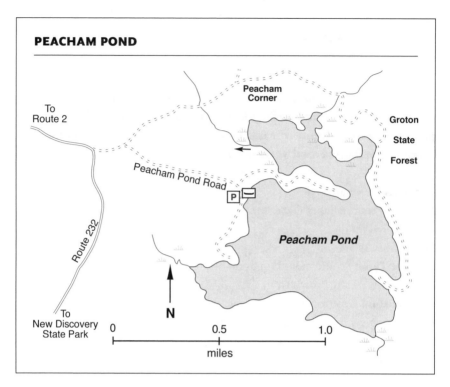

PEACHAM POND

To
Route 2

Peacham
Corner

Groton

State

Forest

Peacham Pond Road

Route 232

P

Peacham Pond

To
New Discovery
State Park

N

0   0.5   1.0

miles

By paddling around to the northern end, you can get away from most of the motorboats and nearly all the houses. This much shallower section has deep marshy coves, islands, and superb wildlife habitats to explore, especially the large horsetail (*Equisetum*) marsh in the northeastern cove. Two loon pairs nest regularly, one here and one in the south cove. Because Peacham is one of the few Vermont bodies of water with successful loon breeding, we fail to understand why the Vermont Natural Resources Board allows personal watercraft and high-speed boating on this pond.

72 | Mollys Falls Pond

Although road noise impinges on parts of the pond, this is still a good place to paddle. You will likely see loons, and look here in the evening for beaver. In spring, Mollys Brook cascades down the hillsides with a roar.

Location: Cabot, VT
Maps: *Vermont Atlas & Gazetteer,* Maps 41: A14, 47: K13; USGS Marshfield
Area: 411 acres
Time: 5 hours
Habitat Type: Large mountain reservoir
Fish: Smallmouth bass, yellow perch, pickerel, northern pike; brook, brown, and rainbow trout
Camping: New Discovery State Park, Stillwater State Park, Ricker Pond State Park, Big Deer State Park; see Appendix A, #31, #32, #33, #34

GETTING THERE

From Montpelier, go northeast on Route 2. From the junction with Route 14 north, go 12.7 miles east on Route 2 to the access on the right. *GPS coordinates:* 44° 21.790′ N, 72° 18.196′ W.

WHAT YOU'LL SEE

Nestled among forested hillsides, Mollys Falls Pond (also known as Marshfield Lake, although it actually lies in the town of Cabot, not Marshfield) is the largest body of water in the area. Protected from development by Green Mountain Power, only one house appears along its shoreline. Although we paddled here on Memorial Day, there were only a few motorboats on the water and about the same number of canoes and kayaks. Near the access, you can hear cars and trucks on Route 2, but that soon fades as you paddle south down the lake. Quiet coves provide protected nooks to explore, and gorgeous Mollys Brook cascades down over a boulder-strewn streambed into the lake. In spring, the creek's roar, audible from afar, helps drown out road noise.

A pair of loons nested behind a closed-off section, and a solitary loon called out from another section of the lake when we paddled here. Signs warn boaters away from the loon nesting area, but we believe that speed limits should also be established.

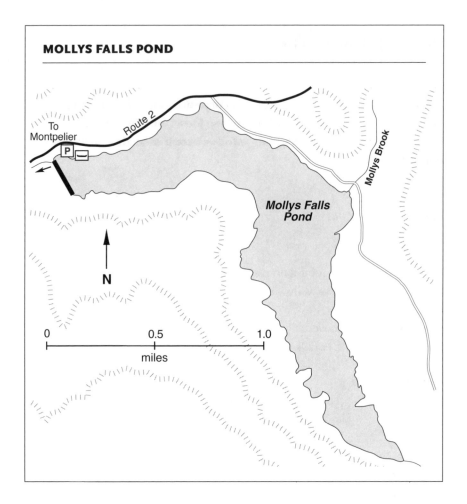

MOLLYS FALLS POND

To Montpelier

Route 2

P

N

0   0.5   1.0
miles

Mollys Falls Pond

Mollys Brook

Nowhere else have we seen as much beaver activity as we saw here, with white birch appearing to be the preferred food. Given that beaver prefer deciduous trees—probably because of the resins in conifers—one wonders why they eat so much resinous paper birch. Several massive beaver lodges poke up here and there. Seeing all of this activity, it is hard to believe that beaver were once nearly extirpated in the Northeast.

A large conifer-clad island harbors a picnic area that has a nice view of the lake's southern end. No camping or overnight parking is allowed.

73 | Lower and Upper Symes Pond

Nestled among the pointed spires of the northern boreal forest, the two small Symes ponds present a good opportunity to look for moose. You will likely see loons here, as well as myriad other birds, and you might see beaver.

Location: Ryegate, VT
Maps: *Vermont Atlas & Gazetteer,* Map 42: D4; USGS Barnet, Woodsville
Area: Lower Symes Pond, 57 acres; Upper Symes Pond, 20 acres
Time: 3 hours for both ponds
Habitat Type: Small wilderness ponds with forested hillsides
Fish: Pickerel
Information: Roy Mountain Wildlife Management Area, www.vtfishandwildlife.com/wma_maps.cfm
Camping: New Discovery State Park, Stillwater State Park, Ricker Pond State Park, Big Deer State Park; see Appendix A, #31, #32, #33, #34
Take Note: Personal watercraft prohibited; Upper Symes Pond, gasoline motors prohibited

GETTING THERE

From I-91, Exit 17 northbound, go 0.9 mile west on Route 302, and turn right onto Boltonville/South Bayley-Hazen roads. Go 3.0 miles (3.9 miles), and turn right onto East Road. Go 0.6 mile (4.5 miles), and veer left onto Symes Pond Road. Go 1.5 miles (6.0 miles), and turn left onto Hunt Mill Road (easy to miss). Go 0.8 mile (6.8 miles) to the access. Low-clearance vehicles should watch for stones. *GPS coordinates:* 44° 14.392′ N, 72° 5.992′ W.

WHAT YOU'LL SEE

We visited these scenic, little-used ponds on weekends in June and July, and saw only one other boat each time. We also saw deer down for midday drinks, and a loon called from the far side. Bird life was incredible, including thrushes calling from the woods, lots of cedar waxwings feeding in small flocks, two kingfishers diving for fish to feed a growing brood, a great blue heron stalking the shallows, common yellowthroats calling from the dense shrubs lining the shore, a red-tailed hawk wheeling overhead, and a red-breasted merganser shooing her brood away from the intruders.

Swamp rose bloomed seemingly everywhere, including on floating islands covered with feathery tamarack. The hillside's northern coniferous forest stood in contrast to the brushy shoreline and diverse aquatic vegetation. Spire-like balsam fir stood sentinel as we paddled through the entrance to Upper Symes Pond, which is quite a bit smaller than the lower pond. In some places, smooth granite boulders line the shore.

This wonderful, remote setting—truly the country of the pointed firs—makes getting there worth the struggle. The Roy Mountain Wildlife Management area includes most of the shoreline around Upper Symes and all of the west shoreline of Lower Symes, and the Vermont Land Trust acquired 75 acres at the access.

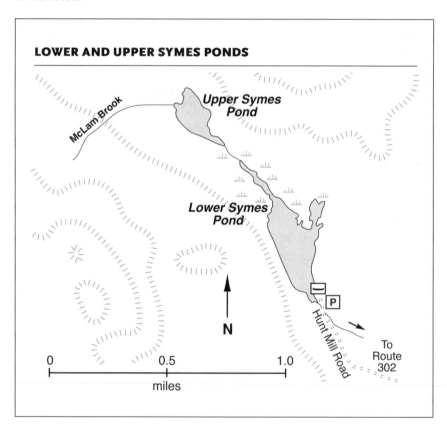

LOWER AND UPPER SYMES PONDS

McLam Brook

Upper Symes Pond

Lower Symes Pond

N

0   0.5   1.0

miles

P

Hunt Mill Road

To Route 302

MOOSE: THE NORTHERN FOREST GIANT

Coming across a huge bull moose as you round the bend of a marshy stream or watching a cow and calf swim across a lake is often the high point of trips into the Northern Forest. We see most moose in early morning and early evening, although one can see them at any time. One October evening, we saw eight moose as we drove over the Kancamagus Highway in central New Hampshire.

The moose (*Alces alces*) is the world's largest member of the deer family. Bull moose can stand 7 feet tall at the shoulders and range in weight from 900 to 1,400 pounds, with cow moose typically three-quarters as large. Among North American land mammals, only bison and Alaskan brown bear (a grizzly bear subspecies) commonly exceed the moose in weight; none approaches it in height.

The typical moose ranges over a small territory, usually just a few square miles. Well adapted to the marsh environment, moose often forage for aquatic plants in ponds and streams, sometimes standing neck-deep in water to escape hordes of biting flies. We have even seen moose completely submerged. Long legs allow moose to reach tree branches and wade into bogs and snow. Thick, dense fur—sometimes 6 inches long around the neck and shoulders—helps protect from biting flies. Moose have a keen sense of hearing and smell, but poor vision. When frightened, they can run at speeds up to 35 MPH for short distances. They swim slowly but have been known to swim as far as 12 miles.

Moose derive most of their nourishment by browsing on trees and aquatic vegetation, but they also graze on grasses, mosses, lichens, and low herbaceous plants. Because of their long legs and short necks, they often need to bend or spread their front legs or even drop to their knees to feed. They may rear to feed on tree branches, and they sometimes "ride down" saplings by straddling them and walking forward to bring upper branches into reach.

The rutting season extends from September through October and may range into November and even early December. After an eight-month gestation period, cows bear one or two calves in May or June. Younger cows generally produce just one offspring. As one might expect, a direct correlation exists between the incidence of twins and the availability of forage.

The moose population in the Northeast fluctuated considerably in the last

two centuries. During colonial days, moose provided an important food source for early settlers. Because they were so easily killed, populations plummeted; by the mid-1800s, fewer than 15 moose populated New Hampshire, and even fewer lived in Vermont. With protection from hunting and changes in land use that have caused a proliferation of low-growing browse, moose populations have rebounded dramatically, to the point where about 300 moose die each year in collisions with cars in the two states. The moose population in New Hampshire and Vermont has reached more than 10,000.

Brainworm infestations, fatal to moose, keep populations from building in southern areas. Deer in those areas carry brainworm; unaffected by these parasites, deer deposit them in their feces, upon which land snails feed. If moose browse on plants hosting snails—a likely occurrence at lower elevations in southern New Hampshire and Vermont—they contract the disease and die.

Many wonderful paddling destinations exist in remote sections of New England, where you have a good chance of seeing moose. We never tire of that exhilarating feeling we get paddling into a marshy cove and coming suddenly upon an enormous bull moose or cow with calf. We have seen many dozens of these majestic mammals, and we hope you see as many on your travels.

6 | NORTHERN VERMONT

This area includes Green River Reservoir, Vermont's premier paddling destination. You can camp here and possibly see osprey, loon, moose, otter, mink, beaver, and black bear. We prefer to visit in the spring and fall, when there are fewer paddlers.

The Northeast Kingdom east of I-91 provides wonderful paddling on Holland, Norton, and Little Averill ponds near the Canada border and on Nulhegan, Long (Westmore), Dennis, and May ponds farther south. Most draw few paddlers, increasing the likelihood of seeing wildlife. The Clyde River provides a many-hour, marshy, meandering traverse through farm country.

Just west of I-91, you can paddle Flagg and the Hosmer ponds. If you're willing to walk in, Long Pond (Greensboro) is also a great place to paddle. From Newport, you can paddle down into South Bay of Lake Memphremagog and into the winding Barton and Black rivers. You could paddle for a few days here amid the abundant aquatic vegetation and wildlife.

On the west side, Waterbury Reservoir is a great place to paddle; the northern half has a 5 MPH speed limit, which keeps that half much quieter. A lot of environmental education takes place on Shelburne Pond, which lies just south of Burlington. Colchester Pond and Indian Brook Reservoir, both fairly small, also lie right outside Burlington.

Farther north lies Fairfield Swamp, Arrowhead Mountain Lake, and Jewett and Stevens brooks. The Rock River, flowing down out of Canada, can occupy you for hours. But the really major paddling destination in the northwest corner is the Missisquoi River delta on Lake Champlain. A floodplain swamp harbors huge amounts of wildlife. You can reliably see the rare black tern here.

74 | Shelburne Pond

Shelburne Pond is used by many groups for outdoor education, and with good reason. It lacks development, and its limestone outcroppings harbor populations of several rare ferns and of northern water snakes. You will likely see great blue heron here, and you might see beaver.

Location: Shelburne, VT
Maps: *Vermont Atlas & Gazetteer,* Map 45: K8; USGS Burlington
Area: 450 acres
Time: 4 hours
Habitat Type: Undeveloped pond with small limestone cliffs
Fish: Largemouth and smallmouth bass, northern pike, yellow perch, walleye
Information: Ecology, University of Vermont Environmental Program, www.uvm.edu/~envprog/; The Nature Conservancy, www.nature.org/wherewework/northamerica/states/vermont/
Camping: Mt. Philo State Park; see Appendix A, #29

GETTING THERE
From Route 2 in Burlington, go 6.9 miles south on Route 116, and turn right onto Pond Road. Go 1.5 miles (8.4 miles) to the access on the right. *GPS coordinates:* 44° 22.610′ N, 73° 9.738′ W.

WHAT YOU'LL SEE
Shelburne Pond, surrounded by limestone ledges and cliffs, provides a home to some very rare ferns: maidenhair spleenwort, mountain spleenwort, walking

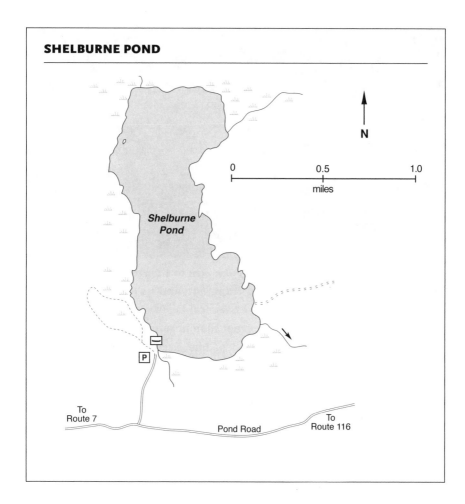

SHELBURNE POND

Shelburne
Pond

N

0   0.5   1.0
miles

P

To
Route 7

To
Route 116

Pond Road

fern, and purple-stemmed cliffbrake. You can see these by paddling along the pond's perimeter or by exploring the surrounding area. Please do not harm any of the rare ferns.

As you paddle the shoreline, keep an eye out for northern water snakes (*Nerodia sipedon*). Apparently, thousands of these attractively patterned nonpoisonous snakes used to appear here, but the population has declined in recent years. You may see them swimming in the water, basking on rock ledges, or hiding in limestone crevices with just their heads sticking out. We spotted at least a half-dozen in a few hours.

In addition to limestone cliffs along the shoreline, explore the extensive marshy areas, particularly at the northern end and at the several inlets to the pond. Cattail, swamp loosestrife, and various rush, sedge, and grasses

A harmless northern water snake, *Nerodia sipedon*, suns on a dense patch of aquatic vegetation. It swims underwater to catch small fish.

proliferate here. You should see great blue heron, green heron, various ducks, and painted turtle. At the northern inlet, paddle back in and explore the marsh more closely. Expect to see signs of beaver along the shore and piles of mussel shells scattered here and there, probably left by raccoons. Near the northern end of the pond, a small, rocky island provides a place to enjoy a picnic lunch.

Along the limestone shoreline, northern white cedar—with its lower branches sweeping out over the cliffs, dipping down to the water—predominates. On a trail extending around part of the pond from the access, you will see many other tree species: white pine, basswood, red oak, hemlock, red and sugar maple, white birch, elm, white ash, beech, hophornbeam, a few white oak, and smooth-bark hickory.

In addition to the pond's fascinating natural history, the area harbors evidence of early human history. Dr. Hub Vogelmann, longtime chair of the University of Vermont botany department and cofounder of the Vermont Chapter of The Nature Conservancy, came upon what he thought was a floating log on one of his many paddling trips to Shelburne Pond. Because he thought it looked a bit odd, he stuck his hand underneath and found it hollow—a dugout canoe. He believes that accumulating marsh gas floated it to the surface from its resting place in the mud. Radiocarbon dating showed that it had lain on the pond bottom for 4,000 years! Loads of other archaeological evidence from the pond's environs show human occupancy for at least 5,000 years. So where is the canoe? Dr. Vogelmann weighted it down and sent it to the bottom for safekeeping until the large amount of money needed to preserve it can be raised.

Shelburne Pond suffers from eutrophication caused by fertilizer runoff and augmented by limestone. The resultant algae blooms and lush aquatic vegetation eventually die, depleting oxygen as they decompose, causing anaerobic conditions and periodic fish die-offs. This promotes anaerobic bacterial growth and production of methane and hydrogen sulfide gas. Nonpoint source pollution—primarily fertilizer runoff—has received much attention in Vermont, and steps have been taken to reduce runoff into Shelburne Pond. Over time, eutrophication should decrease here.

Unfortunately, the pond also suffers from the use of motors. The Vermont Natural Resources Board, in its wisdom—or should we say in its inability to stand up to the consumptive users' lobby—allows motors and personal watercraft on the pond, with no speed limit. On this ecologically sensitive area, personal watercraft and water-skiing should be banned, and a speed limit should be implemented. With Lake Champlain just next door, Shelburne Pond should be reserved for nondestructive uses.

Shelburne Pond's unique ecosystem and its immediate environs remain undeveloped, protected in part by The Nature Conservancy and the University of Vermont, which own more than 1,000 acres here. When they own or have conservation easements on the entire shoreline, we sincerely hope that they will convince the Natural Resources Board to ban personal watercraft and limit speeds—if not ban motors altogether.

---

75 | Waterbury Reservoir

This large reservoir offers an extended paddling opportunity, but we prefer to avoid the reservoir's two southern arms because they suffer from high-speed boating. You should see both loon and osprey here.

Location: Waterbury, VT
Maps: *Vermont Atlas & Gazetteer,* Map 46: K3; USGS Bolton Mountain, Stowe
Area: 823 acres
Time: All day
Habitat Type: Large, deep reservoir
Fish: Smallmouth bass, yellow perch, brown and rainbow trout
Camping: Little River State Park; see Appendix A, #36

Take Note: Best paddling is at the north end because of a 5 mph speed limit

GETTING THERE
Northern access. From I-89, Exit 10 northbound, go 7.0 miles north on Route 100, and turn left onto Moscow Road. Go 2.1 miles (9.1 miles), and turn left onto Cotton Brook Road. Go 1.0 mile (10.1 miles) to the access. *GPS coordinates*: 44° 25.819′ N, 72° 44.552′ W.

    Blush Hill access. From I-89, Exit 10 northbound, go 0.1 mile north on Route 100, and turn left onto Blush Hill Road. Go 2.6 miles (2.7 miles) to the access. *GPS coordinates*: 44° 22.919′ N, 72° 44.474′ W.

    Dam and Little River State Park access. From Route 100 in Waterbury, go 1.3 miles east on Route 2, and turn right onto Little River Road. Go 2.8 miles, and turn right onto the dam access. You can also launch a little farther along at Little River State Park. *GPS coordinates*: 44° 23.007′ N, 72° 46.459′ W.

WHAT YOU'LL SEE
No development crowds the shores of Waterbury Reservoir, a body of water large enough for a lot of paddling—which is good, because you might have to work off some calories accumulated at Ben & Jerry's home in Waterbury. The reservoir is also narrow enough that you always feel fairly protected. The tall surrounding mountains of Mount Mansfield State Forest provide a picturesque setting. In summer, water-skiers and personal watercraft populate the lake, substantially detracting from its peacefulness. On the positive side, though, the lake offers both car- and primitive-camping opportunities. Also, the northern arm, starting about a mile south of Cotton Brook, has a 5 mph speed limit, as do the far portions of the eastern arm.

    The Little River State Park campground, located at the junction of the lake's two arms, sports many campsites and lean-tos, most set in deep woods, providing a fair amount of privacy. Most campsites perch well above the water on a wooded bluff. Unless you choose a site near the water, you will need to drive or carry your boat to one of two launching areas in the campground. Because the campground fills in summer, you should reserve a site in advance. Primitive sites around the reservoir, some in truly gorgeous settings, should be reserved as well. The park office also rents canoes. In 2000, because of safety concerns, the reservoir level was dropped 40 feet to allow dam repairs that took a few years.

    The water itself, unfortunately, can get somewhat dirty, probably from erosion along the shoreline caused by wakes of big motorboats. By the looks of it, this erosion occurs at an alarming rate, causing stretches of shoreline to appear very unnatural.

WATERBURY RESERVOIR

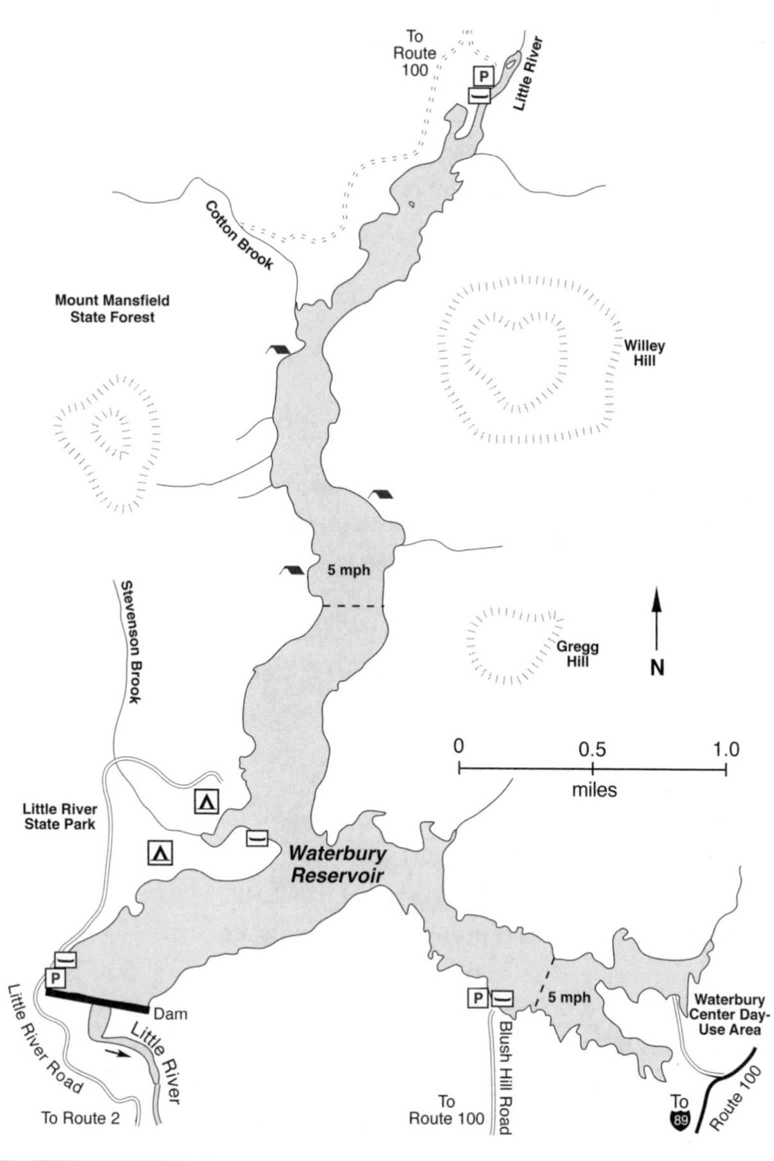

To Route 100

Little River

P

Cotton Brook

Mount Mansfield
State Forest

Willey
Hill

5 mph

Stevenson Brook

Gregg
Hill

N

0   0.5   1.0
miles

Little River
State Park

Waterbury
Reservoir

P

Dam

Little River Road

Little River

To Route 2

To
Route 100

Bush Hill Road

5 mph

Waterbury
Center Day-
Use Area

To
89

Route 100

Deciduous trees, primarily, populate the wooded shoreline, although they give way to stands of white pine and hemlock every so often. Songbirds filled the trees as we paddled along in the early morning light. Broad sections of mica schist protruding into the water provide dramatic rest areas and picnic locations. You will also find some quiet, protected swimming beaches along the shoreline.

As you travel the waterways of Vermont and New Hampshire, warnings appear everywhere about nuisance aquatic invaders. No one seems to be paying attention, however, to the huge invasion of Japanese knotweed that is taking over the reservoir's drainage area. This invasive plant, as it spreads its tentacles rapidly, crowds out native species necessary for wildlife. Bringing this loosed-upon-the-environment ornamental shrub under control will take a massive effort.

76 | Indian Brook Reservoir

This small, popular pond offers a great opportunity for combining camping, hiking, paddling, and nature observation. Look for marshland species, particularly at the pond's northern end.

Location: Essex, VT
Maps: *Vermont Atlas & Gazetteer*, Map 45: E9; USGS Essex Center
Area: 47 acres
Time: 2 hours
Habitat Type: Small, shallow pond
Fish: Smallmouth bass, brown and rainbow trout
Information: Essex Town Office, 802-878-1341
Camping: On-site, Indian Brook Park, 802-878-1342
Take Note: Gasoline motors prohibited; park pass required

GETTING THERE
From Route 2A in Essex Junction, go 1.9 miles east on Route 15, and turn left onto Old Stage Road. Go 0.4 mile (2.3 miles), and turn left onto Indian Brook Road. Go 1.4 miles (3.7 miles) to the access. *GPS coordinates:* 44° 31.848′ N, 73° 5.805′ W.

WHAT YOU'LL SEE
Although very small, Indian Brook Reservoir offers a nice mix of quietwater paddling, fishing, hiking, picnicking, nature observation, and camping.

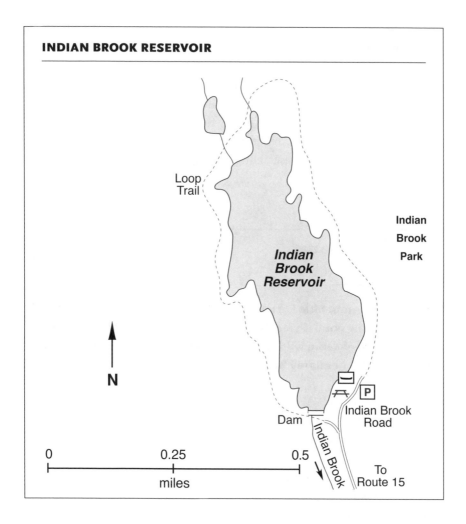

INDIAN BROOK RESERVOIR

Indian Brook Park

Loop Trail

Indian Brook Reservoir

N

Dam

Indian Brook Road

P

Indian Brook

To Route 15

0   0.25   0.5

miles

On warm, sunny days, this small pond can get overrun with people. The unde-veloped reservoir's shoreline consists mostly of rock—a fine-grain metamor-phic schist—with hemlock and white pine boughs overhanging the water. Many areas afford an opportunity to climb onto rock outcroppings to picnic or bask in the sun. At the northern end, in a number of marshy inlets, look for herons, kingfishers, and beaver in early morning and evening.

A superb trail—upgraded by the Youth Conservation Corps—circumscribes the reservoir, and several side trails provide opportunities for further explorations. One of these little trails splits off at the northern end (where it passes over a small inlet brook), and leads to a smaller and much more remote pond, where you will see nesting ducks and other wildlife—species that choose to keep their distance from people. Although it is just a short walk to the pond, to minimize encroachment on wildlife we recommend against bringing your boat along.

The mixed hardwood and softwood forest—sugar and red maple, white and yellow birch, cherry, basswood, hemlock, and white pine—invites exploration because it is so open. Anglers enjoy fishing for plentiful rainbow trout and bass. The town of Essex owns the reservoir and surrounding Indian Brook Park, keeping them open to most uses, although it strictly forbids the use of alcohol and gasoline motors.

77 | Colchester Pond

We have seen great blue heron, muskrat, and beaver while visiting this shallow, marshy pond. Protected from development, it offers a great opportunity to observe wildlife and to study wetland plants. You might see a bald eagle or osprey here.

Location: Colchester, VT
Maps: *Vermont Atlas & Gazetteer,* Map 45: E9; USGS Essex Center
Area: 182 acres
Time: 3 hours
Habitat Type: Marshy pond
Fish: Smallmouth bass, yellow perch, northern pike
Information: Winooski Valley Park District, www.wvpd.org/
Camping: Underhill State Park; see Appendix A, #35
Take Note: Motors prohibited; parking limited to precisely 18 cars

GETTING THERE
From I-89, Exit 16 northbound, go 3.3 miles north on Routes 2/7, and turn right onto Route 2A/Main Street. Go 0.9 mile (4.2 miles), and turn left onto East Road. Go 0.2 mile (4.4 miles), and turn right onto Depot Road. Go 1.0 mile (5.4 miles), and veer left onto Colchester Pond Road. Go 0.3 mile (5.7 miles) to the access. *GPS coordinates*: 44° 33.045′ N, 73° 7.508′ W.

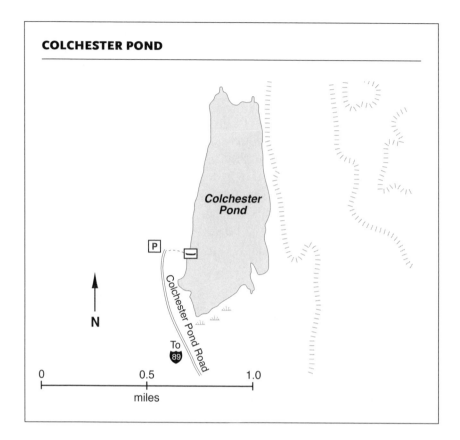

COLCHESTER POND

Colchester
Pond

P

N

Colchester Pond Road

To
89

```
0              0.5              1.0
|----|----|----|----|----|
          miles
```

WHAT YOU'LL SEE

At first glance, with a large power line looming off in the distance, Colchester Pond does not look all that inviting. Allowing that impression to keep you from paddling here would be a mistake. Overseen by the Winooski Valley Park District, with no motors allowed, this biologically productive oblong body of water harbors an amazing assortment of plants and wildlife. Because you have to carry your boat a distance to the water, the Park District has thoughtfully provided a couple of wheeled canoe carriers.

Paddling down to the cattail marsh at the south end, we watched tree and barn swallows skim the surface for a drink and listened to a bittern oompahing from its concealed location in the swamp. Because of the pond's proximity to Lake Champlain, we were not surprised to see ring-billed gulls and a half-dozen double-crested cormorants. Alas, there were no ospreys nesting on the provided platform. If they do nest here, there will be no dearth of fish for them to feed to their young; we have rarely seen so many small fish near shore. A boy we met had caught a 29-inch northern pike on a fly rod.

Indeed, the sheer productivity of Colchester Pond impressed us mightily. Even in May, an algae bloom and tons of aquatic vegetation covered the water's surface. We managed to pluck a snapping turtle out of the vegetation to check its underside for leeches; three had latched on. We wondered how the leeches might affect the resident beaver and muskrat population—we saw two muskrats harvesting grass and a small beaver on the bank stripping bark from a sapling. The beaver did not concern itself with our presence, but the fat raccoon we saw did amble out of sight as we approached.

A Canada goose pair prepared to nest, and we spotted many mallards as well. Columbine clung to the small cliffs along the northern shores, and droves of tiger swallowtail butterflies sipped nectar from the abundant honeysuckle that bloomed along the shore. As we listened to a hermit thrush singing off in the woods, we knew that we would come back to this wonderful spot again.

78 | Arrowhead Mountain Lake

We prefer to paddle the marshy northern section and the gorge-like central section of this elongated reservoir. Osprey nest here, and you might see beaver, otter, and mink.

Location: Georgia and Milton, VT
Maps: *Vermont Atlas & Gazetteer,* Maps 45: A9, 51: K9; USGS Milton
Area: 732 acres
Time: 5 hours
Habitat Type: Large reservoir; marshy sections on north end
Fish: Largemouth and smallmouth bass, yellow perch, walleye, northern pike
Take Note: 5 MPH speed limit on northeast arm

GETTING THERE
From I-89, Exit 18, go 0.1 mile south on Route 7, and turn left on Route 104A. Go 1.4 miles (1.5 miles) to the access on the right. *GPS coordinates*: 44° 40.934′ N, 73° 5.219′ W.

WHAT YOU'LL SEE
We include Arrowhead Mountain Lake in this quietwater guide, despite the state of Vermont's failure to protect it adequately from high-impact uses

ARROWHEAD MOUNTAIN LAKE

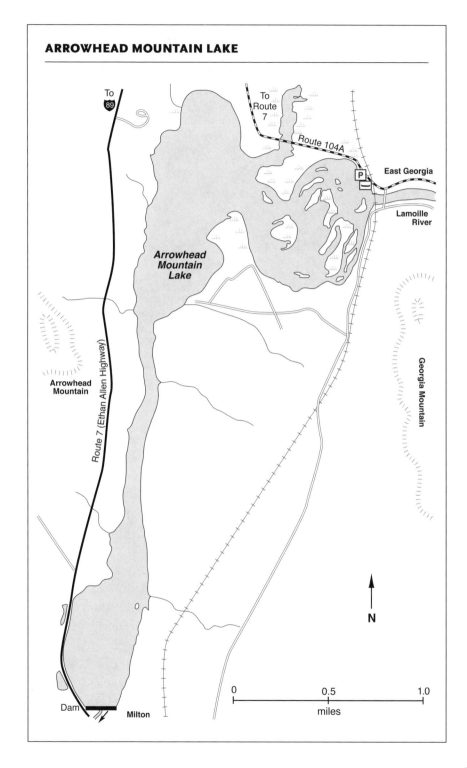

The American bittern tries to look inconspicuous in the marshland grass. Normally the bittern remains well hidden.

and development. Although the lake always had a few motorboats and some limited development, it had retained a certain wilderness feel, especially in the marshy northeast and in the gorgelike central section. The insidious invasion of personal watercraft, upon which the Vermont Natural Resources Board places few restrictions on most larger lakes, is insult enough. But the state invited the Canadian company Husky Injection Molding Systems Ltd. to build an intrusive plastics manufacturing plant on its shores and then a bridge (never built) across the lake! This seemingly constant degradation of the state's waters will not stop until the public demands better treatment for these precious resources.

A dammed-up section of the Lamoille River, Arrowhead Mountain Lake has much to offer. The wide, marshy northern part contains many islands and superb wildlife habitat. Osprey has nested here since 1998, and you should see lots of water birds, including wood duck, merganser, bittern, great blue heron, green heron, and kingfisher. Anglers catch smallmouth bass and northern pike among the marshy islands and pond vegetation. Although the water remains fairly open in spring, by midsummer you will have to restrict your paddling to the open channels that weave through the thick marshes.

As you progress south, the lake narrows and feels much more like the wide river it really is. A few houses perch along the western shore, mostly far above the water, near Route 7. The formerly undeveloped eastern shore, stretching for about three miles, sports a variety of tree species: hemlock, basswood, red oak, silver maple, sugar maple, white ash, American elm, box elder, cottonwood, white pine, ironwood, beech, hickory, and alder. The banks also grow thick with fern. We saw some freshwater mussels and signs of beaver, and it would not surprise us to see mink or otter, who would be just as curious to know why an injection-molding plant has invaded this once-pristine shoreline.

79 | Fairfield Swamp

Fairfield Swamp is part of an extensive wildlife management area where many wetland species breed. Besides the abundant waterfowl, you will likely see osprey and great blue heron, and possibly beaver.

Location: Fairfield, St. Albans, and Swanton, VT
Maps: *Vermont Atlas & Gazetteer,* Map 51: H11; USGS Fairfield, St. Albans
Area: 1,293 acres
Time: 5 hours
Habitat Type: Extensive marshland
Fish: Pickerel
Information: Fairfield Swamp Wildlife Management Area, www.vtfishandwildlife.com/wma_maps.cfm
Camping: Lake Carmi State Park; see Appendix A, #38
Take Note: 5 MPH speed limit; personal watercraft prohibited

GETTING THERE
From Route 104 in St. Albans, go 3.9 miles east on Route 36 to the access on the left. *GPS coordinates*: 44° 47.301´ N, 72° 59.883´ W.

WHAT YOU'LL SEE
To see rich and varied plant life, waterfowl, frogs, and aquatic insects, one could spend days exploring each of the hundreds of underappreciated swamps

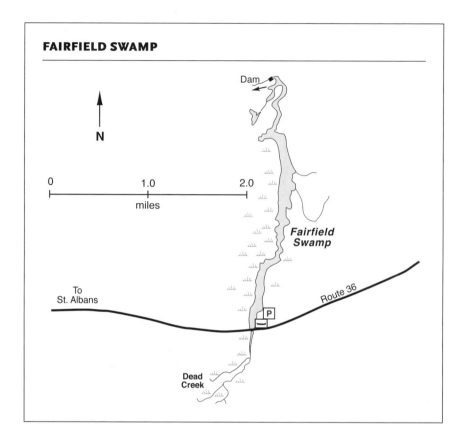

FAIRFIELD SWAMP

Dam

N

0   1.0   2.0

miles

Fairfield Swamp

To St. Albans

Route 36

P

Dead Creek

and marshes of Vermont. Located just a few miles east of St. Albans and I-89, Fairfield Swamp is a great place to experience the changing of the seasons at one of these marshes.

From the access, you can paddle either north or south, although the latter necessitates snaking your way through the culvert under Route 36 (which may not be possible at times of high water). If you head north (downstream) with the imperceptible current, you can paddle nearly three miles through gradually changing vegetation until you reach a small concrete dam that maintains the level of this swamp on Dead Creek.

Cattail and the slivered spikes of long-dead trees, killed when the dam was built, dominate the swamp near the access. Tamarack, a conifer that loses its needles in winter and can survive in water-saturated soils, is gradually coming in here. On higher ground, you will see hemlock, white pine, and assorted hardwood trees. Thick masses of yellow pond lily and—farther north—water shield, pondweed, and pickerelweed impede paddling. After narrowing somewhat as you paddle north, the swamp opens up again about a mile downstream. The cattail gradually disappears, and the woodland at the north end extends right down to the water, providing suitable habitat for the resident beaver.

South of Route 36, Fairfield Swamp feels somewhat more remote, with extensive stands of cattail, black spruce, and tamarack. Wood duck nesting boxes represent the only evidence of humans. Yellow pond lily and pondweed cover the surface of this very wide marsh, with shores and hummocks lined with aromatic shrubs such as sweet gale. We delighted in seeing wild calla (*Calla palustris*) in bloom, the bloom spike clothed in a bright white sheath. Beaver keep the channels open, making paddling through the primordial abundance of vegetation relatively easy.

We saw frogs galore, and the late-spring chorus was almost deafening in some sections. Great blue heron, wood duck, eastern kingbird, ring-billed gull, and the ever-present red-winged blackbird abound. We watched an osprey feed young and much smaller blackbirds hassle a red-tailed hawk. A handful of duck-hunting blinds argue for avoiding this paddling spot during fall waterfowl hunting season.

The northern leopard frog, *Rana pipiens*, is one of several frog species that you could see in Fairfield Swamp.

80 | Jewett Brook and Stevens Brook

These two brooks flow through the Black Creek Wildlife Management Area and continue to the shore of Lake Champlain. You could see great blue heron, and maybe black-crowned night heron and map turtles.

Location: St. Albans, VT
Maps: *Vermont Atlas & Gazetteer,* Map 51: G8; USGS St. Albans Bay
Length: Jewett Brook, 2.3 miles; Stevens Brook, 1.4 miles
Time: Half a day for both
Habitat Type: Slow-flowing, shallow, marshy streams
Fish: No game fish
Information: Black Creek Wildlife Management Area, www.vtfishandwildlife.com/wma_maps.cfm
Camping: Lake Carmi State Park; see Appendix A, #38

GETTING THERE
From Route 7 in St. Albans, go 3.6 miles west on Route 36 to a pullout on the right, just before the bridge over Jewett Brook. *GPS coordinates:* 44° 48.633′ N, 73° 9.049′ W.

WHAT YOU'LL SEE
Jewett Brook, flowing into Lake Champlain at St. Albans Bay, and the smaller Stevens Brook that flows into it provide a relaxing morning or afternoon of quiet paddling through portions of the Black Creek Wildlife Management Area. The murky water—due in part to the silty soils found in the Champlain Valley—suffers from high nutrient loading from surrounding farmland. We suspect that it could become fairly eutrophic in late summer—with a thick layer of algae on the surface and high levels of decomposing organic matter in the water. Breakdown of organic matter robs the water of oxygen, making it uninhabitable for all but so-called coarse fish, such as carp.

Paddling north from the muddy access, you pass through a thick cattail marsh. Tall silver maples cling to the marsh's edge; these can survive water-saturated soils that would kill most trees. We saw a number of common map turtles (*Graptemys geographica*)—a species that is anything but common in New England. In fact, the marshy, muck-bottomed shallows of Lake Champlain and

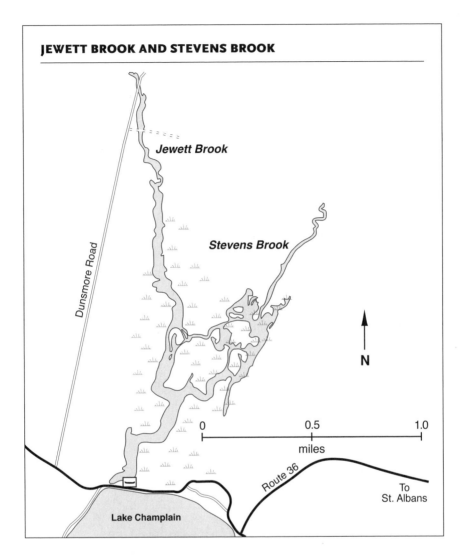

JEWETT BROOK AND STEVENS BROOK

Jewett Brook

Stevens Brook

Dunsmore Road

N

0   0.5   1.0
miles

Route 36

To
St. Albans

Lake Champlain

its tributaries comprise the eastern extension of the range for this midwestern and southern species. The females get quite large; we saw some with top shells (carapace) that were nearly 10 inches in length—quite a bit bigger than our more common painted turtle. To see these turtles out sunning, you must be quiet, though. Map turtles are slightly flatter than painted turtles and significantly flatter than snapping turtles—the only other species here that could be as large. The rear end of the carapace flares out slightly.

We saw wood ducks in the marsh, lots of great blue herons, several black-crowned night herons, mallards, and a blue-winged teal during our midday paddle in late May. Swamp sparrows called with a metallic chip, and marsh wrens flitted about, building nests in the cattails. You undoubtedly will be startled, as we were, as you paddle over some of the huge carp that help make the water murky as they root around the shallows.

If you stay to the left (western shore), you can follow the main channel about two miles upstream, with the marsh gradually narrowing to a creek. Downed trees might block your way here; after maneuvering around a few, a tree finally blocked our way at an old railroad-tie-and-concrete-slab bridge on a farm road.

Along the eastern shore, you can explore some marshy inlets, but the thick cattail growth restricts paddling considerably. About three-quarters of a mile from the access, the smaller (but generally clear) Stevens Brook angles off to the right (northeast), and you can paddle up it at least a mile. You may pass grazing cows along the brook as you leave the marsh and get into farmland. We turned around where a pipe was spewing some foul liquid into the creek—something that we hope will have ended by the time you read this. (If it is still there, you too might want to contact Vermont environmental officials.)

Despite the nutrient loading, the mystery pipe inflow, and some smells from nearby farms wafting into the marsh, Jewett and Stevens brooks offer pleasant paddling and wildlife observing opportunities less than an hour from Burlington.

81 | Missisquoi National Wildlife Refuge

This huge wetland wildlife refuge on Lake Champlain is an extraordinary paddling destination. Numerous channels course through the refuge, much of which is inundated during times of high water. You will likely see waterfowl, black and common terns, and great blue heron, and possibly whitetailed deer, mink, beaver, otter, and bald eagle.

Location: Highgate and Swanton, VT
Maps: *Vermont Atlas & Gazetteer,* Maps 50: B7, 51: B8; USGS East Alburg
Area: 6,500 acres
Time: All day

Habitat Type: Large inlet on Lake Champlain
Fish: Largemouth and smallmouth bass, yellow perch, pickerel, northern pike, walleye; brook, brown, and rainbow trout
Information: Missisquoi National Wildlife Refuge, www.fws.gov/northeast/missisquoi/
Camping: Lake Carmi State Park; see Appendix A, #38

GETTING THERE

Louie's Landing. From I-89, Exit 21 northbound, go 5.8 miles west on Route 78 to the access on the right. *GPS coordinates*: 44° 57.513′ N, 73° 9.977′ W.

Campbell Bay Road. Go 1.1 miles (6.9 miles) farther on Route 78 to the access to the spectacular marsh south of Route 78. *GPS coordinates*: 44° 58.222′ N, 73° 10.883′ W.

WHAT YOU'LL SEE

Even a relatively light wind on Lake Champlain can produce swells of a foot or more, and a breeze of more than 15 MPH can produce dangerous whitecaps. But the lake should not be totally off-limits, either. A few places—including Missisquoi Bay and the Missisquoi River delta—offer protected areas for open-boat paddlers.

In Vermont's northwestern corner, virtually a stone's throw from Canada, sits Missisquoi National Wildlife Refuge, established in 1943. The Abenaki word *missisquoi* means "great grassy meadow." Over the years, at least twenty different spellings have appeared. Two paddleable channels exist here: Missisquoi River proper, with its divided channels near its terminus, and Dead Creek, which branches off the Missisquoi near refuge headquarters.

On a calm day, you can make a loop of these channels; on a windy day, stick to the channels. From the access, paddle the river downstream, then around the eastern side of the peninsula and up Dead Creek to its intersection with the Missisquoi and back to the landing. One could also make the trip in the opposite direction.

On Shad Island, notice the several hundred large great blue heron nests in the trees, belonging to one of the largest rookeries in New England—you may hear loud croaking in spring and early summer. Look for cormorants off Shad Island point. Missisquoi harbors one of the largest nesting black tern populations in New England, and it is one of the few places in Vermont where you can see threatened common terns and can find soft-shelled turtles.

While the Missisquoi River can suffer from heavy motorboat traffic on a

MISSISQUOI NATIONAL WILDLIFE REFUGE

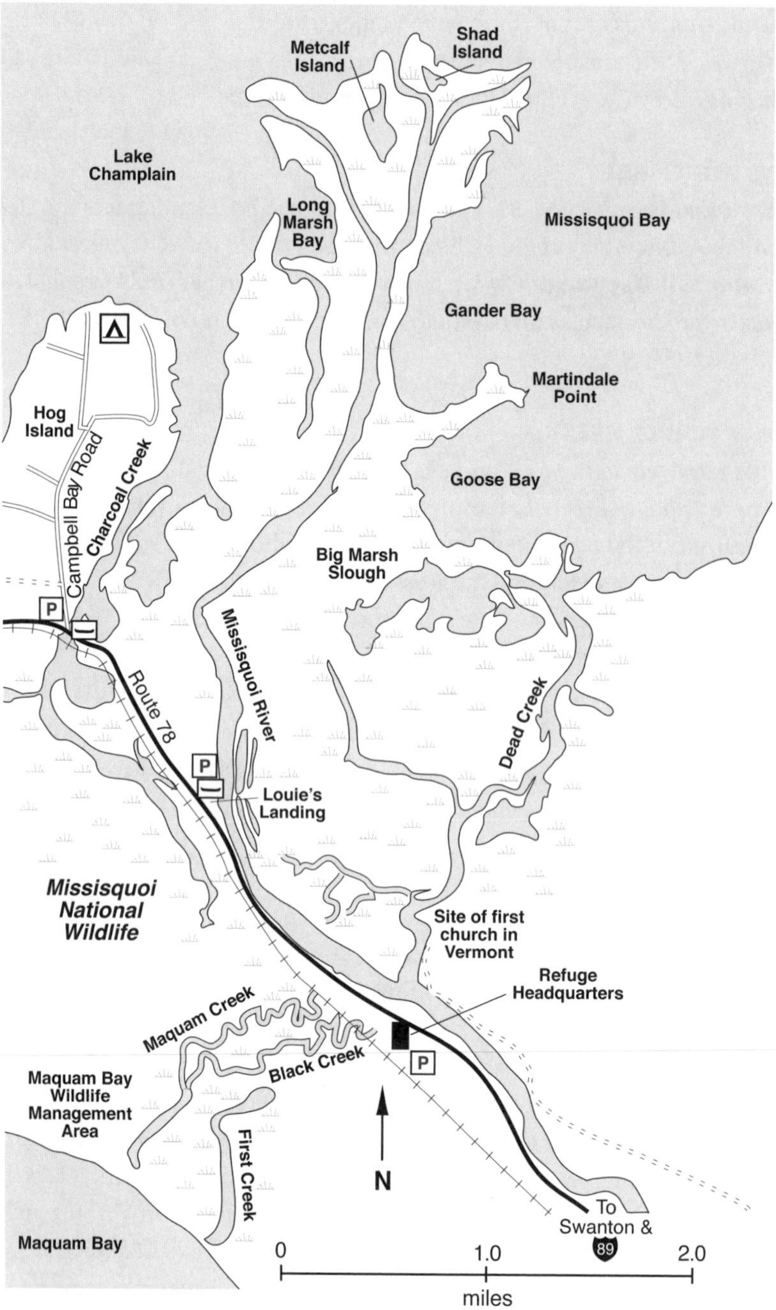

Metcalf Island

Shad Island

Lake Champlain

Long Marsh Bay

Missisquoi Bay

Gander Bay

Martindale Point

Hog Island

Goose Bay

Campbell Bay Road

Charcoal Creek

Big Marsh Slough

Missisquoi River

Dead Creek

Route 78

P

Louie's Landing

Missisquoi National Wildlife

Site of first church in Vermont

Refuge Headquarters

Maquam Creek

P

Maquam Bay Wildlife Management Area

Black Creek

First Creek

N

To Swanton & 89

Maquam Bay

0   1.0   2.0

miles

busy weekend, Dead Creek can be much quieter. On a windless May afternoon, we watched a mink move furtively along the bank of Dead Creek—with one eye on us. Nearby we watched a deer splash through the shallow water.

Silver maple dominates the Missisquoi River and Dead Creek shores; its winged seeds—the largest of any maple—serve as an important wildlife food source. With the maple growing right out of the water, the area reminds us of a Louisiana cypress swamp. Out near Lake Champlain—depending on lake water level—you can actually weave a twisted course through these trees, encountering an occasional wood duck. Be sure not to paddle in restricted areas.

When we paddled here in late summer, we saw clematis, butter-and-eggs, and a vinelike yellow aster in bloom. Arrowhead bloomed along the banks, and we reveled in the abundance of birds.

One other area worth paddling, on the south side of Route 78, is just across from Campbell Bay Road. The broad expanse of marsh here, while home to a lot of waterfowl, has somewhat lower species diversity than the delta on the north side of the road.

If you care to hike, two short trails leave from park headquarters and pass along Black Creek and Maquam Creek, covering roughly 1.5 miles. Just across from the refuge headquarters, where Dead Creek splits off from the Missisquoi River, is the site of the first church in Vermont.

Thick silver-maple swamps, including one with a great blue heron rookery, lend an eerie feeling to the Missisquoi River delta on Lake Champlain.

82 | Rock River

Keep an eye out for the peregrine falcons that nest on Highgate Cliffs on this river. You will likely see great blue heron and numerous songbirds here, and you might see osprey, beaver, otter, and mink.

Location: Highgate, VT
Maps: *Vermont Atlas & Gazetteer,* Map 51: A9; USGS Highgate Center
Length: 6 miles or longer round-trip
Time: 4 hours
Habitat Type: Narrow, canopied river
Fish: Largemouth and smallmouth bass, yellow perch, pickerel, northern pike
Information: Rock River Wildlife Management Area, www.vtfishandwildlife.com/wma_maps.cfm
Camping: Lake Carmi State Park; see Appendix A, #38

GETTING THERE

From I-89, Exit 22 northbound, go 1.6 miles south on Route 7 to the access on the left. *GPS coordinates*: 44° 59.302′ N, 73° 5.296′ W.

WHAT YOU'LL SEE

This meandering tributary to Lake Champlain's Missisquoi Bay, part of the Rock River Wildlife Management Area, can provide hours of secluded paddling away from the clamor, bustle, and wind that can beset an outing on the big lake. We paddled about three miles upriver, although one could go much farther. Expect to portage around an occasional logjam. As with most bodies of water in the lowland North Country, silver maple lines the shores, forming a canopy over this wide, slow river. A consequence of the canopy, however, is that it provides an infinite number of launch pads for deer flies, a dipteran predator (genus *Chrysops*) that locates its prey by sight. We strongly recommend wearing a hat when you paddle here to reduce the aggravation.

Some enormous bur oak appears here and there, along with a very occasional shagbark hickory, both near the northeastern extent of their ranges here. We were surprised at finding bur oak; we would have expected to find swamp white oak on this floodplain.

We listened to hermit thrushes whistling their flutelike notes from the forest floor, and a Baltimore oriole (*Icterus galbula*, recently once again split off from Bullock's oriole, *Icterus bullockii*, with which it had been lumped into northern oriole) sang its melodious song from the treetops. In spring, the woods here are alive with a chorus of bird songs. Barn swallows nest under the bridges, and great blue heron and red-winged blackbird patrol the marshlands where the river spills over into the adjacent lowlands in spring.

We also saw several raptors, including red-tailed hawk, osprey, and turkey vulture. If you have time, visit the nearby Highgate Cliffs Natural Area, where peregrine falcons nest and you can explore an undisturbed cobble beach.

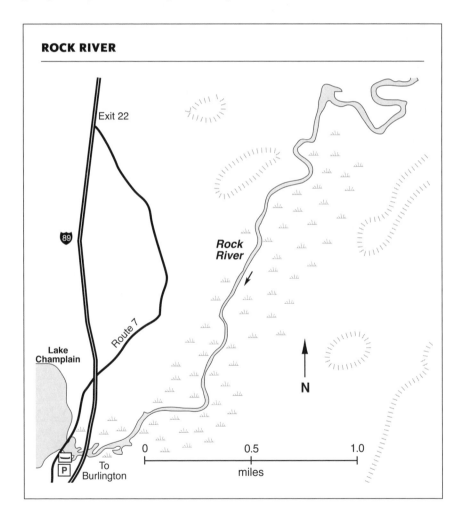

ROCK RIVER

Exit 22

89

Rock River

Lake Champlain

Route 7

N

0   0.5   1.0
miles

P

To Burlington

Silver maples, *Acer saccharinum*, form a canopy over the wide, slow Rock River as it meanders down from Canada to Lake Champlain.

83 | Green River Reservoir

This large reservoir is the premier paddling destination in Vermont, so it is best to avoid it on summer weekends. On our trips here, we have seen black bear, moose, whitetailed deer, mink, otter, beaver, loon, osprey, and much more. Several wilderness campsites dot the area.

Location: Eden and Hyde Park, VT
Maps: *Vermont Atlas & Gazetteer,* Map 47: B8; USGS Eden, Morrisville
Area: 863 acres
Time: 2 days minimum
Habitat Type: Large lake with many islands and inlets
Fish: Smallmouth bass, pickerel, yellow perch
Information: Green River Reservoir State Park,
www.vtstateparks.com/htm/grriver.cfm
Camping: Green River Reservoir State Park; see Appendix A, #37
Take Note: Gasoline motors prohibited

GREEN RIVER RESERVOIR

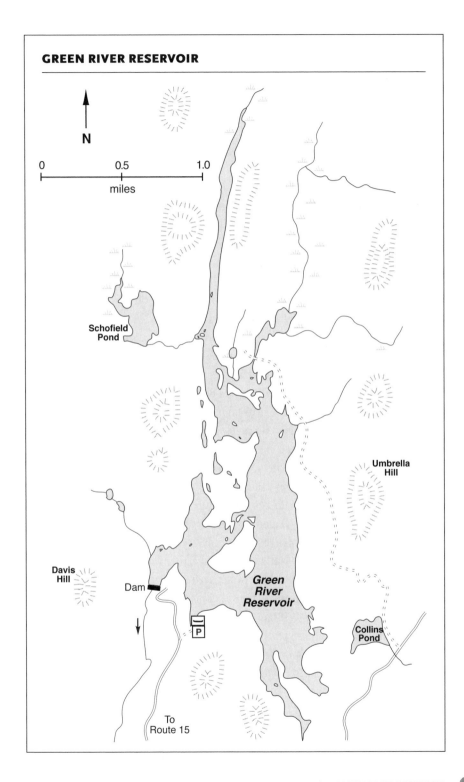

N

0   0.5   1.0
miles

Schofield
Pond

Umbrella
Hill

Davis
Hill

Dam

P

Green
River
Reservoir

Collins
Pond

To
Route 15

GETTING THERE

From Route 100 in Morrisville, go east on either Route 15 or 15A. Right after Routes 15 and 15A join, turn left onto Garfield Road, and go 3.1 miles to the T. Turn right, go 0.1 mile (3.2 miles), and turn left onto Green River Dam Road. Go 1.3 miles (4.5 miles) to the access. *GPS coordinates*: 44° 37.287′ N, 72° 31.559′ W.

From Route 14 in Hardwick, go 10.9 miles west on Route 15, turn right onto Garfield Road, and continue as above.

WHAT YOU'LL SEE

Green River Reservoir, located in north-central Vermont, remains the premier paddling destination in Vermont and a real treasure for remote-camping enthusiasts. The Nature Conservancy purchased the reservoir, formerly used by Morrisville for power generation, and transferred it to the state for management as a state park. The conservancy retained a conservation easement to ensure that the reservoir remains undeveloped and wild

The park includes 5,110 acres of surrounding forest, managed for recreation and as habitat for moose and bear. Indeed, we have seen both while paddling here. It contains deer wintering areas, and the Catamount Trail passes through. The reservoir seems much larger than its 863 acres because of its many long inlet arms and fourteen islands. The total paddleable perimeter of more than 19 miles makes it Vermont's largest undeveloped shoreline. Campers concentrate on and around the large island near the center. By exploring the long fingers and inlets, you can sometimes get away from other people.

The lake's long, northernmost arm offers especially great paddling. We saw a family of six otter, along with several beaver and a number of wood ducks near the northern tip, which becomes marshy and narrows to a slow-moving, winding stream. A beaver dam eventually blocks your way; we carried above the dam, but you really cannot paddle too much farther because of shallow water.

Red maple, yellow birch, white pine, hemlock, balsam fir, sugar maple, and white birch populate most of the lake's heavily wooded shoreline. Look for mountain ash, with its brilliant orange berries in fall, and hophornbeam, along with lots of understory viburnum and other shrubs. In the northern marshlands, tamarack and spruce mix in with the other species. In some areas, exposed metamorphic schist, usually covered with a carpet of polypody fern, forms large outcroppings.

Ospreys nest here, and a tributary creek hosts a great blue heron rookery. Green River Reservoir is one of the few bodies of water in Vermont where loons have nested successfully since the 1970s. The state marks off nesting

A beaver dam will block your passage at the far northern inlet on Green River Reservoir. We saw a black bear near here.

sites, and we all should stay well away from these areas.

Although the waterway does suffer somewhat from overuse—we counted eighteen touring kayaks and only slightly fewer canoes on a warm, bright mid-September Saturday—at least the state prohibits personal watercraft and motors. Queuing up to unload your boat and finding a place to park along the rut-filled access road also provides a challenge. Reluctantly, we have to recommend that you stay away on popular summer weekends; better yet, visit in spring or after Labor Day.

84 | Great Hosmer Pond and Little Hosmer Pond

If you like multisport recreation, Hosmer Ponds and Craftsbury offer great choices. You can go paddling, mountain biking, cross-country skiing, rowing, running, and hiking there. While paddling, we have seen loon, kingfisher, muskrat, and many more species here.

Location: Albany and Craftsbury, VT

Maps: *Vermont Atlas & Gazetteer,* Maps 47: A12, 53: K12; USGS Albany, Craftsbury

Area: Great Hosmer Pond, 155 acres; Little Hosmer Pond, 183 acres (!)

Time: All day for both

Habitat Type: Long, narrow ponds; marshy areas on Little Hosmer

Fish: Smallmouth bass, yellow perch, and pickerel; Great Hosmer also large-mouth bass

Camping and Lodging: Craftsbury Outdoor Center, 802-586-7767, www.craftsbury.com; ask permission to launch on Great Hosmer Pond

Take Note: Personal watercraft prohibited; Little Hosmer Pond, 10 HP limit, 5 MPH speed limit

GETTING THERE

Little Hosmer Pond. From Route 15 in Hardwick, go 7.2 miles north on Route 14, and turn right onto South/North Craftsbury Road. Go 3.9 miles (11.1 miles), and go straight onto Wylie Hill Road. Go 0.1 mile (11.2 miles), and turn right onto Mill Village Road. Go 0.4 mile (11.6 miles), and turn left into the access on Boat Dock Road. *GPS coordinates:* 44° 39.987′ N, 72° 22.568′ W.

Craftsbury Outdoor Center and Great Hosmer Pond. From Boat Dock Road, go 0.7 mile (12.3 miles), and turn right onto Lost Nation Road. Go 0.6 mile (12.9 miles) to the center. Just past the center, go left down to the access. *GPS coordinates:* 44° 40.868′ N, 72° 21.875′ W.

WHAT YOU'LL SEE

Looking for a pleasant weekend of paddling but prefer to be pampered a bit with hot meals, showers, and lodging? Consider the two Hosmer Ponds, located in scenic Craftsbury, in the heart of Vermont's Northeast Kingdom. Great Hosmer and Little Hosmer ponds offer great paddling and lodging. The Craftsbury Outdoor Center started out as a cross-country ski area but expanded into summer sports to make it a year-round operation, where people can hone their rowing, mountain biking, and running skills. Guests can camp or stay in simple lodging with shared baths and have access to a workout room, sauna, massage therapist, and expert instruction in running and sculling—in numerous camps for all levels of skill. Wholesome buffet-style meals include vegetarian dishes.

Great Hosmer Pond

About a dozen cottages dot the shoreline of this 2-mile-long, 0.25-mile-wide pond, but most activity is connected with the Craftsbury Outdoor Center. During an early morning paddle, a flotilla of rowing shells passed us by as if

GREAT HOSMER POND AND LITTLE HOSMER POND

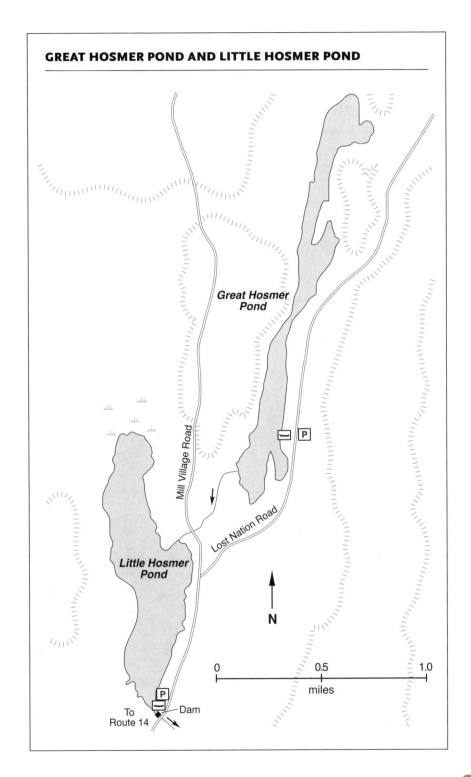

Great Hosmer Pond

Mill Village Road

Lost Nation Road

Little Hosmer Pond

P

N

0   0.5   1.0
miles

To
Route 14

Dam

P

we were standing still. Of course, we had more interest in listening to the oven-bird, white-throated sparrow, and winter wren calling from the undergrowth than in a keeping up with these sleek craft. We also wanted to appreciate a major caddis fly hatch, as thousands of these flies flew in an erratic mating dance. The aquatic larvae build a cylindrical case of twigs, leaves, sand, or small stones cemented together, from which they feed on vegetation. To pupate, they attach the case to an underwater rock, close the open end, pupate, and then climb out of the case and out of the water as adults, with tentlike wings folded over their backs.

Paddling up the shoreline, one cannot help but notice the dominance of northern white cedar (*Thuja occidentalis*), a type of arborvitae. *Arborvitae* means "tree of life"; historians believe that French explorer Jacques Cartier gave the tree that name after learning from Native Americans that a tea made from its needles cures scurvy. Note the conspicuous browse line on the cedars that hang out over the water. Deer often yard up in cedar stands in winter, and they browse the shoreline cedars up to head height as they walk along the ice in winter. The seeds and cones are important winter food for pine siskins and red squirrels.

Deer feeding from the pond's winter ice have carved a conspicuous browse line on shore-line northern white cedars, *Thuja occidentalis*.

Little Hosmer Pond

Located less than a mile away, Little Hosmer is wider but shorter and with more surface area than Great Hosmer; it also boasts more varied habitat, with marshy areas to explore and a shoreline dominated by northern white cedar and tamarack, giving the pond a wild northern feel. The shoreline vegetation consists mostly of sweet gale and fern, and yellow pond lily covers the shallows with a fairly thick mat. As with Great Hosmer, the dozen or so cottages do not intrude too severely into the pond's solitude. We saw mallard, wood duck, loon, and a pair of ring-necked ducks here in late May. During a September visit, we watched a muskrat in one of the cattail marshes on the pond. We saw old evidence of beaver activity here, but nothing current.

85 | Long Pond (Greensboro)

Besides forested hillsides and a northern white cedar swamp, you might see beaver, otter, and moose in this remote location.

Location: Greensboro, VT
Maps: *Vermont Atlas & Gazetteer,* Map 47: B14; USGS Caspian Lake, Craftsbury
Area: 99 acres
Time: 3 hours, including hiking in and out
Habitat Type: Small wilderness pond with a few marshy areas
Fish: Yellow perch, pickerel
Information: The Nature Conservancy, www.nature.org/wherewework/northamerica/states/vermont/
Take Note: Gasoline motors prohibited; camping prohibited

GETTING THERE

From Route 16 in Hardwick, go 8.4 miles north on Route 16, and turn left onto Taylor Road. Go 1.4 miles (9.8 miles), and turn right onto Jaffin Flat Road. Go 0.4 mile (10.2 miles), and turn left onto Hill Road. Go 0.8 mile (11.0 miles), and turn right onto Town Highway 8. Go 1.0 mile (12.0 miles) to Long Pond Road. Park along the gravel road. Do not drive down the access road. Even if you have high ground clearance, you should still carry in to avoid damaging

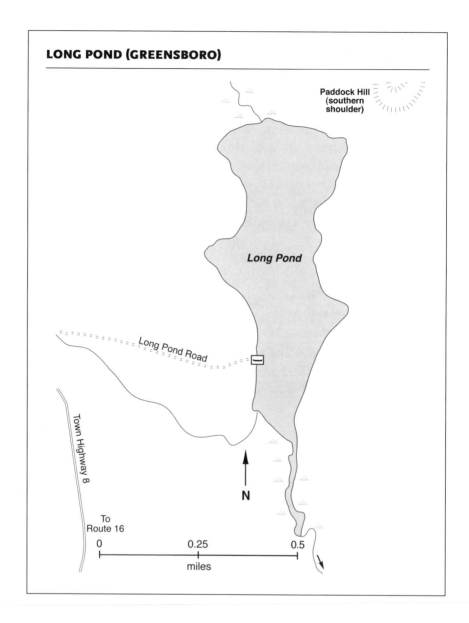

LONG POND (GREENSBORO)

Paddock Hill
(southern
shoulder)

Long Pond

Long Pond Road

Town Highway 8

To
Route 16

N

| 0 | 0.25 | 0.5 |

miles

the road. The mile-or-so carry takes about twenty minutes if you hoof it. When you reach the pond, a nice grassy clearing beneath some large cedars makes an ideal picnic spot. *GPS coordinates*: 44° 37.404′ N, 72° 16.591′ W.

WHAT YOU'LL SEE

Northwest of St. Johnsbury, pretty much in the middle of nowhere in Vermont's Northeast Kingdom, lies undeveloped Long Pond. The Nature

Conservancy protects the southern end of Long Pond as well as 1,500 feet of shoreline on the eastern side—some 767 acres total. The state prohibits gasoline-powered motors on this pristine, difficult-to-find, and hard-to-reach pond.

Northern white cedar lines the pond's southern perimeter and represents one of the finest cedar swamps in the state. When northern white cedar dominates the shore, deer usually trim the lower branches to a perfectly horizontal plane. During winter, deer feed on the lower branches from the ice—as far up as they can reach—creating a conspicuous browse line. Further inland, cedar gives way to balsam fir, hemlock, maple, and other deep-woods species.

Marshy areas with cattail, floating pondweed, and various grasses and sedges line the north inlet and the south outlet. Look for wood ducks here and for the resident beaver in late afternoon. Also keep an eye out for otter. We watched one lazily fishing here on a midafternoon in September. Seeing an otter at midday gives testimony to the remoteness of this pond; usually, in order to see otter, mink, and beaver, you need to get out early in the morning or around dusk.

A tiger swallowtail, *Papilio glaucus*, sucks nectar from a viburnum along the shore.

86 | Flagg Pond

Northern bog vegetation fills the hummocks and shore of this small out-of-the-way pond. This is a great place to study bog plants, and you might see osprey, beaver, otter, mink, black bear, moose, and other animals.

Location: Wheelock, VT
Maps: *Vermont Atlas & Gazetteer,* Map 48: D1; USGS Stannard
Area: 108 acres
Time: 2 hours
Habitat Type: Small, shallow pond
Fish: Largemouth bass, pickerel, yellow perch
Information: The Nature Conservancy,
www.nature.org/wherewework/northamerica/states/vermont/
Take Note: Gasoline motors prohibited

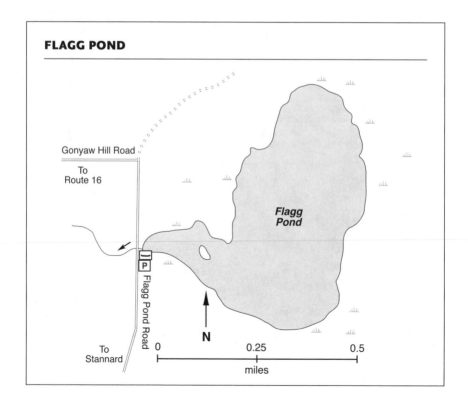

FLAGG POND

Gonyaw Hill Road

To
Route 16

Flagg
Pond

To
Stannard

Flagg Pond Road

P

N

0   0.25   0.5
miles

GETTING THERE

From Route 15 in Hardwick, go 6.5 miles northeast on Route 15, and turn right onto Gonyaw Hill Road. Go 1.9 miles (8.4 miles), and turn right onto Flagg Pond Road. Go 0.2 mile (8.6 miles) to the access on the left along the road. *GPS coordinates*: 44° 33.852′ N, 72° 12.902′ W.

From I-91, Exit 23, go south on Route 5 a short distance, and turn right onto South Wheelock/Stannard Mountain Road. Go 0.7 mile past Stannard, and turn right onto Flagg Pond Road. Go 1.5 miles (2.2 miles) north to the pond.

WHAT YOU'LL SEE

Located in the heart of Vermont's Northeast Kingdom, small, out-of-the-way Flagg Pond rarely sees many visitors, even on a nice summer weekend. Paddling along the pond's perimeter at the end of May, we saw a remarkable number of American toads (*Bufo americanus*) inundating the hummocky shoreline, particularly at the northeast end—literally hundreds were either clinging to the branches of shrubs or sitting in the water. We heard a veritable cacophony of high-pitched trilling, made by toads inflating their throat sacks—and this was a little past their typical breeding season!

As you paddle along here, notice the royal fern, sweet gale, thick hummocks of sphagnum moss, and occasional pitcher plant, along with several members of the heath family—leatherleaf, bog rosemary, and beautiful bog laurel with bright pink blooms—that comprise the thickly vegetated shoreline. Tamarack and northern white cedar, species that do not mind getting their feet wet, also grow here. Several active beaver lodges cling to the pond's edge, and we saw a few great blue herons plying the waters for tasty fish (or toad?). Extensive stands of bulrush grow along the eastern shore. The Nature Conservancy now owns 100 acres around the pond, including 70 acres of cedar swamp.

87 | May Pond

Protected by The Nature Conservancy because of its unique ecological character, this small, little-known pond presents a wonderful opportunity for viewing wildlife. We have seen otter, along with many other species. Look for osprey, beaver, and moose here.

Location: Barton, VT

Maps: *Vermont Atlas & Gazetteer,* Map 54: I3; USGS Sutton
Area: 116 acres
Time: 2 hours, longer if you study plants and observe wildlife
Habitat Type: Small, marshy pond
Fish: Brook trout
Information: The Nature Conservancy, www.nature.org/wherewework/ northamerica/states/vermont/
Camping: Brighton State Park; see Appendix A, #39
Take Note: Gasoline motors prohibited

GETTING THERE

From I-91, Exit 25, go 2.7 miles north on Route 16, and turn right onto May Pond Road. Go 2.1 miles (4.8 miles) to the access road on the left. *GPS coordinates*: 44° 44.525′ N, 72° 7.395′ W.

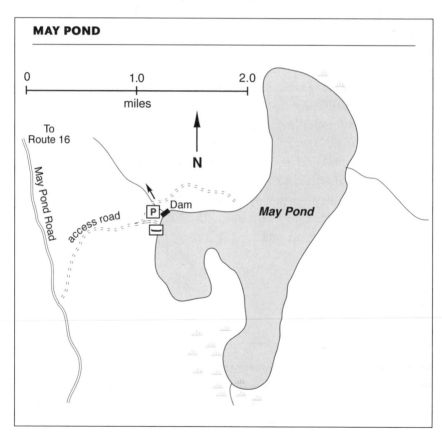

Protected by The Nature Conservancy, the wooded shoreline of May Pond is a good place to see river otter and osprey.

WHAT YOU'LL SEE

Located in Vermont's Northeast Kingdom about a half-hour drive from Lake Willoughby, this little-known pond offers great wildlife viewing in a relatively pristine environment. Although small, May Pond sports a highly varied shoreline and seems much larger. Try to visit here early morning or late afternoon, when wildlife-viewing opportunities peak. For about an hour here one August evening around dusk, we watched a family of four otter diving for crayfish and munching on them at the surface. Look for beaver, nesting loons, and osprey.

The two cabins located near the access and the nearby rolling farmland do not spoil the remote feeling of the pond. The marshy shoreline supports lots of pond vegetation (water shield, waterlily, cattail, sedge, and the like), backed by densely grown and fairly impenetrable shrubs (heath, winterberry, and alder). Farther back on solid ground grow red spruce, balsam fir, white and yellow birch, red maple, and hemlock. At the shallower, more fenlike southern end of the pond, tussocks of sphagnum moss, sundew, and the thick muck of decomposing vegetation stirred up by your paddle stand ready to greet you. In spring, laurel blooms in the understory, and in midsummer you may be able to enjoy a snack of wild blueberries. Look for the huge beaver lodge here—likely the home of many generations of beaver.

Recognizing May Pond's pristine ecological character, The Nature Conservancy's Vermont Chapter many years ago purchased 740 acres around the pond, including 5,000 feet of frontage. In 2003, the conservancy and the state acquired another 6,500 feet of frontage. As you paddle around May Pond, respect its fragile character and avoid disturbing nesting loons, otter, and other wildlife.

88 | Long Pond (Westmore)

Located in the shadow of the much larger Lake Willoughby, Long Pond receives much less traffic. Picturesque views and limits on motorboats make up for the cottages on the northern end. Look for loons and wood ducks on this aptly named long, narrow pond.

Location: Westmore, VT
Maps: *Vermont Atlas & Gazetteer,* Map 54: I6; USGS Sutton, Westmore

Area: 103 acres
Time: 3 hours
Habitat Type: Small, clear, deep lake
Fish: Brook and lake trout
Camping: Brighton State Park; see Appendix A, #39
Take Note: 5 MPH speed limit, personal watercraft prohibited

GETTING THERE

From Route 16 at Lake Willoughby's north end, go 1.5 miles south on Route 5A, and turn left onto Long Pond Road. Go 2.1 miles (3.6 miles) to the access on the right. *GPS coordinates*: 44° 45.370′ N, 72° 1.190′ W.

WHAT YOU'LL SEE

In the heart of Vermont's Northeast Kingdom just east of Lake Willoughby, Westmore's Long Pond enjoys a picturesque setting and offers a pleasant morning or afternoon of paddling amid gorgeous views of surrounding hillsides. About a dozen cottages populate the north end, near the access, but otherwise no development impinges on the long, narrow pond.

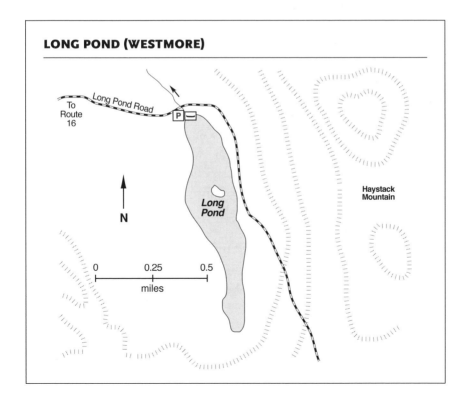

As with many northern Vermont lakes, northern white cedar dominates the shoreline. Note the browse line from deer, which feed on lower branches that they reach from the ice in winter. Loons have nested successfully here in recent years, and you are likely to see (and hear) this fascinating ancient bird. We also saw wood duck here.

The privately owned island remains undeveloped. Here and around the pond's shoreline you will see moss-covered rocks, ferns, clintonia, and many other woodland wildflowers.

89 | South Bay, Lake Memphremagog

South Bay starts in Newport, close to the Canada border, but you quickly leave the sounds of the city behind as you paddle south into the bay and into the slowly meandering Barton and Black inlet rivers. This is a great area to observe many wetland species. You should see the rare black tern here.

Location: Newport and Coventry, VT
Maps: *Vermont Atlas & Gazetteer,* Map 54: C1; USGS Newport, Orleans
Area: 745 acres, not including the Barton and Black rivers
Time: All day
Habitat Type: Large, shallow bay with river inlets
Fish: Largemouth bass, yellow perch, pickerel, smelt, walleye, rainbow trout
Information: South Bay Wildlife Management Area, www.vtfishandwildlife.com/wma_maps.cfm
Camping: Brighton State Park; see Appendix A, #39

GETTING THERE
Coventry Street. From Main Street in Newport, go 0.6 mile south on Coventry Street to the access on the left. *GPS coordinates*: 44° 55.741′ N, 72° 12.779′ W.

Glen Road. From Main Street, go east on Mount Vernon Street, and turn right onto Glen Road. Go 2.6 miles to the small parking area on the right; a dirt track leads down to the water on the left. *GPS coordinates*: 44° 54.222′ N, 72° 11.559′ W.

SOUTH BAY, LAKE MEMPHREMAGOG

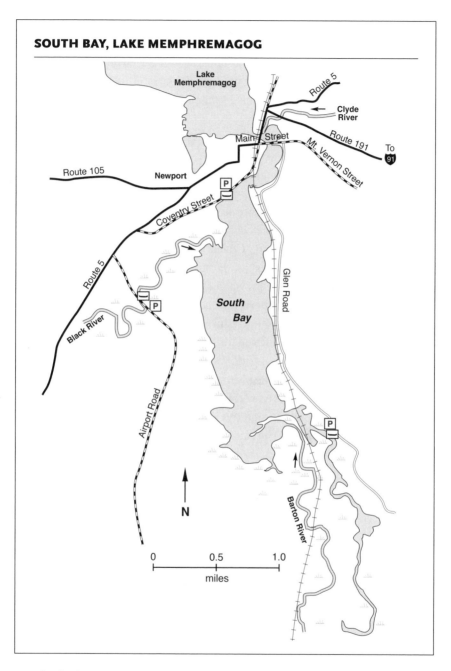

Black River. From Route 105, go 1.1 miles south on Route 5, and turn left onto Airport Road. Go 0.3 mile to the bridge; parking on the right 0.1 mile farther. *GPS coordinates:* 44° 55.081′N, 72° 13.445′W.

WHAT YOU'LL SEE

South Bay of Lake Memphremagog and two of its inlet streams, Black and Barton rivers, are an extraordinary paddling resource. Newport's sirens, trucks, heavy equipment, and cars on nearby streets do not lend an air of solitude. But as you paddle into the long, sinuous channel that extends three or four miles south, most of that noise fades away.

When it is windy, it makes sense to put in at the Glen Road access—our favorite—or on the Black River. You can paddle up the meandering Black River, which flows into South Bay about a quarter-mile below the access, or you can paddle it down from Airport Road. Silver maple and willow, dipping their lowest branches into the water, line parts of the shore, while other stretches are marshy. You may have to carry around some snags.

As you paddle south from the Coventry Street access, the water remains quite open for a distance. Farther south, the open water disappears into thick marshes of pickerelweed, waterlily, water shield, rush, sedge, grass, and cattail. In fact, most of the bay's southern end is not even paddleable by midsummer. Wending your way through marshy islands, you may find yourself in the winding, slow-moving Barton River, lined with silver maple. While you might have difficulty paddling here, at least you will be a lot farther from the city—out with the wood ducks, not the pigeons. Look for beaver here as well.

Curiously, the Barton River roughly parallels another, much wider channel. Follow either one through the South Bay State Wildlife Management Area (portions protected by The Nature Conservancy), one of the few sites in Vermont where the black tern nests and a great haven for wood ducks. We have not explored much of the Barton River, but we have paddled all the way down the more eastern channel. To get to this channel from the Barton River, you may have to paddle back to the main lake and then north a bit; the marshes vary so much that we can't give precise directions. But you should recognize this wide and relatively deep unnamed channel when you get to it. We found it lined with marsh plants and home to a wide assortment of water birds. Fairly soon after getting into the channel, you will pass under a railroad bridge. (Some of the cut-off older wooden posts lurk just below water level—paddle slowly through here.) From the railroad bridge, you can paddle several miles south through increasingly beautiful country. We rarely have seen as many wood ducks in one place—maybe a hundred, mostly in groups of a half-dozen or so. We saw bittern, black duck, kingfisher, great blue heron, northern harrier, lots of painted turtles, and a few snapping turtles—just the triangular noses sticking up above the water. Feathery larch mix with silver maple, white birch, spruce, and other trees along the shores.

A muskrat harvests streamside grasses.

90 | Clyde River and Pensioner Pond

This slow-flowing marshy section of the Clyde River twists and turns through farm country. Be prepared to maneuver around silver maples that, because of beavers, topple into the water. Many bird species inhabit this area, and you might see otter and mink as well as the resident beaver.

Location: Charleston, VT
Maps: *Vermont Atlas & Gazetteer,* Map 54: E5; USGS Island Pond, West Charleston, Westmore
Length/Area: Clyde River, 8 miles one way; Pensioner Pond, 170 acres
Time: 6 hours
Habitat Type: Slow-moving, meandering, farm-country stream
Fish: Yellow perch, pickerel

Information: Clyde River Paddling and Fishing Guide, www.northwoodscenter.org/book.html
Camping: Brighton State Park; see Appendix A, #39
Take Note: Personal watercraft prohibited

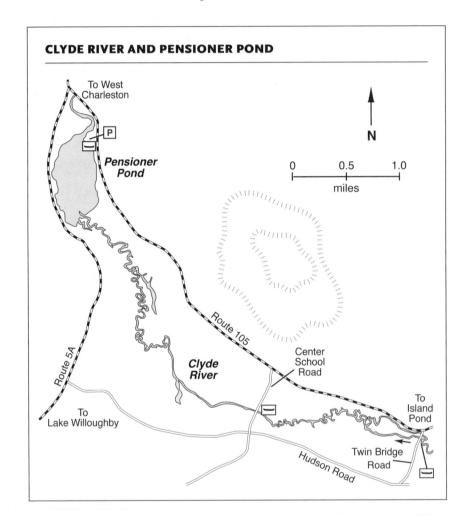

CLYDE RIVER AND PENSIONER POND

GETTING THERE

From West Charleston, go south on Routes 5A and 105. At the split, go 0.7 mile south on Route 105 to the access on Pensioner Pond on the right. *GPS coordinates*: 44° 52.644′ N, 72° 3.144′ W.

Alternate access points are at bridges on Center School Road, Twin Bridges Road, and Route 105.

WHAT YOU'LL SEE

The Clyde River section covered here courses northwest from East Charleston to West Charleston in the heart of Vermont's Northeast Kingdom. The best access lies along the northeast shore of Pensioner Pond, although alternate put-ins occur at the bridges to the southeast. Pensioner Pond itself—totally visible from the road, round, and relatively uninteresting—serves primarily as an access at its southwest corner to the Clyde River.

The river winds through farm country, with silver maple and alder dominating the shoreline. Northern white cedar, an occasional willow, and a variety of shrubs line the 40-foot-wide waterway, and vegetation dips right into the water. Even during spring high water, the barely perceptible current presents no obstacle. The same cannot be said for the beaver that undercut the streamside silver maple, toppling them into the water to make logjams. Be prepared to portage around their handiwork.

The surrounding marshland and side coves support large numbers of wood and black ducks. We also saw tree swallow, red-winged blackbird, great blue heron, a red-tailed hawk, and many other birds. Besides the beaver activity, we spotted a mink moving furtively along the shore and many piles of mussel shells—leftovers from raccoon or otter feasts.

91 | Nulhegan Pond

This tiny pond, with its two outlet streams, is a great place to study marshland plants. We have seen raven, great blue heron, and two orchid species here.

Location: Brighton, VT
Maps: *Vermont Atlas & Gazetteer,* Map 55: H10; USGS Spectacle Pond
Area: 37 acres
Time: 2 hours if you study the plants
Habitat Type: Very small, shallow, marshy pond with inlet and outlet streams
Fish: Pickerel
Camping: Brighton State Park; see Appendix A, #39
Take Note: Gasoline motors prohibited

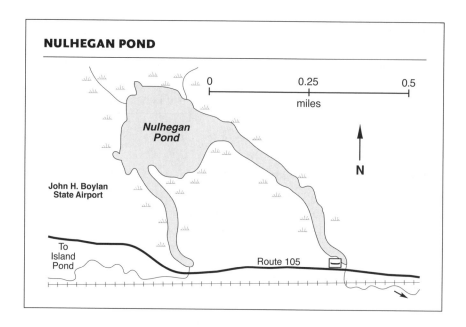

NULHEGAN POND

Nulhegan Pond

John H. Boylan
State Airport

To
Island
Pond

Route 105

0   0.25   0.5
miles

N

GETTING THERE

From Route 114 in Island Pond, go 4.6 miles east on Route 105, just past Boylan Airport, to the access on the right at the bridge over the outlet. Carry your boat across the road. *GPS coordinates*: 44° 47.162′ N, 71° 48.550′ W.

WHAT YOU'LL SEE

Nulhegan Pond, although shallow and small, presents a wonderful place to study aquatic and bog plant life. Its inlet (southeast) and outlet (southwest) streams provide more habitat to explore and make the pond seem much larger. When we paddled here in mid-July, two orchid species were in bloom, along with rafts of pickerelweed, water shield, sundew, pitcher plant, and yellow pond lily. We also found a white waterlily with very small blossoms, perhaps the smallest we have seen on a plant of this type. This could be dwarf waterlily (*Nymphaea leibergii*), recently split off from *N. tetragona* of the Northwest and critically imperiled in the Northeast, but more likely it's a diminutive fragrant waterlily (*N. odorata*).

We also enjoyed identifying bog rosemary, leatherleaf, sweet gale, and a yellow pea that bloomed in profusion. In addition to exploring the pond, take some time to explore the inlet and outlet channels, but watch out for submerged logs.

As in much of the Northeast Kingdom, the northern boreal forest surrounds Nulhegan Pond. Balsam fir, red spruce, northern white cedar (see Trip 84), white birch, and red maple dominate, while tamarack and black spruce tolerate growing on sphagnum hummocks.

Nulhegan Pond is part of the 740-mile Northern Forest Canoe Trail. The northern forest is also moose country. If you do not see moose standing in the local ponds and streams, you can often see them by the road in early morning and evening.

92 | Dennis Pond

Even though the road to the pond can be a challenge, a visit to isolated Dennis Pond is worth the visit, as it is a great place to look for moose and to study wetland plants. We have watched osprey fish here, and you might see otter, mink, and beaver.

Location: Brunswick, VT
Maps: *Vermont Atlas & Gazetteer,* Map 55: J14; USGS Maidstone Lake
Area: 185 acres
Time: 2 hours, more if you study the wetland plants
Habitat Type: Small, shallow, marshy pond
Fish: Yellow perch, pickerel
Camping: Brighton State Park; see Appendix A, #39
Take Note: High-clearance vehicle recommended; gasoline motors prohibited

GETTING THERE
From Route 105 in Bloomfield, go 1.8 miles south on Route 102, and turn diagonally right into the West Mountain Wildlife Management Area. Go 0.6 mile (2.4 miles), and take the right fork. Go 0.2 mile (2.6 miles), cross the bridge, and turn right. Go 0.4 mile (3.0 miles) to the access on the right. Park along the road. *GPS coordinates*: 44° 43.478′ N, 71° 39.250′ W.

WHAT YOU'LL SEE
A few unobtrusive hunting cabins huddle along the northeastern shore of Dennis Pond, land once owned by International Paper, but now protected by The Nature Conservancy and other conservation organizations. Despite the cabins' presence, this boggy pond exudes the essence of the northern coniferous

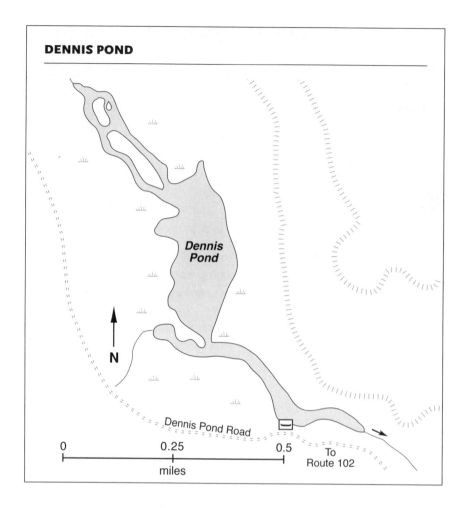

DENNIS POND

Dennis Pond

N

Dennis Pond Road

| 0 | 0.25 | 0.5 |
miles

To
Route 102

forest. Access to the pond, unfortunately, requires carrying about 100 feet over
a rather spongy sphagnum bog. If you want dry, unmuddied feet, stay away
from Dennis Pond.

A paddle here is definitely worth it, especially in early morning or evening
when you have the best chance of spying moose. Sphagnum hummocks, many
sporting stands of stunted tamarack, occur everywhere out in the water and
along the shore. Typical bog plants abound, including leatherleaf, sheep laurel,
cattail, and yellow pond lily; nodding flower heads of pitcher plants poke up
everywhere.

As you dip your paddle in the water, note the yellowish-brown cast from
tannic and other organic acids, the product of decaying vegetation. This very
shallow lake is filling in; even if you push your paddle down very lightly into
the silty bottom, it will penetrate quite far. Before long, this pond will fill in

Adults and children should always wear PFDs when paddling.

completely; indeed, it would be best to paddle this shallow pond in spring, during high water and before emergent vegetation takes over.

We spent a lazy afternoon here in June, enjoying the scenic hillsides all around, along with myriad wildlife: tree swallow, kingfisher, wood duck, red-winged blackbird, kingbird, hermit thrush, cedar waxwing, goldfinch, bittern, great blue heron, painted turtle, and beaver. Tiger swallowtail butterflies appeared in abundance, and two osprey fished the shallow waters.

93 | Norton Pond

Norton Pond's long, narrow aspect and inlet streams can take a long time to explore fully, and you should look for otter, mink, beaver, and moose. You should also see loons here, along with ducks, herons, and other wetland species. The few cottages do not impinge on feelings of solitude.

Location: Norton and Warren Gore, VT

Maps: *Vermont Atlas & Gazetteer,* Map 55: C9; USGS Morgan Center, Norton Pond
Area: 583 acres
Time: 5 hours
Habitat Type: Long, narrow, shallow pond with marshy inlets
Fish: Northern pike
Camping: Brighton State Park; see Appendix A, #39
Take Note: Personal watercraft prohibited

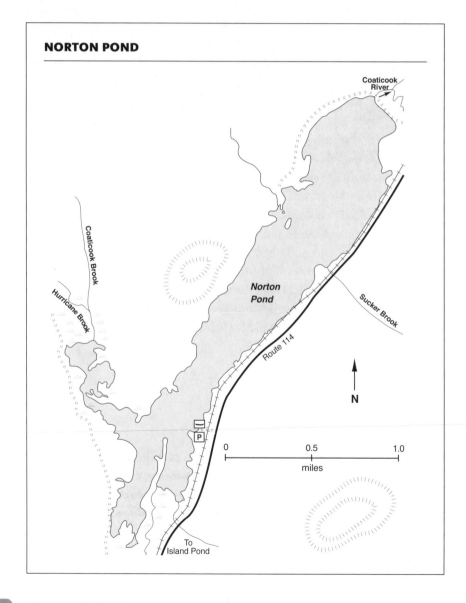

NORTON POND

GETTING THERE

From Route 105 in Island Pond, go 8.8 miles north on Route 114, and turn left into the access. *GPS coordinates*: 44° 55.440′ N, 71° 52.271′ W.

From Route 147 at the Canadian border, go 7.2 miles south on Route 114, and turn right into the access.

WHAT YOU'LL SEE

Norton Pond, less well known than the Averill ponds, Lake Willoughby, and some other lakes in Vermont's Northeast Kingdom, has some real advantages for paddlers. The pond stretches out southwest-to-northeast, providing many coves and inlets to explore. Some—but not much—development mars its otherwise wild and remote-feeling shoreline. Islands, deep coves, and long, winding inlet brooks fill the entire southern end of this large pond. Be sure not to disturb the nesting loons; the chicks have a hard enough time evading the large northern pike that inhabit this pond.

While we enjoyed paddling the northern reaches of Norton Pond, we much preferred the southern end and especially the marshy inlet to the west, where Hurricane Brook and Coaticook Brook flow in. Wildlife abounds here; we saw wood duck, black duck, heron, and deer. Look carefully for otters cavorting along the banks. Judging from tracks along the swampy shores, moose must browse this area in considerable numbers.

Even in late summer, with water levels down and pond vegetation at a peak, you can paddle surprisingly far up the inlet creeks. Higher water in late spring makes the area much more accessible. Where the Hurricane and Coaticook inlet joins the main pond, you can explore a number of different channels through and around the various islands. At the far southern end you will find some gorgeous little coves and just a few summer cottages.

94 | Holland Pond and Turtle Pond

Holland Pond has some development, but that won't stop you from enjoying this remote pond that lies about a mile from the Canada border. Moose abound in this area, which also harbors a good population of black bear. Look for loon, beaver, and osprey here as well.

Location: Holland, VT

Maps: *Vermont Atlas & Gazetteer*, Map 55: A8; USGS Morgan Center
Area: Holland Pond, 334 acres; Turtle Pond, 27 acres
Time: 4 hours
Habitat Type: Ponds with marshy inlets
Fish: Holland Pond—pickerel, brook and rainbow trout; Turtle Pond—brook trout
Information: Bill Sladyk Wildlife Management Area, www.vtfishandwildlife.com/wma_maps.cfm
Camping: Brighton State Park; see Appendix A, #39

GETTING THERE

From I-91, Exit 29, turn right onto Holland/Valley Road, go 5.2 miles, and turn left onto Holland Pond Road as Holland/Valley Road goes right. Go 2.9 miles (8.1 miles), and turn right, staying on Holland Pond Road. Go 2.3 miles (10.4 miles) to the access. *GPS coordinates*: 44° 59.140′ N, 71° 56.077′ W.

From Island Pond, Route 114 north, turn left onto Route 111. Go 6.7 miles, and turn right onto Valley Road. Go 4.7 miles (11.4 miles), turn right onto Holland Pond Road, and continue as above.

WHAT YOU'LL SEE

Holland Pond sits about a mile, as the crow flies, from the Canadian border, in the Northeast Kingdom. The pond has moderate development along its western shore, but these summer cottages (approximately 40) are much different from ones farther south. Few big docks and few huge motorboats loom in front. Further development should be limited because, except for the immediate western shore, all of Holland Pond—and indeed all of the small ponds on the map—fall within the 10,000-acre Bill Sladyk Wildlife Management Area.

Holland Pond's northern and southern ends provide the most interesting areas to paddle. Two southern inlets, as well as a fairly extensive marshy area, await exploration. You can paddle a short distance into the inlets, amid the alders and sphagnum- and grass-covered tussocks—although access to this marshy area may be restricted from May through July because of nesting loons.

The northern end feels a little more remote and wild. You can paddle into the northeast inlet a little ways, and if you feel really adventurous, you can carry your boat from here a couple of hundred yards into small, beautiful, totally remote Turtle Pond. The trail to Turtle Pond starts on the inlet's northwestern side, where it narrows to a rock-strewn channel. Judging from the tracks, moose do most of the trail maintenance.

Farther around Holland Pond's northern end, to the west, a large, flattish rock protruding into the pond makes a great picnic spot. Another occurs at the other inlet where the small creek flows over huge, flat rocks beneath a stand of large northern white cedar. You may find trails here to several other small ponds to the north. Dense stands of cedar, balsam fir, larch, white and yellow birch, and red spruce grow along the rest of the shoreline.

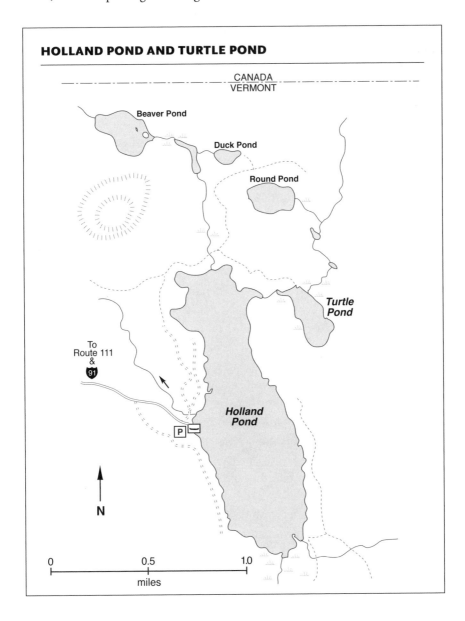

HOLLAND POND AND TURTLE POND

CANADA
VERMONT

Beaver Pond

Duck Pond

Round Pond

Turtle Pond

To Route 111 & 91

Holland Pond

P

N

0   0.5   1.0
miles

95 | Little Averill Pond

This deep lake harbors four species of salmon and trout, which draw in area fishermen. You will likely see loon here, and many moose inhabit this area. If you spend enough time here, you should catch a glimpse of the peregrine falcons that nest on cliffs just to the northwest.

Location: Averill, VT
Maps: *Vermont Atlas & Gazetteer*, Map 55: B13; USGS Averill
Area: 483 acres
Time: 4 hours
Habitat Type: Round, deep lake
Fish: Smelt, landlocked salmon; lake, brook, and rainbow trout
Camping: Brighton State Park; see Appendix A, #39
Take Note: Personal watercraft prohibited

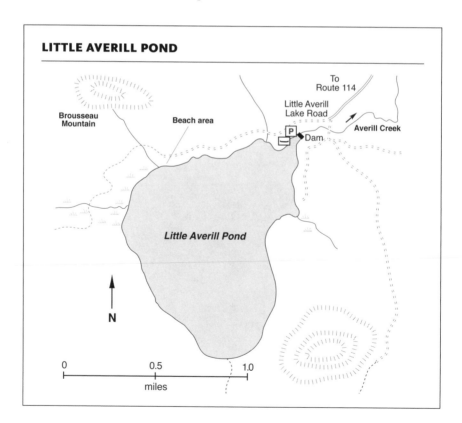

LITTLE AVERILL POND

GETTING THERE

From Route 147 entering from Canada in Norton, go 3.4 miles east on Route 114, and turn right onto Little Averill Lake Road. Go 3.2 miles (6.6 miles) to the access on the left. *GPS coordinates*: 44° 57.845′ N, 71° 42.383′ W.

WHAT YOU'LL SEE

Little Averill Pond lies just south of the Canadian border, in Vermont's Northeast Kingdom. Like Great Averill Pond, its larger brother to the north, Little Averill sits in a deep northern forest of spruce, fir, cedar, red maple, and white and yellow birches. Beautiful Brousseau Mountain, with an extensive cliff area with nesting peregrine falcons, overlooks the pond from the northwest. Some camps occur around the pond, although much less than at Great Averill.

Round and deep, Little Averill boasts excellent fishing for landlocked salmon and lake, rainbow, and brook trout. The densely wooded and generally rocky shore includes a few sandy beaches. The Nature Conservancy manages a tract of land around the pond's northwestern end, including a deep inlet, to protect loon nesting habitat. You will see wispy horsetails and grasses in the water in this gorgeous inlet, amid the whitened snags of long-dead trees. From May through July, some areas may remain off-limits to paddlers to protect nesting loons, which may be using an artificial nesting platform in the south cove.

A trail extends west from the access, around the northern end of the pond, south to the Black Branch of the Nulhegan River, and northwest toward Norton. Another trail extends south from the southern tip of the pond, along the East Branch of the Nulhegan River. (See the *Vermont Atlas & Gazetteer*, or better yet, use the USGS topographical map.)

THE PLAYFUL RIVER OTTER

The river otter (*Lutra canadensis*) inhabits New England's remote lakes and rivers. We have seen dozens throughout New Hampshire and Vermont, mostly in the less-populated North Country, but some near the Massachusetts border. Look for them in early morning and late afternoon.

The river otter once inhabited virtually every U.S. watercourse, from sun-warmed southwestern rivers to icy far-northern lakes and streams. Today, because of 250 years of trapping, water pollution, and encroaching development, the otter has retreated to the far corners of its former range. Because it eats at the top of the food chain, the otter also suffers from pollution and

toxic chemicals in the environment, such as heavy metals, DDT derivatives, dioxin, and PCBs.

With its long, thin body and relatively thick, sharply tapered tail, it can reach 4 feet in length and weigh up to 25 pounds. Long prized by trappers, its dense dark-brown fur above gives way to lighter colors on the belly and throat.

The otter has adapted well to its aquatic environment. Nose and ears close when underwater, and webbed toes aid in swimming. Although it swims fast enough to catch trout, it usually preys on slower-moving suckers, minnows, crayfish, tadpoles, and salamanders. It often thrusts its head way up above the surface, looking around and exhaling loudly.

Although adapted for water, the otter does well on land, with its typical weasel-family undulating gait. Clocked at up to 18 MPH on land, it can travel 100 miles overland in search of new territory. It generally places dens—abandoned beaver lodges or natural cavities under tree roots—at the water's edge, with an underwater entrance.

The otter consumes smaller fish and crayfish in the water and larger prey on shore or on a protruding rock. An ingenious hunter, it sometimes herds fish into shallows or punches a hole in a beaver dam—allowing water to escape—then wades in and feasts on flopping fish. Because it hunts so successfully, it has plenty of time to play—a famous otter trait. Animal behaviorists believe that play among young mammals provides practice for future hunting, territorial interactions, and courtship. But the adult otter continue to play, chasing one another or climbing a snow- or mudbank repeatedly and sliding down into the water.

The otter mates in late winter, but birth follows almost a year later. As with many weasel-family members, it delays embryo implantation, stopping development until the following winter, followed by birth of two to four cubs anytime between November and April. Cubs emerge fully furred, but with eyes closed and no teeth. They venture outside the den after about three months. Although the mother provides initial care, the father may rejoin the family to help with rearing after the cubs reach about six months.

Although the otter is curious and relatively bold, keep your distance. Interference from humans may cause it to move away and search for more remote locations.

Appendix A: Camping

NEW HAMPSHIRE

White Mountain National Forest, 603-447-5448,
www.fs.fed.us/r9/forests/white_mountain/recreation/camping
New Hampshire State Park Reservations, 877-647-2757,
www.reserveamerica.com

	Campground	Address	Reservations	Delorme Atlas & Gazetteer

SOUTHERN NEW HAMPSHIRE STATE PARKS

	Campground	Address	Reservations	Delorme Atlas & Gazetteer
1	Monadnock State Park	Route 124 in Jaffrey	603-532-8862	NH, Map 20: F2
2	Greenfield State Park	Route 31 or Route 136 in Greenfield	603-547-3497	NH, Map 20: B7
3	Pillsbury State Park	Route 31 in Washington	603-863-2360	NH, Map 26: D2
4	Bear Brook State Park	Deerfield Road in Allenstown	603-485-9869	NH, Map 28: H5
5	Pawtuckaway State Park	Route 156 in Nottingham	603-895-3031	NH, Map 29: 19
6	Hampton Beach State Park	Route 1A in Hampton	603-926-8990	NH, Map 31: J10

	Campground	Address	Reservations	Delorme Atlas & Gazetteer
CENTRAL NEW HAMPSHIRE STATE PARKS				
7	Mt. Sunapee State Park	Route 103 in Newberry	603-763-5561	NH, Map 26: A3
8	White Lake State Park	Route 16 in Tamworth	603-323-7350	NH, Map 41: E8
NORTHERN NEW HAMPSHIRE STATE PARKS				
9	Coleman State Park	Off Route 26 on Little Diamond road in Stewartown	603-237-5382	NH, Map 50: A5
10	Mollidgewock State Park	Route 26 in Errol	603-482-3373	NH, Map 51: G10
11	Umbagog Lake State Park	Route 26 south of Errol	603-482-7795	NH, Map 51: I12
12	Lake Francis State Park	Off Route 3 on River Road in Pittsburg	603-538-6707	NH, Map 52: G6
13	Deer Mountain State Park	Route 3 in Pittsburg	603-538-6965	NH, Map 53: C8
14	Long Pond State Park	Off Route 116 on Long Pond Road in Benton	603-536-6100	NH, Map 42: I7
15	Lafayette Campground	I-93 in Lincoln	603-823-9513	NH, Map 43: F11
16	Dry River Campground	Route 302 in Crawford Notch State Park	603-374-2272	NH, Map 44: E5

VERMONT

Green Mountain National Forest, 802-362-2307,
www.fs.fed.us/r9/forests/greenmountain
Vermont State Park Reservations, 888-409-7579, www.vtstateparks.com

	Campground	Address	Reservations	Delorme Atlas & Gazetteer
SOUTHERN VERMONT STATE PARKS				
17	Woodford State Park	Route 9 in Woodford	802-447-7169	VT, Map 21: G11
18	Molly Stark State Park	Route 9 in Wilmington	802-464-5460	VT, Map 22: H2
19	Fort Drummer State Park	Off Route 5 on Old Guilford Road in Brattleboro	802-254-2610	VT, Map 22: 17
20	Jamaica State Park	Route 30 in Jamaica	802-874-4600	VT, Map 26: J3
21	Emerald Lake State Park	Route 7 in Dorset	802-362-1655	VT, Map 25
CENTRAL VERMONT STATE PARKS				
22	Bomoseen State Park	Off Route 4 on Bomoseen Lake, west shore	802-265-4242	VT, Map 28: B6
23	Half Moon State Park	Off Route 4 north of Glen Lake	802-273-2848	VT, Map 28: A6
24	Quechee Gorge State Park	Route 4 in Hartford	802-295-2990	VT, Map 31: C11
25	Banbury State Park	Route 53 in Salisbury	802-247-5925	VT, Map 33: E10
26	Gifford Woods State Park	Route 100 in Killington	802-775-5354	VT, Map 30: B2
27	Button Bay State Park	Off Route 22A on Button Bay Road in Ferrisburgh	802-475-2377	VT, Map 38: F3
28	D.A.R. State Park	Route 17 in Addison	802-759-2354	VT, Map 38: K2

	Campground	Address	Reservations	Delorme Atlas & Gazetteer
29	Mt. Philo State Park	Route 7 in Charlotte	802-425-2390	VT, Map 38: C6

NORTHERN VERMONT STATE PARKS

	Campground	Address	Reservations	Delorme Atlas & Gazetteer
30	Elmore State Park	Route 12 in Elmore	802-888-2982	VT, Map 47: E8
31	New Discovery State Park	Off Route 302 on Route 232 in Peacham	802-426-3042	VT, Map 41: B13
32	Stillwater State Park	Route 302 on Route 232 in Peacham	802-584-3822	VT, Map 41: C14
33	Ricker Pond State Park	Off 302 on Route 232 in Peacham	802-584-3821	VT, Map 41: D14
34	Big Deer State Park (register at Stillwater Park)	Off Route 302 on Route 232 in Peacham	802-584-3822	VT, Map 41: C14
35	Underhill State Park	Off Pleasant Valley Road on Mountain Road in Underhill	802-899-3022	VT, Map 46: F1
36	Little River State Park	Off I-89 in Waterbury on Little River Road	802-244-7103	VT, Map 46: J3
37	Green River Reservoir State Park	Off Route 15 on Garfield Road in Hyde Park	802-888-1349	VT, Map 47: B8
38	Lake Carmi State Park	Off Route 105 on Route 236 in Franklin	802-933-8383	VT, Map 51: B14
39	Brighton State Park	Route 105 east of Island Pond	802-723-4360	VT, Map 55: G9
40	Ball Mountain Dam State Park	Route 30 in Jamaica	802-874-4881	VT, Map 26: J3

VERMONT STATE FORESTS

	Campground	Address	Reservations	Delorme Atlas & Gazetteer
41	Grafton/Mollie Beattie, primitive camping	Off Route 121 on Hinckley Brook Road	802-885-8845	VT, Map 26: H6

Appendix B: Outfitters

New Hampshire

Alden of Sunapee
71 Main Street
Newport, NH 03773
1-800-287-9660
www.aldenofsunapee.com

Contoocook River Canoe Company
9 Horse Hill Road
Concord, NH 03303
603-753-9804
www.contoocookcanoe.com

Kayak Country
27 Kearsarge Valley Road
Wilmot Flat, NH 03287
603-381-8685
www.kayakcountry.com

Lopstick Outfitters
45 Stewart Young Road
Pittsburg, NH 03592
800-538-6659
www.cabinsatlopstick.com/
Outfitters.html

Miller Outdoors
1185 Route 16
Dummer, NH 03588
603-449-2333
www.milleroutdoors.com

Mountain Road Trading Post
68 Mountain Road
Raymond, NH 03077
603-895-3501
www.mrtp.net

North Star Canoes
1356A Route 12A
Cornish, NH 03745
603-542-6929
www.kayak-canoe.com

Northern Waters
29 Upton Road
Errol, NH 03579
603-482-3817
www.beoutside.com

Outback Kayak
104 Main Street
Lincoln, NH 03251
603-745-2002
www.outbackkayak.org

Plymouth Ski and Sports
97 Main Street
Plymouth, NH 03264
603-536-2338
www.plymouthski.com

Portsmouth Kayak Adventures
185 Wentworth Road
Portsmouth, NH 03801
603-559-1000
www.portsmouthkayak.com

River Run Deli and Kayak Rentals
Route 28 South
Alton Bay, NH 03180
603-875-1000
www.rrdeli.com

Saco Bound
2561 East Main Street
Conway, NH 03813
603-447-2177
www.sacobound.com

Saco Canoe Rental Company
328 White Mountain Highway
Conway, NH 03818
866-897-2940
www.sacocanoerental.com

Sam's Outdoor Outfitters
74 Monadnock Highway
North Swanzey, NH 03431
603-352-6200
www.samsoutdooroutfitters.com

Ski Fanatics
23 Vinntinner Road #6
Campton, NH 03223
603-726-4327
www.skifanatics.net

Ski Works
2265 Route 16
West Ossipee, NH 03890
603-539-2246
www.skiworksnh.com

Summers' Backcountry Outfitters
16 Ashuelot Street
Keene, NH 03431
603-357-5107
www.summersbackcountry.com

Sunapee Outfitters
104 Route 103
Newbury, NH
603-938-5292
www.sunapeeoutfitters.com

Suncook River Canoe and Kayak
13 Parade Road
Barnstead, NH 03218
603-269-5185

Village Sports
394 Main Street
New London, NH 03257
603-526-4948
www.villagesportsllc.com

Wild Meadow Canoes
Route 25
Center Harbor, NH 03226
603-253-7536
www.wildmeadowcanoes.com

Vermont

Canoe Imports
370 Dorset Street
South Burlington, VT 05403
802-651-8760
www.canoeimports.com

Clearwater Sports
4147 Main Street
Waitsfield, VT 05673
802-496-2708
www.clearwatersports.com

Clyde River Recreation
2355 Route 105
West Charleston, VT 05872
802-895-4333
www.clyderiverrecreation.com/

East Burke Sports
439 Vermont 114
East Burke, VT 05832
802-626-3215
www.eastburkesports.com

Equipe Sport
(multiple locations)
Junction of Routes 30 and 100
Rawsonville, VT 05155
802-297-2847

Village Square
Stratton Mountain, VT 05340
802-297-3460

Mount Snow Access Road
West Dover, VT 05356
802-464-2222

207 Main Street
Ludlow, VT 05149
802-228-6200
www.equipesport.com

Green River Canoe
4807 Route 15
Jeffersonville, VT 05464
802-644-8336

Middlebury Mountaineer
2 Park Street
Middlebury, VT 05753
877-611-7802
www.mmvt.com

Mountain Travelers Hike and Ski Shop
147 Route 4 East
Rutland VT, 05701
802-775-0814
www.mtntravelers.com

North Hero Marina
2253 Pelots Point Road
North Hero, VT 05474
802-372-5953
www.northheromarina.com

Sam's Outdoor Outfitters
(two locations)
74 Main Street
Brattleboro, VT 05301
802-254-2933

78 Rockingham Street
Bellows Falls, VT 05101
802-463-3500
www.samsoutdooroutfitters.com

Umiak Outdoor Outfitters
849 Sout Main Street
Stowe, VT 05672
802-253-2317
www.umiak.com

Vermont Adventure Tours
223 Woodstock Avenue
Rutland, VT 05701
802-773-3343
www.vermontadventuretours.com

Vermont Canoe Touring Center
451 Putney Road
Brattleboro, VT 05301
802-257-5008

Appendix C: Further Reading

Buchsbaum, Robert. *Best Day Hikes in the White Mountains*. Boston: Appalachian Mountain Club Books, 2006.

Connecticut River Joint Commission. Connecticut River maps. www.crjc.org/boating/boating1.htm.

Connecticut River Watershed Council. *The Connecticut River Boating Guide*: *Source to Sea*, 3rd edition. Guilford, Conn.: Falcon, 2007.

Daniell, Gene, and Steven D. Smith. *White Mountain Guide*, 28th edition. Boston: Appalachian Mountain Club Books, 2007.

Hampton, Bruce, and David Cole. *Soft Paths: How to Enjoy the Wilderness without Harming It*, 3rd edition. Mecanicsburg, Pa.: Stackpole Books, 2003.

Hutchinson, Derek. *Basic Book of Sea Kayaking*, 2nd edition. Guilford, Conn.: Falcon, 2007.

Jacobson, Cliff. *Canoeing and Camping, Beyond the Basics*, 3rd edition. Guilford, Conn.: Falcon, 2007.

Monkman, Jerry, and Marcy Monkman. *Discover the White Mountains*, 2nd edition. Boston: Appalachian Mountain Club Books, 2009.

New Hampshire Atlas & Gazetteer, 15th edition. Yarmouth, Maine: DeLorme Mapping Company, 2005.

Roberts, Harry, and Steve Salins. *Basic Essentials Canoe Paddling*, 3rd edition: Guilford, Conn.: Falcon, 2006.

Roberts, Harry, and Steve Salins. *Basic Illustrated Canoe Paddling*. Guilford, Conn.: Falcon, 2008.

Seidman, David. *The Essential Sea Kayaker*, 2nd edition. Ragged Mountain Press, 2001.

Smith, Steven D., and Gene Daniell. *Southern New Hampshire Trail Guide*, 3rd edition. Boston: Appalachian Mountain Club Books, 2010.

Vermont Atlas & Gazetteer, 12th edition. Yarmouth, Maine: DeLorme Mapping Company, 2003.

List of Waterways

About the Authors

John Hayes, a former professor of biochemistry and environmental science at Marlboro College in Vermont, is now Dean of Arts and Sciences at Pacific University in Oregon. Besides exploring the lakes and rivers of his new home in the Northwest, he has paddled Minnesota's Boundary Waters Canoe Area, Georgia's Okefenokee Swamp, and Florida's Everglades, as well as throughout the Northeast. Hayes has written for *National Geographic Traveler* and has edited numerous solar energy conference proceedings. He was book review editor of the *Passive Solar Journal* and served as vice chair of the American Solar Energy Society. He has led natural history field trips to Central America, Mexico, Southwest deserts, Rockies, Everglades, Borneo, and Africa. He and Alex Wilson are co-authors of paddling guides to all New England states and New York.

Alex Wilson is founder of BuildingGreen, LLC, in Brattleboro, Vermont, a 25-person company dedicated to reducing environmental impacts of the built environment. BuildingGreen has published *Environmental Building News* since 1992, publishes the most comprehensive directory of green building products (GreenSpec), and offers various other print and online resources on green building. Wilson also writes widely for other magazines, including *Fine Homebuilding, Architectural Record*, and *Landscape Architecture*, and he is author or coauthor of *Consumer Guide to Home Energy Savings*, 9th ed. (ACEEE, 2007); *Green Development: Integrating Ecology and Real Estate* (Wiley, 1998); and *Your Green Home* (New Society, 2006). Wilson served on the board of the U.S. Green Building Council for five years and is currently a trustee of The Nature Conservancy, Vermont Chapter. He has long been an avid quietwater paddler and naturalist.

About The AMC New Hampshire Chapter

The AMC New Hampshire Chapter offers a wide variety of hiking, backpacking, climbing, paddling, and skiing trips each year, as well as social, family, and young member programs and instructional workshops. The chapter also maintains trails throughout the state. The AMC maintains the Appalachian Trail (AT) in the White Mountains from Woodstock, New Hampshire, to Grafton Notch in Maine, as well as huts, campsites, and shelters along the AT. To view a list of AMC activities in New Hampshire and other parts of the Northeast, visit trips.outdoors.org.

AMC Books Updates

AMC Books strives to keep our guidebooks as up-to-date as possible to help you plan safe and enjoyable adventures. If we learn after publishing a book that trails are relocated or that route or contact information has changed, we will post the updated information online. Before you hit the trail, check for updates at www.outdoors.org/publications/books/updates.

If you notice discrepancies in the descriptions or maps while hiking or paddling, or if you find other errors in the book, please let us know by submitting them to amcbookupdates@outdoors.org or in writing to Books Editor, c/o AMC, 5 Joy Street, Boston, MA 02108. We will verify all submissions and post key updates each month.

AMC Books is dedicated to being a recognized leader in outdoor publishing. Thank you for your participation.

AMC BOOKS & MAPS

EXPLORE THE POSSIBILITIES

Appalachian Mountain Club

Founded in 1876, the AMC is the nation's oldest outdoor recreation and conservation organization. The AMC promotes the protection, enjoyment, and understanding of the mountains, forests, waters, and trails of the Appalachian region.

People

We are more than 100,000 members, advocates, and supporters; 16,000 volunteers; and more than 450 full-time and seasonal staff. Our 12 chapters reach from Maine to Washington, D.C.

Outdoor Adventure and Fun

We offer more than 8,000 trips each year, from local chapter activities to major excursions worldwide, for every ability level and outdoor interest—from hiking and climbing to paddling, snowshoeing, and skiing.

Great Places to Stay

We host more than 140,000 guests each year at our lodges, huts, camps, shelters, and campgrounds. Each AMC destination is a model for environmental education and stewardship.

Opportunities for Learning

We teach people the skills to be safe outdoors and to care for the natural world around us through programs for children, teens, and adults, as well as outdoor leadership training.

Caring for Trails

We maintain more than 1,500 miles of trails throughout the Northeast, including nearly 350 miles of the Appalachian Trail in five states.

Protecting Wild Places

We advocate for land and riverway conservation, monitor air quality and climate change, and work to protect alpine and forest ecosystems throughout the Northern Forest and Mid-Atlantic Highlands regions.

Engaging the Public

We seek to educate and inform our own members and an additional 2 million people annually through AMC Books, our website, our White Mountain visitor centers, and AMC destinations.

Join Us!

Members support our mission while enjoying great AMC programs, our award-winning *AMC Outdoors* magazine, and special discounts. Visit www.outdoors.org or call 800-372-1758 for more information.

Appalachian Mountain Club
Recreation • Education • Conservation
www.outdoors.org

More Books from the Outdoor Experts

River Guide New Hampshire and Vermont, 4th Edition

EDITED BY JOHN FISKE

This guide features thousands of miles of paddling routes in New Hampshire and Vermont, making it the most comprehensive paddling guide to the states. Inside you will find descriptions of the most popular rivers in the area, as well as their tributaries.

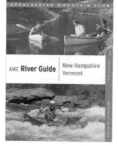

ISBN: 1-934028-05-3
$16.95

Discover the White Mountains, 2nd Edition

BY JERRY AND MARCY MONKMAN

Explore 50 of the best hiking, biking, and paddling trips in the Whites, with everything from short walks to challenging day-long adventures. Includes hikes on Mount Washington, bike trips on the Franconia Notch Bike Path, and paddling on Chocurua Lake.

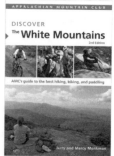

ISBN: 978-1-934028-22-3
$18.95

Quiet Water Maine, 2nd Edition

BY ALEX WILSON AND JOHN HAYES

Quiet Water Maine reveals more than 100 spectacular ponds and lakes ideally suited for canoeing and kayaking. Each trip includes a detailed tour description with summaries of the time, distance, difficulty, and special features of each area, as well as notes about flora and fauna.

ISBN: 1-929173-65-2
$18.95

Discover Maine

BY TY WIVELL

For active travelers seeking the best outdoor adventures the state has to offer, this guide describes 60 hiking, biking, and paddling trips from the southern coast to the Northern Forest. Features coverage of Baxter State Park, Saco River, and lesser-known pockets of wilderness.

ISBN: 1-929173-70-9
$17.95